Autonomy Is in Our Hearts

KAIROS

In ancient Greek philosophy, *kairos* signifies the right time or the "moment of transition." We believe that we live in such a transitional period. The most important task of social science in time of transformation is to transform itself into a force of liberation. Kairos, an editorial imprint of the Anthropology and Social Change department housed in the California Institute of Integral Studies, publishes groundbreaking works in critical social sciences, including anthropology, sociology, geography, theory of education, political ecology, political theory, and history.

Series editor: Andrej Grubačić

Kairos books:

Practical Utopia: Strategies for a Desirable Society by Michael Albert

In, Against, and Beyond Capitalism: The San Francisco Lectures by John Holloway

Anthropocene or Capitalocene? Nature, History, and the Crisis of Capitalism edited by Jason W. Moore

Birth Work as Care Work: Stories from Activist Birth Communities by Alana Apfel

We Are the Crisis of Capital: A John Holloway Reader by John Holloway

Archive That, Comrade! Left Legacies and the Counter Culture of Remembrance by Phil Cohen

Beyond Crisis: After the Collapse of Institutional Hope in Greece, What? edited by John Holloway, Katerina Nasioka, and Panagiotis Doulos

Re-enchanting the World: Feminism and the Politics of the Commons by Silvia Federici

Occult Features of Anarchism: With Attention to the Conspiracy of Kings and the Conspiracy of the Peoples by Erica Lagalisse

Autonomy Is in Our Hearts: Zapatista Autonomous Government through the Lens of the Tsotsil Language by Dylan Eldredge Fitzwater

The Battle for the Mountain of the Kurds: Self-Determination and Ethnic Cleansing in the Afrin Region of Rojava by Thomas Schmidinger

Autonomy Is in Our Hearts

Zapatista Autonomous Government through the Lens of the Tsotsil Language

Dylan Eldredge Fitzwater

KAIROS

PM

Autonomy Is in Our Hearts: Zapatista Autonomous Government through the Lens of the Tsotsil Language
Dylan Eldredge Fitzwater
© 2019 PM Press.

ISBN: 978-1-62963-580-4
Library of Congress Control Number: 2018931534

Cover by John Yates / www.stealworks.com
Cover art "Autonomía es Vida / Sumisión es Muerte," screenprint, 2013, by Fernando Marti www.justseeds.org/artist/fernandomarti/
Interior design by briandesign

10 9 8 7 6 5 4 3 2 1

PM Press
PO Box 23912
Oakland, CA 94623
www.pmpress.org

Printed in the USA by the Employee Owners of Thomson-Shore in Dexter, Michigan.
www.thomsonshore.com

"La autonomía está en nuestros corazones."
"Autonomy is in our hearts."
Elena, member of the autonomous *consejo*, autonomous municipality
Ricardo Flores Magón, Caracol III La Garrucha[1]

Contents

Acknowledgments

I would like to thank my teachers: the education promoters of the Oventik Escuela de Lenguas, the amazing people from Bats'il K'op, and of course Margaret, Lisa, and Roosbelinda for being the best editors I could ever hope for. Thank you to Kaden for all the linguistics help, to Maya for the edits and comments, to Gustavo for translating my work and for answering my translation questions, to Alix for the diagrams, and to Quincy for breathing new life into the whole project.

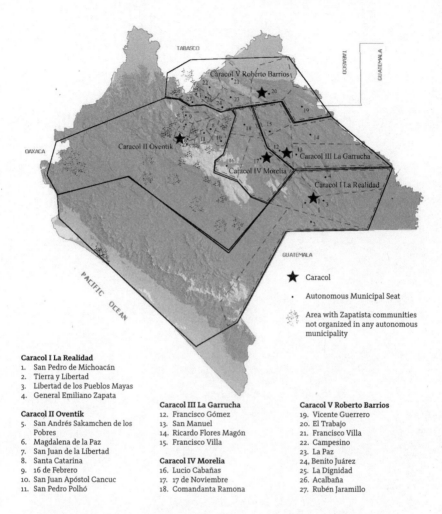

Caracol I La Realidad
1. San Pedro de Michoacán
2. Tierra y Libertad
3. Libertad de los Pueblos Mayas
4. General Emiliano Zapata

Caracol II Oventik
5. San Andrés Sakamchen de los Pobres
6. Magdalena de la Paz
7. San Juan de la Libertad
8. Santa Catarina
9. 16 de Febrero
10. San Juan Apóstol Cancuc
11. San Pedro Polhó

Caracol III La Garrucha
12. Francisco Gómez
13. San Manuel
14. Ricardo Flores Magón
15. Francisco Villa

Caracol IV Morelia
16. Lucio Cabañas
17. 17 de Noviembre
18. Comandanta Ramona

Caracol V Roberto Barrios
19. Vicente Guerrero
20. El Trabajo
21. Francisco Villa
22. Campesino
23. La Paz
24. Benito Juárez
25. La Dignidad
26. Acalbaña
27. Rubén Jaramillo

A note on the map: it should become apparent when reading this book that it is close to impossible to draw a "map" of Zapatista autonomous government. The autonomous government system is not a state with set administrative boundaries, passports, and postal codes. A map of Zapatista autonomous governance is really a map of collective decisions, shared work, and the complex shifting relationships between life and land. This web of relationships cannot be captured within sharp territorial boundaries. However, it is also true that the communities that are located in the highland region of Chiapas send authorities to serve on the Good Government Council of Caracol II Oventik and are in turn attended to by those authorities. Even though there are no borders or border crossings, each Caracol and municipality covers a certain geographical area. To put it succinctly, the lines on this map represent the collective agreements of communities that, as the Zapatistas would say, have organized themselves in a certain "geography." Although for convenience I represent them as straight lines on a map, their reality is fuzzy, shifting, and changeable.

FOREWORD
by John P. Clark

A Politics of Heart and Spirit

For many years, I have been conducting an experiment to investigate the dominant ideology. I have asked people if there was any famous statement by Marx that they could quote from memory. I have found that there has been one almost universal response, namely, that Marx said that "religion is the opiate of the masses." What is so striking about this reply is that it cites only part of Marx's famous saying and, rather suspiciously, leaves out what is quite possibly the most important part. The missing part states that "religion is the sigh of the oppressed creature, the heart of a heartless world, and the spirit of spiritless conditions."[1] Marx implies that religion has been and remains a powerful force in society, because it is a source of "heart" and "spirit."[2]

If we think deeply about the implications of Marx's statement, we may learn something very important. It is something that has not been grasped very well by radical and revolutionary movements (including, and perhaps even especially, by those movements called "Marxist"). If one wants to replace traditional religion with something else, the result will be a disaster if that "something else" does not contain at least as much *heart* and *spirit* as what is being replaced. The history of the Zapatista movement, as revealed in Dylan Fitzwater's eloquent and illuminating account, is the history of learning precisely that truth.

One of the most important lessons of the history of the Zapatista movement is the need to give up presuppositions of the dominant hierarchal, dualistic society and to learn from the wisdom of indigenous people. The EZLN, or Zapatista Army of National Liberation, grew out of the FLN, or Forces of National Liberation, which was a traditional Marxist vanguardist organization that focused on the seizure of state power and the reorganization of the economy under centralized control. The FLN militants inherited this patriarchal authoritarian model, which professes egalitarianism in theory but operates in practice as an ideological justification of the power of an elite that rules in the supposed interest of the masses. A small group of FLN militants were sent to Chiapas to organize the peasants according to the tenets of this ideology.

What happened instead was an extraordinary dialectical reversal that has had world-historical implications. The self-proclaimed organizers were themselves "reorganized" or transformed through their encounter with the indigenous culture and values of Chiapas. The precise term for the deep change that they underwent is "conversion." The militants were converted from a view of revolution as the imposition of an ideological paradigm led by an enlightened vanguard to a vison of revolution as a socially and ecologically regenerative activity that is deeply rooted in history, tradition, culture, and place. As the EZLN began to emerge from this process of transformation its focus was no longer on seizure of state power and the leading role of the vanguard party, but rather on "local autonomy and self-determination" for the indigenous people themselves. One aspect of this transformation was that the Zapatista conception of the political shifted from the traditional Western leftist privileging of social ideology and social institutional structure to a larger problematic that emphasizes very heavily the social ethos and the social imaginary as forms of communal self-expression.

Making Connections

Central to this revolutionary ethos and radical imaginary are the concept of "heart" and the closely connected concepts of "soul" and "spirit." "Heart" appears almost two hundred times in Fitzwater's text, most often taken from indigenous Zapatista testimonies. The Zapatista movement brings to the center of radical political thought and practice these and related concepts that have generally remained on the margins of the Western left, though they have been important in certain strands of communitarian anarchism and so-called "utopian socialism" and became familiar as the result of the forms of radical spirituality associated with liberation theology. Thus, in addition to offering invaluable lessons for a generally disoriented left in what Vandana Shiva has called the "maldeveloped" world, the Zapatista revolution can help that left recover some of its own most important but largely neglected and submerged traditions.

These dissident currents have drawn upon all the sources of heart and spirit that were embodied in traditional religion, transforming them into a means for communal liberation and realization. For example, the concept of "heart" is quite central to Gustav Landauer's communitarian anarchism. He observed that "the more capitalism blossoms, the weaker the heart and spirit of the proletariat become."[3] This heart and spirit must be revived and the disintegrative effects of atomizing bourgeois society reversed for the people to regain hope and creative energy. He states that "the community should not concern itself with efforts other than those that derive from its heart—a heart formed by the hearts of all of its members, united in a common will."[4] At least as important for Landauer was the concept of *Geist* or spirit, which he describes as a "communal spirit," a "drive to the whole, to associate with others, to community, to justice," that "never rests."[5]

A similar radical spirituality is expressed powerfully in eco-socialist philosopher of liberation Joel Kovel's classic work *History and Spirit*. Kovel describes spirit as "*what happens to us as the boundaries of the self give way. Or we could say that it is about the 'soul,' by which we shall mean the form of 'being' taken by the spiritual self.*"[6] It is this liberated spiritual self that is most capable of becoming the subject of revolution. It is significant that Kovel's work was profoundly influenced by his experience of radical spirituality in Central America, the Sandinista Revolution in particular, and reflects the confluence of indigenous wisdom and liberation theology that also shaped the Zapatista revolution. For thinkers like Landauer and Kovel, as for the Zapatistas, revolution must be a movement of spiritual regeneration in which the greatest wealth of the community is found in the flourishing of its collective heart and spirit. These realities are the basis on which social and ecological regeneration can begin to emerge.

The Language of Heart and Spirit

As Fitzwater explains, these crucial realities are expressed in the indigenous culture of Chiapas through the interconnected concepts of *o'on* and *ch'ulel*. In the course of his studies, he learned that the former term means "collective heart," while the latter connotes both "soul" and "potentiality." The collective heart is fundamental to the community because of its ability to "give rise to common thoughts and feelings." Fitzwater explains that these two concepts should really be expressed through the single idea of "thoughts/feelings," since they "are understood as one and the same" and are interconnected as "realizations of the inherent potentialities of the heart," in which thinking and feeling are not separate. This account contrasts markedly with the reigning Western (and increasingly global) dualism exhibited classically in Hume's famous fact-value dichotomy, in which thought, which is supposed to be based on experience of an objective world, and feeling, which is supposed to be based on subjective, relativistic responses to that world, are relegated to entirely separate realms.

The dominant hierarchical and dualistic ideology of civilization, and especially its manifestation in Western modernity, expresses abstractly and fantastically the actual conditions of social alienation in a hierarchical and dualistic society. Under civilization, the society of separation and domination, the "what is," that is, the existing system of domination, cannot really be challenged by the "what ought to be," that is, by any alternative to that system. "What is," no matter how irrational it may be, is perceived as self-evident, a priori truth that becomes a de facto categorical imperative. The discovery of the non-dualistic Tsotsil and Tzeltal cultural concepts and the social practice based on them has the power to destabilize this conventional wisdom. We might say that in a sense "all that is solid melts into spirit." Alternatively, we might say that all that has been deadened and objectified is reanimated and reenspirited.

Another pivotal indigenous concept with deep ontological implications that is discussed by Fitzwater is *ch'ulel*. According to a study of Tzeltal usage carried out in the municipality of Cancuc, "a person is composed of a body (*bak'etal*), made up of flesh and blood, and a group of 'souls' (*ch'ulel*; plural *ch'uleltik*) residing within the heart of each individual." This implies that selfhood is a multiplicity, a kind of unity in diversity, rather than the "simple substance" favored in Western egocentric metaphysics. Fitzwater suggests that references to this momentous reality as "soul" must be taken with a grain of salt, since the indigenous concept does not correspond to what we expect when we hear that Western term. It derives from the Tzeltal and Tsotsil root *ch'ul*, which means "holy" or "sacred," and "in a strict sense" it "denotes a thing's radical 'other.'"

This explanation immediately recalls Rudolf Otto's famous description of "the holy" or "the sacred" in *The Idea of the Holy* as a powerful and numinous reality that is "wholly other." However, even more pertinent is what Kovel uncovers in diverse spiritual traditions in *History and Spirit*. Kovel says that "the self is not only its positive self; there is also its Otherness in relation to being, and the things we call spiritual take place in the zone of Otherness that links the self to being."[7] It is the discovery of this Otherness that leads us beyond the bounds of the ego to the community of humanity and nature. It also leads us to recognize the need for revolution against a system of domination and separation that tears that community apart.

Attaining Greatness of Heart

It might not be immediately clear to those accustomed to the dominant Western models of politics (whether right or left) how the discourse of "heart" and "spirit" is a specifically political discourse. This is because the prevailing views focus heavily on social institutional structures, the ideologies that legitimate or challenge these structures, and the problematic of either defending or overturning them. The language of "heart" and "spirit" does not neglect these spheres, but it is also in a very strong sense a communitarian language that is grounded in a *communal ethos* and a *communal imaginary*. One of the weaknesses in standard radical thought is the weak connections that are made between ideology and institutions, on the one hand, and ethos and imaginary, on the other, so there is much to learn from indigenous cultures in which there is a stronger dialectical interrelation between such spheres.

One of the most personally, communally, and politically significant concepts that illustrates how these dimensions intersect is "*ichbail ta muk'*." This Tsotsil phrase is defined by Fitzwater as "to bring (*ichil*) one another (*ba*) to largeness or greatness (*ta muk'*) and implies the coming together of a big collective heart." The reader may be surprised when Fitzwater reveals that the phrase can also be translated simply as "democracy." Obviously, the Zapatistas impart a much fuller and deeper meaning to this term than that found in the impoverished conception of democracy inherited from the Western liberal tradition. The Zapatista concept is a profoundly social-ecological one, since it implies "respect" for and "recognition" of all beings in both the natural and social worlds, which are really seen as one continuous world. It combines aspects of the ethics and politics of care with an ethics and politics of social and ecological flourishing. In this sense, it is one of the most radical and far-reaching conceptions of democracy yet to appear.

The process of ichbail ta muk', or "carrying one another to greatness" through the creation of "a big collective heart," aims at the achievement of a non-dominating unity in diversity. This process presupposes the existence of a communal subjectivity, "the inclusive we (ko'ontik) that does not subsume the different exclusive 'our hearts' (ko'onkutik) that compose it." Such an analysis refutes typical anti-communitarian arguments, which assume that communal institutions must entail a regression to reactionary and repressive, if not explicitly fascistic, concepts of homogeneity and identity.

The use of such repressive mechanisms is not, however, typical of indigenous communities and horizontalist organizations. Rather, they are usually the result of the contradictions that arise within highly atomized statist and capitalist societies or within evolving societies going through the traumatic process of integration into the statist and capitalist global order. In these societies, highly participatory traditional communities have either dissolved or are disintegrating under severe stress. The longing for the security that they once provided is co-opted for authoritarian and exploitative purposes. The increasingly atomized masses are offered a fantasized identity through mythic, ideological, and highly manipulative concepts of unity based on nationality, race, ethnicity, or religious background. What the commodity per se has failed to achieve is marketed as "identity," the powerful and alluring commodity of last resort.

The Zapatista "big collective heart" is diametrically opposed to such regressive tendencies. It is a creative, rather than reactive, response to the destructive and alienating tendencies of the corporate capitalist economy, the liberal political order, and the nihilistic culture of mass consumption. It responds to such threats through organic forms of solidarity, rather than mechanistic ones.[8]

A Change of Heart

A final and extremely crucial aspect of the politics of heart concerns the nature of the transformative experience, the deep change of heart, or fullness of heart, that is necessary. Three passages from Fitzwater address this issue very pertinently. First, he says that heart (o'on) denotes "the space inhabited by a certain ch'ulel," or soul, including "a ch'ulel that traverses an entire community, and thus brings them together into the shared space of a single heart." Thus, the politics of heart has a goal of communal wholeness and draws on an inherent potentiality within the community to "bring itself to greatness" collectively.

Second, Fitzwater explains that "in Tsotsil the wholeness or fragmentation of the heart describes the positive or negative emotional, physical, and spiritual state of a collective or an individual." Thus, there is a

connection between the condition of the heart of the person and the condition of the heart of the community, the heart of the world. Depression,
addiction, anxiety, alienation, aggression, and nihilism on the part of the
person are symptoms of a deranged and diseased state of the world. Love,
compassion, joy, enthusiasm, hope, and creative energy on the part of the
person are symptoms of a sane and healthy state of the world or of a new
world that is coming into being, in which one is taking part.

Third, Fitzwater points out the importance in the indigenous community of "the process of sadness overflowing the heart." He explains that
"the spreading of shared sadness, and thus of shared ch'ulel" is "the first
step in a process of self-organization, what might be called 'creating political consciousness' in English or Spanish." This shows an awareness within
the indigenous culture of the ways in which suffering and trauma can be
the beginning of liberation. This point is particularly thought-provoking,
since it addresses the question of what initial step could lead one to engage
in personal and social transformation.

This analysis of transformative experience parallels the teaching
in Buddhism (the "First Noble Truth") that the beginning of wisdom and
compassion is awakening to the suffering in the world and its relation to
one's own suffering. Buddhist philosophy concurs with Marx that most of
religion is an opiate, rather than a curative treatment, but adds that most
of everything else is too, and often without even the palliative effects that
religion offers. Buddhism points out the need to move on to a cure. The
truth of suffering only attains fulfillment when it becomes part of the
comprehensive practice of a community of liberation and solidarity (the
sangha, the revolutionary base community) that aims at getting to the
causes of suffering and effecting a cure for it.

Such insights are not, of course, limited to Buddhism (except to the
degree that Buddhism is taken simply as a generic term for the "awakened
mind"). More generally and cross-culturally, there is an experience of a
"Dark Night of the Soul," or transformative trauma, that signals the break
with egocentric, patriarchal, hierarchical, dominating consciousness and
leads toward personal and communal liberation. The function of a revolutionary movement is to assure that the transformed consciousness does
not retreat into some comforting but illusory solution in the narrowly
personal realm (the opiate of the person), but that it is expressed in effective social transformative practice of a flourishing community of liberation and solidarity.

Celebrating the People and Earth

One of the most revelatory aspects of this book is its account of the indigenous ontology of self and world. We are confronted with the implicitly revolutionary implications of the teaching of "no separate selfhood" and the indigenous practice of communal selfhood. Many passages are reminiscent of Dorothy Lee's analysis in her classic essay "The Conception of the Self Among the Wintu Indians."[9] Lee presents one of the most illuminating analyses of the contrast between the non-dualistic, integral, yet differentiated Native American indigenous conception of the self and the civilized, domineering, egocentric conception. Her essays explore the ontological and epistemological aspects of selfhood and the ways in which they are related to a reciprocal and nondominating relationship to the world.

Its spirit is conveyed simply and concisely in the words of Lee's respondent Sadie Marsh, who informed Lee that the Wintu word for body was "*kot wintu*," meaning "the whole person." When Lee asked her for her autobiography, she recounted what she called "my story." Lee says that "the first three quarters of this, approximately, are occupied with the lives of her grandfather, her uncle and her mother before her birth; finally, she reaches the point where she was 'that which was in my mother's womb,' and from then on, she speaks of herself, also."[10]

This same spirit of relatedness and transpersonal selfhood is found in the worldview expressed in the testimonies cited by Fitzwater. The Zapatistas are a movement of storytelling par excellence, and when they tell their stories these are always stories that are "our stories." The members of every culture and subculture have a fundamental fantasy, and it is always a collective fantasy. Even when the fantasy is a fantasy of individualism it is still a collective fantasy. There is nothing so boringly monotonous as the self-justifying tales of "rugged individualists" telling how ruggedly individualist they are. The members of some cultures might well be embarrassed if they had to reveal in explicit terms the story of their deepest egocentric and avaricious longings. Others, such as the members of the indigenous cultures of Chiapas, can express their fundamental fantasies openly and joyfully through beautiful and poetic stories celebrating the people and the earth.

And it is not only in words that they are celebrated. "The question of the party" is an inevitable one for radical politics. However, the Zapatista answer to the question might surprise many. When local people explained to Fitzwater that "the party" has been important in nurturing "a sense of collectivity," they were not referring to the leftist vanguardist institution that the Zapatistas abandoned long ago. Rather, they had in mind the fiestas that the indigenous communities understand as central to building and strengthening the Zapatista movement. The celebration in question has subtleties of meaning that are perhaps conveyed better by the English term "festival," which connotes not only a time for collective jubilation but also harks back to ancient rites in which sacred beings, places, and objects are honored. As Fitzwater notes, the members of the community not only "have fun" at Zapatista parties, they also, as the Tsotsil phrase expresses it, make an offering to or have a festival for "the territory/earth/world."

It is a "celebration," both in the sense of a shared experience of joy and in the sense of a tribute to that which is the source of joy. This is one of many important ways in which the Zapatista movement puts the social ethos and the social imaginary at the center of revolutionary transformation. Indigenous people have often understood what few laboring under the yoke of civilization have realized. To paraphrase slightly a famous maxim: "What's a revolution without general celebration?" The radical carnivalesque is one of the most effective catalysts of Landauer's "positive envy" or liberatory desire that will lead masses of people to the free community. Fitzwater notes that "there is a close relationship in Tsotsil between parties or festivals and the bringing of the heart to greatness." Chiapas offers the often missing link between "Carnival against Capitalism" and "Carnival for the Creation of the World." The Zapatista party is a form of deep play, in which the ludic intersects with the political and the ontological.

The Politics of *Poesis*

Autonomy Is in Our Hearts reveals that the Zapatista movement is based on a social ontology that poses fundamental questions about the nature of human social being. Many have looked rightly to the Zapatista revolution as perhaps the most instructive example in the contemporary world of the practice of horizontalist politics. It is important, however, to recognize the *horizonal* dimension of Zapatista *horizontalism*. The movement is deeply revolutionary in large part because it poses *the question of our horizons*. That is, it evokes critical reflection on and rethinking of the boundaries (and the unboundedness) of our social world. It calls on the members of the community (and, ultimately, it calls on all of us) to recognize the natural and, indeed, sacred boundaries that have been transgressed at great cost to both human beings and to all other beings on earth. But further, it urges us to question the artificial, destructive boundaries that have been imposed on the earth's human and non-human inhabitants in the interest of the state, capitalism, and patriarchy. Zapatista horizonalism reminds us of lost and forgotten horizons, while at the same time opening up for us new and transfigurative ones.

The opening up of these horizons is called radical creativity. Fitzwater's account is invaluable for the degree to which it reveals Zapatista political practice to be a creative *politics of poesis*. He notes that the Tsotsil term for "political struggle and revolution" is "*pask'op*," which is "a construction of *pasel*, the verb to do, to make, to create, to produce, and the word *k'op*, a noun meaning word, language, and speech." This conceptualization focuses on the radically creative aspects of political praxis and revolution. Such activities are, above all, the creation of new or renewed, richer, and more compelling meanings. They involve the discovery or rediscovery of a new or renewed logos or expression of the nature of things. One of the great virtues of indigenous cultures is they have so often preserved the transformative and regenerative powers of the word, of speech, and of all forms of non-alienated communal symbolization. This has often been exhibited in the poetic and mythic discourse of Subcomandante Marcos/Galeano, which draws deeply on communal traditions and narratives, and in the celebratory visual arts that are so integral to the Zapatista creation of communal space and place. Such expressions generate a communal social imaginary that pervades and conditions the Zapatista social ethos.

Fitzwater's analysis of how an indigenous language and the values it embodies have contributed to the Zapatista revolution shows how the interaction between traditional culture and institutions and emerging revolutionary and regenerative forces can play a crucial role in liberatory social transformation. He notes that the language he learned "is a particularly Zapatista Tsotsil that is being reflected on through the lens of the Zapatista movement." This is an extremely significant point. Those who taught the language to him, explaining the subtleties of Tsotsil terms and concepts, are participants in a social dialectic between a rich cultural legacy and an ongoing process of creative, revolutionary praxis. Critics of radical indigenism (and other forms of radical communitarianism) reproach it unjustly as a misguided attempt to uncover some perfect, idealized past, or even dismiss it as an absurd quest for an impossible return to that mythical past. Yet the Zapatista experience illustrates strikingly that for self-conscious revolutionaries, it is in large part through the deepest and most intentional exploration of tradition that radical creativity, agency, and autonomy can be unleashed. Like all forms of poesis, such a project is not an impossible effort to regain a lost past but a successful attempt to realize an impossible future.

The Zapatista Critique of Domination

The question of the nature of power is a crucial one for revolutionary politics. If there are to be institutions such as an army, an administrative apparatus, a party, or even a quasi-state apparatus, these must all be subordinated to the self-organized autonomous (self-determining) community. The Zapatista revolution is notable for addressing this issue in relation to an army, just as the Democratic Autonomy Movement in Rojava is significant for broaching it in relation to a party. Both are important for confronting the issue of the quasi-state or proto-state dimensions of federative organization and the ever-present tendencies toward the emergence of more explicitly statist and hierarchical structures.

Since its beginnings, under the influence of indigenous communal egalitarianism, the EZLN has made the critique of hierarchal power central to its revolutionary identity. This has involved an ongoing process of self-criticism. What is extraordinary is that an organization that has had, in effect, a territorial monopoly on the means of coercion could remain resolutely aware of the dangers of its own abuse of power and work actively to check that power. As Fitzwater notes, the EZLN addressed such dangers through the institution of revolutionary laws "creating an explicit separation between these civilian authorities and the armed forces of the EZLN."

For once, the means of coercion were to be at the command of neither capital nor the state bureaucracy but would instead be subordinate to the community organized and mobilized democratically. The function of these means would not be to "command," in the sense of exercising "power over," but rather to "serve" by aiding the community in developing its collective power to flourish and achieve "greatness of heart." In the shift from vanguardist politics to communitarian democracy, a movement consisting (in its beginnings as part of the FLN) of a small cadre of urban mestizo militants was transformed into a large, community-based movement of indigenous people, both female and male, living in many communities and speaking six different languages.

Subcomandante Marcos/Galeano shows the depth of the Zapatista break with all forms of hierarchical power when he states with brutal and compassionate realism that "the military structure of the EZLN in some way 'contaminated' a tradition of democracy and self-government," and "was, so to speak, one of the 'antidemocratic' elements in a relationship of direct communitarian democracy." The EZLN's coming to consciousness of the nature of domination and the corrupting effects of concentrated power can be compared to the primordial political process that we might call *archegenesis*, which Pierre Clastres describes in his classic work of anarchist anthropology, *Society against the State*.[11] Clastres argues that before conquest Amerindian cultures were haunted by the constant threat of the emergence of "the One," that is, the system of hierarchical power and social domination that we now call the state. He shows that these cultures engaged in an ongoing cultural war—an ethotic struggle—against this emergence. The Zapatistas recognize that now, as then, an ongoing battle is necessary to keep this development in check.

The Leader as Servant

Another concept that Clastres shows to be central to the struggle of traditional Amerindian societies against hierarchy and domination is the idea of "the leader as servant." As shown here, this same idea has become fundamental to the Zapatista worldview through the movement's commitment to the guiding precept of "governing by obeying." The precept shapes the Zapatista vision of governing as a form of "good government." According to this outlook, almost all of what we ordinarily think of as "government" (undemocratic, hierarchical, statist, authoritarian, colonialist, technocratic, and bureaucratic government) is judged by the Zapatistas to be "bad government." Zapatista "good government" is reminiscent of Laozi's ancient Daoist concept of "ruling" as a form of *wuwei*, or "acting without acting," meaning nondominating action. Thus, Zapatista "good government" is a kind of "governing without governing."

Fitzwater explains that the Zapatistas see "governance as a particular form of work in service to the community, rather than as the exercise of power through administration or rule." Such governance is nothing like the quest for power and influence and the imposition of a particularistic interest on the community that we see in politics as usual in capitalist and statist society. Fitzwater notes that those who serve the community through positions of responsibility "do not ask the people to elect them and certainly do not run election campaigns." The fact that fines have been imposed for not carrying out official duties indicates that offices are more likely to be looked upon as a burden, albeit a necessary one, than as an opportunity to enjoy the exercise of power or to reap personal benefits.

Positions of leadership are accepted as a *cargo* or charge on behalf of the community. They are a basic responsibility that is fundamental to the democratic functioning of the community and "those who are chosen as authorities by the communities must always obey the agreement of the communities." This process of governing by obeying is a form of "obedience," not in the sense of a subordination to the community but in the form of careful listening to the community, attunement to its needs, and response to those needs. On the deepest level, it is not only a form of service but also a form of awakened or mindful care (close to the Buddhist concept of *appamada*). In fact, Zapatista politics is perhaps the deepest expression of the politics of care in the world today, as this work reveals so eloquently, in the words of those who do the caring.

Despite their heavy emphasis on leadership as a mode of service and care, the Zapatistas remain aware of the danger that "even a group of people who do their work through the strength of their commitment rather than for money could transform into a new form of revolutionary governing elite with disproportionate influence and power." Such a development would reverse all the gains that were made when the ELZN transformed itself from a centralist, hierarchical movement into a horizontalist, participatory movement in service to the community. So significant measures have been taken to avoid hierarchy and concentration of power.

While lengths of terms on decision-making bodies vary from community to community in accord to the principle of respect for diversity, terms are limited and periods of service are rotated, so that leadership functions are widely dispersed among the population, no class of permanent rulers or leaders emerges, and the concentration of power is avoided.

The Zapatistas deep understanding of the dangers inherent in the exercise of power, even in a formal system of grassroots democracy, is also exhibited through the institution of the "comisión de vigilancia." This is an oversight committee that supervises the councils and monitors all expenditures to prevent corruption and abuse of power from creeping in.

The Zapatista Critique of Patriarchy

One of the most revolutionary aspects of the Zapatista struggle against all forms of domination is its rejection of patriarchal authoritarian conceptions of society and social change and its commitment to the liberation of women, equality for women, and full participation by women at all levels of organization and decision-making. This required not only a break with the movement's Eurocentric, hierarchical background but also a radical transformation of existing practice within indigenous communities. Women have a long history not only of being silenced by social pressure but of being subjected to systemic violence. A key element of the struggle for women's equality has been the demand for women not only to be formal members of assemblies but to be active, fully recognized, and respected participants in all democratic processes. Quotas for equality in leadership positions and council membership have gone a long way toward establishing equality, though as Fitzwater points out, progress is still thwarted in practice because of the persistence of "deeply ingrained gender hierarchies."

As important as the formal political structures of assemblies and councils may be, equal participation at this level is not seen by the Zapatistas as the single magic key to the liberation of women. Rather it is only one element of a comprehensive struggle in all areas of society, and advances in this sphere are sometimes dependent on more deeply transformative progress in other spheres in which what is most "deeply ingrained" can be taken on more directly. Fitzwater reports that the great initial step in the process of liberation of women (by women) was their participation not in communal assemblies or councils, but rather in cooperatives. As one respondent remarks, it was there that "women first began to understand that we have rights," in the process of developing a means "to support each other" as they acted "to help the community." This is not surprising, since as long as the legacy of patriarchy persists the assembly has certain inherently masculinist tendencies that are difficult to combat, while a cooperative, especially one that focuses on community subsistence and productive interaction with the earth, has distinctively eco-feminist potentialities that can be developed.

Thus, Fitzwater points out both the far-reaching aspirations of the Zapatistas regarding the equality of women and the failure to attain some goals. There is a rule that half of all council members must be women, but this has not yet been achieved in many, perhaps a majority, of communities.

A proposal to guarantee land rights, including the right of inheritance for women, is part of the Revolutionary Law of Women and has existed for two decades but has still not been ratified. On the other hand, the *trabajos colectivos*, the Zapatista cooperative work projects, have made important advances toward equality by offering women practical control of land through their participation in communal labor. This offers empirical evidence that the movement toward gender equality and justice often proceeds unequally in different social spheres and that the sphere of formal decision-making, though always crucial, is not always the most advanced one in substantive terms.

Beyond Hierarchical Dualisms

The Zapatista political ideal is one that that has long been dreamed of in radical political thought: the withering away of the division between society and the state, so that politics is no longer a mode of domination by any elite, class, sex, or ethnic group. Fitzwater says that the goal of the Zapatistas as "a form of political existence in which there is no separation between the autonomous government and the communities, where everyone participates in governance and is prepared to take a turn in a governing body in the Caracol, the municipality, and the community." This reflects an awareness that social alienation is only in part the result of a separation between the producers and their labor and the products of their labor. It is also the result of the separation between the community and all the products of its communal activity. This is what is addressed in the Zapatista program and the larger social ontological vision that it expresses.

The Zapatistas are undertaking a world-historical and earth-historical project of overcoming the society of separation and domination that was instituted with the beginning of civilization and forms of systemic social domination. It is perhaps only in Chiapas and Rojava today that there is a high degree of consciousness of the manner in which revolutionary political praxis relates to the great developments over geohistory and ethnohistory (the Earth Story and the Human Story), a widespread consciousness of the all-encompassing nature of the society of separation and domination and its underlying hierarchical, dualistic system of values (the Story of Domination), and a pervasive consciousness of the need for a definitive break with that system not only in the sphere of social institutions but also on the level of social ideology, the social imaginary, and, above all, the social ethos (the Story of Freedom).

In Rojava, this consciousness is nurtured by the pervasive influence of Abdullah Öcalan's critique of civilization's five-thousand-year history of domination and alienation and in aspects of traditional Kurdish culture that have resisted the system of domination. In Chiapas, it has even deeper roots in the actually existing communalism of indigenous society and in indigenous peoples' continuing struggle against conquest and imperial domination. Fitzwater cites Subcomandante Marcos/Galeano's recognition of the existence of "self-government" or autonomy in Chiapas long before the coming of the EZLN at "the level of each community." One of the great achievements of the EZLN was to recognize and respect the traditional values and practices that constituted these indigenous roots of autonomy and make them the cultural-material basis for political organization not only at the local level but throughout the regions and zones.

Communal assemblies have a long history in the traditions of indigenous people in Chiapas, as do practices of highly participatory discussion and consensus decision-making. This is a source of the ethical substantiality that makes revolutionary transformation a grounded possibility. To clarify this point, such "ethical substantiality" is "ethical" in the sense that it refers to the "ethos" or historical practice of the community, which is seen as having a deep normative significance. It is "substantial" in that it offers a material basis, and one might say "maternal basis," for the naissance and flourishing of communal autonomy. This process is radically opposed to the model of freedom as an abstract ideal that is imposed on a community as an object of transformation by some liberating agent that has a fundamentally external relation to that community. It is the definitive rejection of all forms of "forcing to be free," no matter how ideologically mystified and leftist these forms may become.

Free Association

The Zapatista political ideal is a society based on voluntary cooperation, with the autonomy and individuality of each person and group protected and expanded through collective action that serves the good of the whole. Fitzwater finds such nondominating unity in diversity embodied in "the single most important commonality in Zapatista autonomous government," the fact that "every community, autonomous municipality, and Caracol does things differently and has the right to do things differently." He illustrates this through examples of diversity in the manner in which the smaller communities organize themselves into municipalities, and municipalities organize themselves at higher levels.

Fitzwater says that "the heart of Zapatista governance is the 'agreement' that is reached between several communities or individuals and that only lasts as long as those communities or individuals remain in agreement." Thus, voluntary agreement or consensus, as opposed to force and coercion, is at the core of all decision-making. The Zapatista goal is consensus at all levels, though they recognize that it cannot always be achieved. What is so striking is that this ideal is made obligatory and is achieved at the federative level, thus realizing in practice the anarchist nonhierarchical ideal. It should be understood that consensus agreement, another term for voluntary association, is the only purely anarchistic form of decision-making, and that divergence from it, if necessary, must still be recognized as a departure from the noncoercive ideal.

The presupposition that either majority rule or consensus will be more effective in all places and at all times is a form of abstract idealism or dogmatism. Consensus processes will be more feasible to the degree that an ethos of voluntary cooperation, mutual aid, and solidarity prevails in a community. To the degree that such a cultural precondition does not exist, majority rule will seem more practical. Western leftists have tended to be skeptical of consensus and to have faith in majority rule, as is to be expected given their experience of living in cultures that do not have a strongly communitarian ethos. Nevertheless, one should not conclude that because consensus does not seem practical in some cultural climates, that it is not an eminently practical possibility, or, indeed, an extensively realized one, in other cultural contexts.

Thus, the existence of a traditional libertarian and communitarian ethos in Chiapas makes possible a degree of consensus that seems utopian to those who take American or generic Western individualism as a cultural norm. Ironically, much of the contemporary (that is post-1960s) left in the United States and some other countries has focused on organizing social strata that are more heavily conditioned to internalize such individualism (albeit in reactive, oppositional ways), while neglecting indigenous, immigrant, and marginalized groups that are more likely to have cultural traditions conducive to cooperative and communal modes of association. There are signs that this tendency is beginning to be reversed, especially as the result of the recognition of indigenous leadership in the water protector and pipeline resistance movements. This may help open the way for the American left and even the global Eurocentric left to learn from the experience of Chiapas and from other communitarian, indigenous-based movements.

The Primacy of the Assembly

The question of the primacy of the communal assembly is an important one for contemporary left libertarian thought, so Fitzwater addresses a key issue when he says that "the assembly is the heart of the Zapatista form of autonomous government." And, indeed, his analysis presents a good case for the validity of this statement. However, he goes on to state that the assemblies and government "must always be aware of the multiple smaller collectives (ko'onkutik) that make up their collective heart (ko'ontik)." So we discover that there is, in addition to the assemblies, another "heart" to the communal social organism. This might seem to be a contradiction, but it is not. Both the unifying processes of the assembly and the differences embodied in small groups and collectives are aspects of the communal "heart." Both must be given adequate recognition and must be allowed to function effectively if a true social unity in diversity is to be achieved.

Fitzwater explains that when the smaller collectives disagree, they are not forced to conform to a kind of artificial "general will" in which differences are submerged or denied. Instead, processes related to the "general heart" come into play. Specifically, the smaller collectives come together in the assembly and engage in a consensus process until an agreement is reached "through mutual recognition and respect (ichbail ta muk')." As has already been mentioned, the voluntary agreement that is "reached between several communities or individuals" can also be looked upon as a third locus of the heart of the Zapatista body politic. The quest for consensus as an expression of communal solidarity must also be associated with the communal heart. And finally (though we know that this account is not exhaustive), a fourth dimension of heart is pointed out. This is the "new form of work" that is understood as *a'mtel*, which is a form of mutual aid and caring labor.

The concept of a'mtel has revolutionary implications that are also found in the materialist ecofeminist concepts of caring labor and the subsistence perspective. Fitzwater shows how the political work of participating in assemblies, serving on councils, and accepting leadership positions are "a form of collective work in service to the collective survival of the community." Thus, "working in a cornfield so that the community can eat and participating in an assembly so that the community can reach an agreement are seen as two manifestations of the same form of 'collective labor for collective survival,'" and "the material work of governance is understood as identical and coequal to physical labor in the fields, emotional labor for rest and relaxation, celebratory labor in preparation for a fiesta, etc."[12] One finds in this concept of a'mtel the basis for a "caring labor theory of value" that challenges not only exploitative capitalist conceptions of exchange value but also instrumentalist patriarchal conceptions of use value that have continued to afflict the dominant left. In the end, one discovers "the greatest wealth for the human being," the community's collective heart and spirit, in all the forms of caring labor through which its members shape communal freedom and solidarity into social realities.

Yet the assembly does, in fact, have a certain kind of qualified primacy in the political system. However, even here there is the important question of what level of assembly decision-making is primary, to the degree that it is primary. Fitzwater says at one point that "the assembly of all the communities of the zone should be the final authority for all decisions of the autonomous government," and that "all new agreements, projects, and governing structures that affect the entire zone must emerge from this assembly." This might lead one to question how such "final authority" on the zonal level can be reconciled with the primacy of the local communities. However, the larger point that Fitzwater is making is that officials at any level have no authority of their own and are bound by the directives of the local assemblies, which are, in fact, structurally primary. If there is a break in consensus at the zonal level, "all the local authorities in the assembly go back to their communities and discuss the problem and come back with proposals until all the communities can agree on how best to solve the problem." Thus, any higher-level (federative) assembly of communities is merely an expression of the will and the solidarity of all the local communities, and its authority is identical with the authority of the social base in these communities.

One of the worst mistakes one could make in regard to Zapatista base democracy would be to transform this subtle and dialectical conception into a new base-superstructure model in which the communal assembly becomes the new material base and other institutions are reduced to mere superstructural expressions of what occurs at that level. In such a problematic, "the forces of decision-making" or, at best, "the forces and relations of decision-making" would occupy the place formerly held by the forces and relations of production. Programmatic politics, including programmatic forms of social ecology or libertarian municipalism, tends to lapse into such reductive base-superstructure thinking (B-S politics). This is precisely the kind of politics that the Zapatistas abandoned when they decided to open themselves up to the wisdom and experience of indigenous cultures. "In the last instance," social determination is deeply dialectical, and the social whole is shaped by the interaction between what goes on in assemblies and councils, in collective labor and cooperative projects, in the language that is spoken, in the rites and rituals that are celebrated, in the symbols and images through which the community imagines itself, and in many other aspects of communal poesis.

So, in the end, we must speak of both the primacy and the nonprimacy of the assembly.

The Restoration of the Commons

Much of the attention that has been given to the Zapatistas focuses rightly on their major achievements in establishing a system of direct democracy and communal autonomy. What is often given less attention is the ways in which the Zapatista revolution has initiated forms of mutual aid and voluntary cooperation with deep and ancient roots in the commons and the gift economy. We might say that these forms contribute as much, or even more, to what we might call the deep structure of democracy. This dimension is manifested perhaps most distinctively through the practice of a'mtel described extensively in the text. As has been mentioned, this term refers to forms of work, or, more precisely, forms of caring labor, that are carried out voluntarily as a cargo, or responsibility, entrusted on behalf of the community or the collective.

In this case, as in so many others, Zapatista communitarian practice finds ethical substantiality through its roots in ancient communal traditions. Democracy in a larger sense is much more than a decision-making process, even one as radical as assembly and council government. It arises as much, or perhaps even more, out of egalitarian, participatory practices that pervade social life. These are not created by any assembly or council but are at most reaffirmed through such bodies, because they have proven their rightness through their contribution over the ages to the community's mode of flourishing or "bringing itself to greatness." The restoration of the commons is part of this process of communal realization. It offers a means of overcoming barriers that seem intractable on the basis of the dominant statist and capitalist forms of decision-making (because they are, in fact, impassable).

An important problem for the Zapatistas has been how to reconcile the autonomy of municipalities with what Fitzwater describes as "an unequal distribution of resources and ultimately an unequal process of development" of these municipalities. The problem of unequal distribution of resources is a classic one for decentralist and horizontalist systems, one that is often used by opponents to discredit these systems. The complexities of this problem are highlighted in relation to the issue of resources stemming from external aid to the Zapatista municipalities. In view of widespread need, the municipalities have looked to NGOs for such assistance. Though this support has benefitted the communities, it has also created significant problems. First, the more advantaged municipalities have received proportionally more aid than the disadvantaged ones, thus exacerbating the existing inequalities. Second, the acceptance of aid, especially to the degree that it means deferring to the priorities of the NGOs, creates a form of dependency that tends to undermine the autonomy of the communities. In Fitzwater's words, the resulting system sometimes "looked more like charity and less like solidarity."

The Zapatistas' response to these problems shows that as challenging as they may be, they are certainly not insoluble for a system that is both deeply libertarian and deeply communitarian. The Zapatista solution to the problem of external aid has been to require that NGOs negotiate aid with authorities at the level of the zone, rather than that of the individual municipalities. The distribution of such resources according to the needs of the individual communities can then be determined by the assemblies of the zones, based on their deliberations and the achievement of consensus among the communities. Through such processes of communal democracy, the Zapatistas are beginning to reestablish the commons and distribution according to need as a means of solving problems of resource inequality. The same principle is applied to the question of communities' unequal endowment with natural resources. If resources are appropriated merely on the basis of physical proximity, this will make the collective labor projects of some communities disproportionally more beneficial than those of other communities, thus creating inequalities. The solution has been to communalize such resources, treating them as a commons at the level of the zone:

> [T]he Good Government Council of Morelia was given control over all the resources from these trabajos colectivos so that they could be distributed equally throughout the zone and create more trabajos colectivos, rather than just being spent on the individual sustenance or development of one community. The zone collectively decided that it was not fair to let a single community reap all the benefits of a very lucrative trabajo colectivo just because they are lucky enough to be located near a beautiful river, gravel mine, or source of salvaged wood.

Another example of the reemergence of mutual aid and the commons comes from the organization of the system of cargos. The communities decided that in order to honor and uphold the spirit of a'mtel political service should always be a voluntary activity. However, the Zapatistas believe that just as those who serve the community were expected to give according to their abilities, they also deserve to be helped by the community according to their needs. Fitzwater observes that "some receive support from their community in work, in staple grains, different forms of support according to how the community comes to agreement." Thus, we see a tendency to introduce the ancient communitarian practice of distribution according to need, a practice that has roots in the gift economy and that has always been typical of indigenous and other traditional communities.

The Community against Empire

The Zapatista attitude toward governmental aid (that is, aid from the "bad government") illustrates the antistatist dimensions of the movement and its vigilance in regard to possible manipulation and co-optation. The movement is highly protective of the freedom and self-determination of local communities and recognizes the fact that dependence on support from the centralized government and state bureaucracies inevitably undermines and destroys communal autonomy. The threat of withdrawal of aid can be used at any time to demand conformity to the alien will of the state and the dominant classes and interests that control it.

Fitzwater shows how the experience of three communities with a major state-sponsored conservation program called ProÁrbol illustrates this danger. According to the glowing words of the program description, it is "a comprehensive programme promoting actions for the conservation, restoration and sustainable use of Mexico's forests" that "works on the premise that sustainable forest management is best achieved by allocating the rights to exploit forest resources to forest owning *ejidos* and communities."[13] However, the reality of the program is like so many tragic stories known by local communities across the globe. In the end, the communities were prevented from cutting trees needed for firewood and construction, while the lumber companies gained control of their woodlands. Moreover, this expropriation of their resources forced the communities to resort to state aid, requiring them to divulge information that was then used to seize their land and displace the local inhabitants.

The Zapatistas have discovered modes of communal self-organization that can resist such deceptions and abuses by the state and by private interests (collectively, the corporate-state apparatus). Fitzwater describes the local alternative that was developed to aid the communities. When citizens in one or more local communities express the need for developmental programs, the Good Government Council meets with local councils and commissions to find out the nature of the need as perceived by the community members themselves. A proposal for a project is then formulated by the local communities. The role of the Good Government Council is to try to find an NGO that will truly fulfill the needs of the communities, to the extent that solutions cannot be found in the community itself or among communities.

Yet, the goal is always to move toward finding all solutions at the level of the autonomous communities and their free associations through mutual aid and solidarity. Fitzwater concludes from his experience in Chiapas that "the center of Zapatista autonomous governance" is "in every Zapatista community." This libertarian and communitarian ideal expresses the radically horizontalist nature of Zapatista politics that also poses the Zapatista challenge to the global political and economic order. Whether locally, regionally, or globally, there will no longer be a powerful "core" and a powerless "periphery." The center is everywhere, in the sacred community and the sacred earth. The Zapatista revolution announces the end of Empire.

•

As this introduction has attempted to show, *Autonomy Is in Our Hearts* presents a wealth of evidence of the ways in which the Zapatista revolution has confronted the most pressing social, political, and even ontological issues of our time and offered hopeful, creative solutions to social, ecological, and spiritual problems that are often met with resignation, denial, and disavowal. This introductory analysis can only hint at the depth and scope of the Zapatista vision and the inspiring creativity with which it has been realized in the lives of people and communities. In the pages that follow, Dylan Fitzwater reveals much more of this depth and scope by allowing the people of Chiapas to tell their own story, largely in their own words and with their own distinctive voice. What they convey through that story is an eloquent and urgent message of justice and liberation of spirit and heart.

Introduction

On December 21, 2012, at the end of the 12th B'ak'tun of the Mayan calendar, the Zapatista Army of National Liberation (Ejercito Zapatista de Liberación Nacional, or EZLN) retook the same cities they had occupied in their 1994 revolution, but this time through the force of organization rather than through the force of arms. Thousands of Zapatistas marched in complete silence into the central squares of the Chiapan municipal centers of San Cristóbal de las Casas, Ocosingo, Las Margaritas, Comitán, and Altamirano. They marched with their faces covered with black balaclavas emblazoned with numbers corresponding to their system of self-organization and autonomous government. The communities of the EZLN filed into each of the central squares and stood in perfect lines as a small group erected a stage. The press prepared for the expected round of speeches by the Clandestine Revolutionary Indigenous Committee (Comité Clandestino Revolucionario Indígena, or CCRI), the military leadership of the EZLN, or perhaps Subcomandante Marcos, the famous masked spokesman of the movement. Instead, every Zapatista from all the different autonomous zones, municipalities, and communities walked across the stage in front of the Zapatista and Mexican flags in silence with raised fists. They then dismantled the stages and marched out of the cities, all in complete silence. On their website *Enlace Zapatista* (Zapatista Link) the CCRI and Subcomandante Marcos published the following communiqué that asked, "Did you listen? It is the sound of your world crumbling. It is the sound of our world resurging."[1]

Silence is the sound of thousands of Zapatistas building a system of autonomous government in the mountains of the Mexican southeast. It is the sound of a world forged through five hundred years of indigenous oppression being broken apart and replaced by a new way of life created through Zapatista self-government. The autonomous government is a system that, in the words of the Zapatistas, "governs by obeying." It is a government that obeys the people not the interests of political and economic elites or the faceless imperatives of global capitalism. The autonomous government provides a means of making decisions that affect the different areas of Zapatista autonomy, such as their collective agricultural projects, their autonomous health and education systems, the autonomous Zapatista radio stations and media collectives, and the autonomous justice system. At the core of the autonomous government are seven guiding principles of "good government" intended to prevent the autonomous authorities from falling into the practices of the "bad government" that currently holds power in Mexico:

1. To serve others not oneself
2. To represent not supplant
3. To build not destroy
4. To obey not command
5. To propose not impose
6. To convince not defeat
7. To go below not above[2]

The principles of governing by obeying imply a form of government where the governing authorities always look "below" to the words of the communities and never "above" toward the accumulation of power. These principles are the heart of the Zapatista struggle. They represent the new world they aspire to create and have tirelessly struggled to build in their own communities throughout the more than thirty-year history of their organization.

The initial seed of the Zapatista organization was the Forces of National Liberation (Fuerzas de Liberación Nacional, or FLN), a Marxist political-military organization that went into the mountains of the Lacandon Jungle in 1983 to organize the EZLN as the peasant wing of their strategy for a national armed uprising.[3] Over the years, this organization was transformed by the Tsotsil, Tzeltal, Chol, Tojolabal, Mam, and Zoque indigenous communities that joined its ranks, and the EZLN eventually severed its ties with the national FLN organization.[4] At the end of ten years of clandestine organizing, the thousands of indigenous EZLN communities throughout the whole state of Chiapas voted to go to war against the Mexican state. On January 1, 1994, the EZLN took five municipal government centers of Chiapas and attacked the main Mexican military positions in the state before withdrawing into the mountains and jungle. Although the Zapatista communities had spent years preparing for an armed revolution, they only spent twelve days in open military confrontation with the Mexican state. Almost as soon as the uprising began, Mexican society rose up in massive popular protests to support the Zapatistas and demand a ceasefire and dialogue with the government. Both sides agreed to a ceasefire on January 12, 1994. This put an end to open military conflict, although the Zapatistas have continued to experience numerous forms of low-intensity military harassment, as well as violence at the hands of government-supported paramilitary groups.[5]

In the course of their revolution the Zapatistas reclaimed and redistributed nearly 250,000 hectares (617,763 acres) of land that had previously made up large farming or ranching estates where generations of the indigenous people of Chiapas had worked in virtual slavery.[6] In the first year after the revolution, the Zapatistas organized themselves into autonomous municipalities, adding newly reclaimed land to existing communities. Since then, the Zapatistas have governed themselves in autonomy from the Mexican state. The Zapatista uprising and the subsequent construction of Zapatista autonomy fundamentally altered the social, political, and economic realities of Chiapas and produced reverberations throughout Mexico and the world. The revolution of 1994 provided the conditions for the continuing struggle to construct a new way of life defined by the self-determination of autonomous government. It provided the initial conditions by reclaiming land from the rich Chiapan landowners and ranchers, and the process of clandestine self-organization provided the foundation of the autonomous government, as well as the schools, health system, and collective agriculture in the Zapatista communities of today.

In 2003, the Zapatistas took a significant step forward in the construction of their autonomy with the inauguration of the five *Caracoles* in the five regions of Zapatista territory, each with its own autonomous Good Government Council. These five Caracoles provided a new level of regional coordination that brought together the autonomous municipalities formed in the first year of the Zapatista uprising. The formation of the Caracoles also sought to redefine the Zapatistas' relationship to the numerous solidarity organizations that arose to support economic development in Zapatista communities by giving the Good Government Councils control over the administration of all projects in the communities. Furthermore, the Caracoles sought to strengthen the Zapatista autonomous health, education, and collective production projects and to coordinate these projects so that they could develop equally in every Zapatista community.

The work of the Caracoles represents the most recent development in the Zapatistas' slow struggle to create autonomous self-government. "Caracol" means snail shell in Spanish and has a multilayered symbolism for the Zapatistas. On the one hand, it literally refers to a snail as a metaphor for the Zapatista description of their struggle as "slow but going forward." On the other hand, according to Subcomandante Marcos, "The caracol is how our peoples call together the collective. When the men are in the cornfields and the women are working, the caracol brings us together to meet in an assembly and thus create a collective. That is why we say that is it 'the call of the collective.'"[7] The caracol represents the silent sound of thousands of Zapatistas organizing themselves to create an autonomous government that governs by obeying.

"This Is Our Work": The Escuelita and the Zapatista Experiences of Autonomous Government

The silent march on December 21, 2012 marked the beginning of a new period in the history of the Zapatista movement in which the Zapatistas extended the silent call of the caracol beyond their territories in Chiapas. Since 2012, the Zapatistas have organized several public initiatives that for the first time shared their experience of autonomous government as an inspiration for anticapitalist movements throughout Mexico and the world. Shortly after the silent march, the Zapatistas organized a new initiative that would bring those of us outside the movement into direct contact with the practice of autonomous government in the Zapatista communities. On February 13, 2013, the Zapatistas announced a new spokesperson for their movement: a Tzeltal man who has participated in the Zapatista military organization for many years named Subcomandante Insurgente Moisés. In his first communiqué written from this new position the following day, Moisés issued an invitation to all those who align themselves with the Zapatista movement's "Sixth Declaration of the Lacandon Jungle" (abbreviated as "*la Sexta*" in Spanish or "the Sixth" in English), which defines their current political analysis and form of struggle:

Now is the time in which we truly make the world that we want, the world that we imagine, the world that we dream. We know how. It is difficult.... But if we don't do it, our future will be even harder and there will never again be freedom.... We are waiting for you here at this door, which it is my turn to watch, to be able to enter into the humble school of my compañer@s who want to share the little we have learned, to see if it will help you there in the places where you work and live. We are sure that those who have already entered into the Sixth will come, or they won't, but as they desire they will enter the *escuelita* (little school), where we will explain what freedom is for the Zapatistas. And in this way they will see our advances and our mistakes, which we will not hide, directly with the best teachers there are, the Zapatista communities.[8]

This invitation took a more concrete form over the next few months. On March 7, 2013, Subcomandante Moisés released a communiqué that announced that the "escuelita" on "freedom according to Zapatismo" would take place from August 1 to August 17, 2013. Those who received an invitation would spend a week in a Zapatista community in one of the five Caracoles where they would learn directly from the people of the community, who, as Moisés emphasized, are the real "leaders" of the Zapatista organization. Moisés also made clear that this week would only be the first grade of the Zapatista escuelita, and that those who completed it could go on to the next levels that would be organized in the future. There were three rounds of the first grade of the escuelita, one in August 2013, another in December 2013, and a final round in January 2014. I was invited and attended the final round of the first grade in January 2014.

This would be my second visit to Zapatista territory. I had first encountered the Zapatistas on a field course through Hampshire College in June 2013 that brought students to the language school in the Zapatista Caracol of Oventik. The school teaches Spanish and Tsotsil, and all proceeds from tuition go toward financing Oventik's autonomous secondary school. While I was there with the cohort of students from Hampshire College, the Zapatistas were in the process of organizing the escuelita. Throughout our time spent in the Caracol, the big assembly hall was filled, seemingly at all hours of the days and night, with hundreds of Zapatistas discussing the organization of the escuelita in Tsotsil and Tzeltal. Although we were not able to listen in on any of the assemblies, after seeing the incredible organizational effort involved in the escuelita I can imagine that a large part of those discussions involved how to bring over two thousand students from all over the world and place each of them in different Zapatista communities in the five Caracoles, as well how to connect with thousands of collectives all over the world that would attend the escuelita via video conference.[9]

On January 1, 2014, I arrived at the University of the Earth (also known as The Indigenous Center for Integral Training, or CIDECI), the Indigenous University that provides their space in San Cristóbal de Las Casas for Zapatista initiatives. Throughout the day, each of the thousands of students were assigned to one of the five Caracoles, given four textbooks and two instructional DVDs, and loaded into the back of a pickup truck or small bus emblazoned with banners proclaiming that they were transporting students of the Zapatista escuelita. After several hours in the back of one of the pickups, I arrived in Caracol IV Morelia. As soon as students arrived in their respective Caracol, each one was assigned an individual Zapatista "guardian" who would accompany us throughout the escuelita and act as our teacher, translate between Spanish and the indigenous languages of Zapatismo, and watch over our safety and security. I arrived in Morelia late at night and spent the following morning packed into the assembly hall with all the other students and guardians listening to a panel of more than twenty Zapatista teachers describe the various processes and systems of Zapatista autonomy in their Caracol.

We did not stay in this classroom for long, because, as Subcomandante Moisés said, the real teachers in the escuelita were to be the Zapatista communities. Although they are all near Zapatista communities, the Caracoles themselves are primarily spaces for assemblies and coordination whose only residents are the autonomous authorities currently serving in positions related to the work of the Good Government Councils. After the teachers finished their speeches, all the students and their guardians again piled into the backs of pickup trucks and left for their individual communities within the zone of Caracol IV Morelia. After a five- to six-hour car ride and a forty-five-minute hike up the mountain, I arrived in the Zapatista community of Nueva Esperanza with my guardian, another student from Guatemala, and her young daughter.

My three days in this community were occupied by three primary activities: harvesting corn and beans from the community's collective fields, studying the textbooks in the afternoons with my guardian while

6

the autonomous radio blared out its programing in Spanish and Tzeltal, the language in that area of Morelia, and receiving explanations of the community's collective projects in health, education, and agriculture. The core lesson of the escuelita was the practice of autonomy. The corn and beans we harvested were planted on land reclaimed in the 1994 revolution, and the whole valley as far as the eye could see in any direction was once part of a single estate where the Tzeltal communities worked as peons with little or no land of their own. I saw that even in this tiny community made up of only two families, there was an autonomous school as well as basic herbal medicines and antibiotics received through the autonomous health system.

Throughout my time in Nueva Esperanza, whenever we would finish with our labor in the fields or our time spent discussing the textbooks, my guardian would turn to me and say, "This is our work." For me, this simple statement was the fundamental lesson of the escuelita. The experience of the escuelita frames the Zapatistas, and in particular the Zapatista base communities, not as objects of study but as teachers. The escuelita rearticulated the relationship between the Zapatista movement and the adherents to the Sixth in Mexico and the world who align ourselves with their movement and form of politics. It defined this politics as a politics of listening. And what were we expected to listen to? To the thousands of diverse Zapatista voices proclaiming in their seven different languages: "This is our work." The four escuelita textbooks—titled *Autonomous Government I*, *Autonomous Government II*, *The Participation of Women in Autonomous Government*, and *Autonomous Resistance*—describe the ongoing process of autonomous self-government that created the new way of life I witnessed in Nueva Esperanza. However, these books do not describe a set model of governance. There are no lists of policies or decision-making flowcharts. Instead, there are only the seven principles of governing by obeying and scores of testimonies from various current and former authorities in the autonomous government that give examples of how these principles are practiced in their communities. They are a collection of multiple voices that describe the diverse forms of painstaking work that bring Zapatista autonomy from imagination to reality.

This book presents my analysis of these testimonies and my own reflection on my experience of the practices of Zapatista autonomous government. I have been back to Chiapas on several other occasions: to attend other Zapatista public initiatives, as a human rights observer, and to study Tsotsil at the language school in Caracol II Oventik. And in August of 2015, I went on to attend the second grade of the escuelita that consisted of an online video with over three hours of testimony from Zapatista elders describing their process of clandestine organizing before the 1994 revolution. All these experiences have contributed to my understanding of what my guardian meant by "our work," as well as my interpretation of the complex descriptions of this collective work in the escuelita textbooks.

The organization of the escuelita was a gift, a complex lesson given to those of us outside the Zapatista organization, but it implies a responsibility: to share this lesson and reflect on it in our own contexts. As Wilbur and Lorena from Caracol I La Realidad said in the Zapatista's collective evaluation of the escuelita students published in their magazine *Rebeldía Zapatista*, "Thanks to those who came here. They got to know us, and so our message can be passed on, the knowledge can go on to everyone else who didn't come to hear our message." With the organization of the escuelita, the Zapatistas opened a small door into their practice of self-organization and autonomous government. This book is my attempt to pass on my knowledge of these practices.

The Study of Social Movements in Tsotsil: Pask'op
While my understanding of the practice of Zapatista organization has come through my experience in the Zapatista escuelita, my way of thinking about these practices has been profoundly shaped by my experience as a student in another Zapatista initiative: the language school in Caracol II Oventik. I first studied Spanish at this school in the summer of 2013 during my first visit to Chiapas and returned to study Tsotsil in the summer of 2015. I took my second classes directly with two of the Zapatista education promoters I had studied with previously,[10] since I couldn't make it to Chiapas while the Oventik language school was in session. During my initial Spanish classes I was introduced to several central Tsotsil political concepts, and these concepts were greatly expanded upon in my subsequent Tsotsil lessons. These concepts are the lens through which the Zapatista education promoters bring students to a deeper understanding of their struggle, which serves to reflect not only the concrete practices of their autonomy but also their own ways of thinking and understanding these processes in one of the indigenous languages of the movement. Tsotsil is predominantly spoken in the zone of Caracol II Oventik, although there are also speakers who have migrated from this region throughout Zapatista territory.

My Tsotsil lessons with the Zapatista education promoters of Oventik have left me with a grasp of several key concepts that I believe are very useful for understanding the politics of Zapatismo. These linguistic concepts represent a collective form of understanding and naming the reality experienced by the Tsotsil Zapatista communities. Certain words in Tsotsil provide a more precise and nuanced way of describing many aspects of Zapatismo than do common English political categories, even those that are often applied to the Zapatistas, such as "democracy" or "autonomy." This is both because many Zapatistas speak Tsotsil, and because the Tsotsil that they speak, and which they taught me, is a particularly Zapatista Tsotsil that is interpreted through the lens of the Zapatista movement. For example, the first time I learned some Tsotsil at the Zapatista language school in Caracol II Oventik, a Zapatista education promoter taught me one of the central concepts used in this book: "*Ich'el ta mu'k*," which literally means "to carry oneself to greatness" but has the connotation of recognizing and respecting everything that is, both in the human community and the natural world. For the Zapatistas it describes a process that is inherently opposed to capitalism. Three years later when I could go back to study again, the same promoter taught me the phrase as "*Ichbail ta muk*," which is changed by the addition of the suffix "*-ba*," which marks reciprocity and specifies that the activity is done by a concrete collective in the world. The promoter's understanding of the Tsotsil concept had changed from a more abstract idea of universal respect to one emphasizing a concrete practice of respect through self-organization. The Tsotsil political concepts taught by the education promoters of Caracol II Oventik do not represent some timeless or unchanging indigenous wisdom, rather they are contemporary political concepts shaped by Tsotsil people's reflections on their participation in the everyday struggles of building Zapatista autonomy.

The Tsotsil Zapatistas of Oventik, just like any other human community, express their ideas in a particular language. Tsotsil reflects a certain ordering of the world in which political ideas come into being and gain meaning. As Carlos Lenkersdorf argues in *Los hombres verdaderos*, which takes a similar approach to understanding culture and politics in Zapatista territory through the medium of the Tojolabal language, "[W]e think that in every language the speakers reveal their way of being, thinking and acting. In general, they do so without realizing it."[11] Languages, and in particular non-European languages, provide a means of understanding a culture and politics very different from those of the West. However, although the structure and vocabulary of a language is a constant, there is never one "inherent" politics or worldview to a language. My interpretation of Tsotsil is not intended as a claim to an inherent meaning or politics of the language itself. Rather, it is an attempt to share the understanding of Zapatismo taught to me by the education promoters of Oventik, an understanding that focuses on several Tsotsil concepts at the core of their understanding of Zapatismo that have no straightforward translation in English or Spanish. Understanding the practice of Zapatista autonomy is an exercise in translations that never quite fit within the various political categories of Western thought. As Subcomandante Marcos puts it, "Our banners are painfully elaborate, struggling to find equivalents for what we in our languages describe in just one word, and what in other languages requires three volumes of *Capital*."[12] This book engages in this same struggle of translation: to convey a politics and worldview that in Tsotsil-speaking Zapatista communities could be meaningfully summed up in a handful of sentences.

The first relevant aspect of the different ordering of the world implied by Zapatista Tsotsil has to do with the approach to understanding, evaluating, and writing about a social movement, particularly the Zapatista social movement. The message of the December 21 mobilization and the escuelita was that practice itself speaks. In the Tsotsil language the word for political struggle and revolution is *pask'op*: a construction of *pasel*, the verb to do, to make, to create, to produce, and the word *k'op*, a noun meaning word, language, and speech. In Tsotsil, to struggle is to create the word, to make it reality, and to speak by doing. This word has a very different connotation than the word "struggle" or "revolution" in English and "lucha" or "revolución" in Spanish. These two words have a connotation of a confrontation between two or more opposed sides with the goal of attaining some form of power, though exactly how that power is attained—through arms, mass mobilization, electoral politics—and where exactly it resides—in the institutions of the state, in civil society, at the local level, in networks of different peoples—is a subject of constant debate. Furthermore, the evaluation of this form of struggle is often in terms of "success" or "failure," even if the criteria of these two terms is based on the "sustainability" of the struggle or its ability to grow and perpetuate itself as a movement, rather than on the definitive seizure of state institutions.

However, these are not the connotations of *pask'op*. A struggle whose meaning is to make the word has a whole different logic, different forms, and different debates, many of which are strikingly apparent in the Zapatista struggle. When "pask'op" is translated into English or Spanish, it can appear as if it has a triple meaning: first to speak by creating or doing, second to create something in the world by speaking, and third to do what you say you will do or to be true to your word in your actions. This triple meaning is a result of the awkward transformation of a single word into three phrases, in the single word "pask'op" these multiple aspects are one and the same. December 21, 2012 and the escuelita were to a certain extent attempts to reconfigure the terms of the debate surrounding the "success" or "failure" of the Zapatista struggle in terms of pask'op, of a struggle that is defined as the single process of creating the word and speaking by creating, rather than one that is evaluated through ideas of "success" or "failure." These initiatives define the Zapatista struggle in terms of the process of making the word inherent in the Zapatista process of self-organization. They focus on the world that has been created since the beginning of the organization in the secrecy of the mountains in the early 1980s. This world began as words, as hopes and dreams spoken in clandestinity, and then publicly proclaimed in 1994. These aspirations have slowly passed from words into the concrete practices of organization that exist in the Zapatista communities of today.

This book traces the history and contemporary practices of the Zapatista pask'op. In Part One, I begin by laying out the history of the Zapatsta movement in terms of pask'op, in other words in terms of the words that crystallized their aspirations and then the practices of organization that brought these words into reality. Chapter One focuses on the beginnings of the Zapatistas' aspirations with the transformation of the original FLN into an organization led by the indigenous communities. The differences between the FLN statutes of 1980 and the EZLN's Revolutionary Laws published in 1994 show that the aspirations of the organization changed from the seizure of state power and redistribution of national resources to a focus on local autonomy and self-determination. In Chapter Two, I frame this transformation using the Tsotsil understanding of the creation of collectivity as the expansion and organization of the collective o'on and ch'ulel, which roughly translate as collective heart and potentiality. I then go on to describe the process of Zapatista clandestine organization detailed in the second grade of the escuelita in terms of the creation of this collective heart and potentiality. Chapter Three traces the history from the revolution of 1994 to the creation of the Caracoles.

I lay out the concrete difficulties faced by the Zapatista organization in the practical implementation of their aspirations for autonomous self-determination. I frame the organizational mechanisms developed to overcome these difficulties in terms of the Tsotsil understanding of difference within the collective heart exemplified by the two forms of the first-person plural in Tsotsil, the "inclusive" and "exclusive" we.

In Part Two, I draw on the written materials from the first grade of the escuelita, as well as my own experience, to analyze the contemporary practice of Zapatista autonomous self-government. In Chapter Four, I introduce the Tsotsil concept of *a'mtel*, or collective work for the community, and frame the two main aspects of the work of autonomous government, democratic decision-making and the administration of justice, in terms of this concept. In Chapter Five, I contrast a'mtel to the Tsotsil word for paid or exploitative work, *kanal*, to clarify the importance of the Zapatistas' collective organization of work as a process of decolonization and constructing a new way of life. Finally, in Chapter Six, I lay out the various challenges faced by the Zapatista autonomous government system and the structures that the five Caracoles have created to address them. In particular, I discuss the challenges of creating accountability, preventing the formation of political elites, and the barriers to women's participation in autonomous government. Throughout this book, my goal is to understand the intertwined process of political aspirations and the concrete organizational practices that propel the Zapatista struggle, or pask'op, down the path of autonomy.

PART ONE
The History of Autonomous Government

CHAPTER ONE

A Genealogy of Zapatista Political Aspirations: From the Dictatorship of the Proletariat to the Self-Determination of Peoples in Struggle

Subcomandante Moisés and Subcomandante Galeano[1] announced the second grade of "freedom according to the Zapatistas" for early August 2015.[2] Admission would only be for those students who received a good evaluation from their guardians during the first grade. In July, they clarified that second grade would consist of a video and that the final test would be six questions, because "As is our Zapatista way, [the questions] are more important than the answers."[3] While the heart of the first grade of the escuelita was the contemporary organization of dignified life in the Zapatista communities, the heart of second grade was the story of the beginnings of this organization before January 1, 1994. If the first grade was the experience of Zapatista organization, the second grade describes the process of beginning to create this organization. Instead of asking, "What is the practice of our organization?" it asks, "What was our way of organizing ourselves?"

The video consisted of over three hours of testimonies from elder *responsables*[4] from all five zones of Zapatista territory who have been with the organization since its beginnings in the early 1980s. They described how they joined the organization, their responsibilities in the organization, and how these responsibilities facilitated the growth of the organization. However, perhaps even more important than what they said was why they said it. At the end of most of the testimonies, the responsable would close by expressing his or her hope that maybe his or her word could serve the compañeros and compañeras of the Sixth in organizing themselves in their own calendars and geographies. Francisco from the zone of Caracol V Roberto Barrios said:

> We invite you students of the national and international Sixth, we invite you to pay close attention. Take this seed, put it in practice, and soon you will be as we are today.[5]

Evider from the zone of Caracol I La Realidad said:

> You should be under no obligation. You yourselves should decide whether to do as we did. Wherever you are, you can see if this helps you or not there, the way in which we did the work and continue doing it.[6]

Daniel from the zone of Caracol II Oventik said:

> You can learn to inspire, to organize in your communities, in your neighborhoods, in your municipalities, wherever they are in your country.[7]

Estel from the zone of Caracol III La Garrucha said:

> Why don't we [women] govern? It's the men, the men silence us. . . . I am not afraid of these men, because the most important thing is the struggle. I give thanks that we are here now, I give thanks that your eyes can see us, I give thanks to the compañeros of the Comandancia [CCRI], and I hope that the whole world will do this as well, compañeros, because it is important. Why? Because women are important, even the young girls who make demands as well, even the children. These are my few words.[8]

Bernabe from the zone of Caracol IV Morelia said:

> Hopefully you of the Sixth will take up the example of how we started in the organization. I am very happy because now we have advanced very far in the organization.[9]

The responsables described how the EZLN came to be, but these closing words show that the proposal of second grade is not a history lesson concerning a past that is meant to remain in the past, it is a proposal for the present and the future: it proposes that others listen to the Zapatista way of organizing, and it offers the hope that by listening others can build their own forms of organization and, ultimately, their own forms of dignified life.

However, listening is not the same as following a blueprint. The Zapatista form of organizing is a "seed," in the words of Francisco; a "way," in the words of Evider; a "hope," in the words of Estel; an "example," in the words of Bernabe. What do these four choices of description say about the nature of the Zapatista form of organizing? First, they say that it is a certain "way," a logic and method that is particular to its own way of doing things that is different from other forms of organizing. Second, they say that it is just one "example" of this form, that it is a way of organizing that arises from a particular context, but that this particularity does not foreclose the ability of others to take up the Zapatista example as inspiration in their own contexts. Third, they say that this example of a form of organizing is a "seed," and when it is taken up and planted in a different place what grows will be similar in form, yet will have its own path of growth, its own branches, its own flowers and fruits. And fourth, it is a "hope" that this seed will undermine the gendered oppression within the community that plants it. Thus, there are four central questions that can guide a reflection on the second grade of the Zapatista escuelita and the Zapatista way of organizing more generally: What is its form and how is this form different than other ways of organizing? What is the social and historical context that shapes the particular example of this form? How was it intertwined with women's liberation in this context? Lastly, how might this form be planted and nurtured as a seed in different contexts?

To understand how the Zapatista form of organizing is different, we have to understand the forms of organizing that it is different from. Although there are as many forms of organizing as there are peoples who struggle for a dignified life, there are certain forms that have particular resonance in different historical moments. In the context of Latin America, many of the most important struggles in the second half of the twentieth century looked to the forms of revolutionary organization promulgated by the successful Cuban Revolution of 1959. The example of Cuba was an important inspiration for the Forces of National Liberation, the Marxist political-military organization that first organized the EZLN in the Lacandon Jungle of Chiapas. However, the EZLN that emerged on January 1, 1994 was organized in a different way and with different aspirations than the original FLN.

The FLN was founded by nine members of the Ejercito Insurgente Mexicano (Mexican Insurgent Army, EIM), which operated very briefly in Chiapas in 1968–1969. The FLN first created a guerrilla nucleus in Chiapas in 1972, inspired by the ideology of focoism promulgated by the Cuban revolution. Focoism held that the presence of an armed guerrilla cadre, no matter how small, could radicalize the exploited rural population and inspire them to take up arms. However, the FLN's first guerrilla nucleus neither developed broad connections with the local Tzeltal and Lacandon populations nor pushed them into armed revolt. It was discovered and destroyed by the Mexican military with the aid of the local indigenous peoples in 1974 after a raid of two urban safe houses in Monterrey and Nepantla revealed the location of the guerrilla encampment.

After this severe repression, which saw many FLN members killed or imprisoned, the organization created a safe house in San Cristóbal de Las Casas in 1978 with the goal of developing more extensive connections among the indigenous population and reorganized in 1980 under a new set of guiding principles in the Statutes of the Forces of National Liberation. In this period the organization was more inspired by the recent triumph of the 1979 Sandinista Revolution in Nicaragua and adopted their more long-range view of guerrilla warfare based in prolonged struggle from organized base communities. In the early 1980s, the FLN established connections with members of the Ejido Lazaro Cardenas in northern Chiapas, which had been very active in land reclamation struggles, and trained several young people from the ejido in the San Cristóbal safe house. In 1983, they sent six members, three mestizo and three indigenous, to begin creating a rural clandestine organization that would create the organized base communities necessary for prolonged guerrilla struggle. With this move they began to grow significantly as an organization beginning in the Lacandon Jungle and Canyons region but eventually spreading throughout most of the eastern half of Chiapas. In 1993, with the organization of the Clandestine Revolutionary Indigenous Committee (CCRI) and the declaration of war, the EZLN definitively broke its remaining ties to the FLN national leadership, abandoned the FLN statutes, and approved the ten Revolutionary Laws that still hold power in the Zapatista communities of today.[10]

Thus, the differences that might reveal the particular form of the Zapatista way of organizing can be found in the history of the organization itself, in this process of change from 1983 to 1994, and in particular by comparing the aspirations implied by the 1980 Statutes of the Forces of National Liberation and the EZLN's ten Revolutionary Laws, which were approved by all the Zapatista communities on the eve of their uprising. While this comparison is necessary in order to begin to tease out the particular Zapatista form of organizing and political imagination, it is ultimately only the first step toward a deeper question: How and why did this change from the FLN to the EZLN occur? What were the particular aspects of the clandestine organization of the EZLN in the mountains of the Mexican southeast that brought about this change? However, these questions can only be answered by first understanding the particularities of the differences between the statutes of the FLN and the Revolutionary Laws of the EZLN—in other words, through an understanding of the particularities of the Zapatista form of liberation.

The Zapatista Form of Liberation

Both the statutes of the FLN and the Revolutionary Laws of the EZLN have the same basic goal of describing the processes of governance that give form to an armed organization as it struggles for national liberation. Both define the decision-making processes of the organization as well as the forms of governance that will be instituted in territory liberated by the organization in the course of the armed struggle. However, the similarities stop there. Each document outlines a fundamentally different form of decision-making and governance. Both express the desire to redistribute land and institute a system of fair wages, to create equality, justice, and dignity; however, they each describe entirely different processes for instituting these aspirations and entirely different actors who would have the power to decide what is fair, what is just, and what is equal.

In the case of the FLN, article six of the statutes, titled "long-range goals," outlines the forms of governance that will be instituted through the triumph of the revolution. Point A of this article states that the first goal of the FLN is to "defeat the bourgeoisie politically and militarily in order to liberate definitively our country from imperialist domination." Points B through D outline the form of governance that would be instituted to replace the old system of domination. The goals of the FLN after the triumph of the revolutionary armed forces are:

a) To install a socialist system that, through social ownership of the means of production, will suppress the exploitation of the workers and distribute among the population the wealth that it creates, according to the principle, "from each according to his ability, to each according to his needs," transferring land to the peasants and factories to the workers.

b) To integrate a popular government with representatives of the revolutionary organizations that have participated in an

outstanding and intransigent way on the various fronts of struggle (military, political, ideological) against the governing oppres-
sor, in order to exercise the dictatorship of the proletariat, so
establishing a workers' state, which will attend to the interests
of the majority of the population, and in which work will be
obligatory.

c) To form a single political party based on the principles of
Marxism-Leninism.[11]

The final point E of Article Six lists the resources that will be expropri-
ated by the workers' state, including big factories and agricultural estates,
credit institutions, means of communication and transportation, private
schools, hospitals, recreational facilities, and large private residences. It
also calls for the abolition of the army and obligatory military service, to be
replaced by the formation of a "People's Army" and closes with the general
promise to expropriate "the bourgeoisie's goods for the full benefit of the
people" and "to stop the plunder of our wealth in natural resources."[12]

This list of long-term goals should be familiar to anyone with a basic
knowledge of the Cuban Revolution or with other similar Latin American
guerrilla movements. The overarching assumption of these goals is that
the agent of postrevolutionary change is a centralized socialist state
organized into a single unified party made up of the triumphant forces of
the revolution.[13] A central state power carries out all the concrete actions
of postrevolutionary change, such as the expropriation of lands and factories, the creation of fair working conditions, and the obligation to work.
The revolutionary state is vested with the responsibility for the creation
of justice and equality and the power to ensure the realization of this
responsibility. The aspirations of good governance in the FLN statutes
follow a model in which the desires of the people are submitted to the revolutionary state, which is conceived as their single legitimate representa-
tive and as the embodiment of their collective revolutionary achievement.
In turn, the revolutionary state enacts the desires of the people for redistribution of resources and the means of production, which are seen as the
material conditions for a dignified life. The statutes of the FLN lay out a
future form of good government organized like the spokes of a wheel: the
desires of all the different peoples and places of the nation radiate toward
a central axle whose rotation is the motor force that moves them all down
the road toward justice, equality, and a dignified life. It is a vision in which

the peoples and places of the nation have the freedom to fully and equally make use of the means of production but do not directly participate in the process of administering their redistribution nor the process of governance over these means of production. This implicit model of power in the revolutionary form of good governance would be fundamentally altered in the Revolutionary Laws of the EZLN.

The Revolutionary Laws were first published in early January 1994 in the EZLN's underground newspaper in Mexico City, *The Mexican Alarm Clock*, after being approved by all the Zapatista communities in March 1993 as part of the collective decision to go to war.[14] However, many of their tenets arose from practices that were already clandestinely in place in the organized Zapatista communities. The Revolutionary Laws lay out many of the same material aspirations as the FLN statutes regarding redistribution of land and the means of production. The Revolutionary Laws are much more specific and concrete regarding agrarian reform, prohibiting individual ownership of good-quality land exceeding 50 hectares (nearly 125 acres) and poor-quality land exceeding 100 hectares (nearly 250 acres). However, the most striking difference is the process for implementing and administering these reforms and expropriations. According to the Revolutionary Laws, all forms of administration and governance must be carried out solely by democratically elected civilian authorities specific to each population. This form of administration is indicative of a unifying theme consistent throughout all ten of the Revolutionary Laws: the source of authority for all significant economic and political decisions are democratically elected civilian authorities specific to each of the places and peoples in struggle. There is no law defining a national revolutionary government,[15] and the military power of the EZLN is explicitly forbidden from having any influence on civilian authority.

This civilian authority is described in the Law of Rights and Obligations of the Peoples in Struggle. According to this document all the peoples in struggle, regardless of political affiliation, religion, or race, are guaranteed the following rights:

a) To elect, freely and democratically, their own authorities in whatever way they consider to be best and to demand that they are respected.

b) To demand that the revolutionary armed forces not intervene in matters of civilian authority or in the expropriation of agricultural, commercial, financial, and industrial capital, which is *the exclusive power of the freely and democratically elected civilian authorities.*[16]

The heart of revolutionary authority and governance is the "free and democratic" election of civilian authorities with final authority over each place and people liberated by the revolutionary armed forces. These authorities have the "exclusive power" to carry out expropriations of land and other forms of capital, as well as the right to levy war taxes in their territories.[17] They have final authority in administering the fundamental economic aspirations of the revolution, namely expropriation of land and resources that enact redistribution and ultimately begin to build a more equal society. And this is just one of the broadest economic powers vested in these civilian authorities. According to the Law of Urban Reform: "The civilian authorities will name neighborhood committees that decide on requests [for housing] and distribute rights to housing according to necessity and available resources." Additionally, the civilian authorities along with "workers, residents, employers, [and] merchants" are given the power to form a "local commission of prices and salaries" with the power to determine the prices of basic products, set wages for Mexican businesses,[18] determine how much they will increase each month, and mandate that all retired persons receive a pension equal to the minimum wage set by the local commission.[19] The local civilian authorities control all basic aspects of economic life. They have authority over taxes, expropriation and redistribution of land, housing, and the means of production, and have the power to determine wages and prices.

The Struggle for National Liberation

Does the EZLN's rejection of forming a national government mean that they do not aspire to a struggle for collective liberation throughout all of Mexico? Not at all. In the "First Declaration of the Lacandon Jungle" they not only explicitly position themselves as the inheritors of five hundred years of indigenous struggle, the independence struggle of 1810, and the Mexican Revolution of 1910 but also legitimize their struggle by referencing article thirty-nine of the Mexican constitution, which states, "National sovereignty resides essentially and originally in the people. All public power arises from the people and is instituted for their benefit. The people have, at all times, the inalienable right to alter or modify their form of government."[20] Furthermore, when the government attempted to eliminate national issues from the agenda of the first peace dialogue, the EZLN constantly insisted on their rights as Mexicans to make demands affecting the entire nation and that they struggle for all Mexicans not just for the peoples of Chiapas.[21] They sing the Mexican national anthem and salute the Mexican flag at all of their public events. Their actions speak to a strong sense of collective Mexican identity and the aspiration to liberate all peoples who find themselves within the territory tied to this identity.

However, their interpretation of the nation comes from their understanding of the true spirit of article thirty-nine of the Mexican constitution, and from their belief that the diverse multiplicity of the Mexican people has the right to decide how they are governed at all times. It is a nationalism without an absolute national authority and a collective national identity that does not seek to prescribe the ways of life of the peoples and places that compose it. The first explicit mention of the formation of a national government by the EZLN comes as a result of their interactions with Mexican civil society during the first peace dialogues in late February 1994. Subcomandante Marcos first publicly addressed the issue of national government on behalf of the EZLN in a press conference the day after the initiation of the first peace dialogues in the cathedral of San Cristóbal de las Casas:

> During an interview of almost two hours the delegates of the EZLN who attended the Conferences for Peace and Reconciliation, especially Subcomandante Marcos, responded to twenty reporters representing various local, national, and international radio stations. There, Marcos spoke to the issue of national democratization.... He observed, "We do not have the moral authority nor the strength to say to the nation: this is the Mexico we want. There are others that do. We say to them: take us into account so it will not be necessary for us to once again kill and die so that we can be heard." ... Concretely, Marcos, almost yelling at reporters, said, "The issue of national democracy goes beyond the dialogue table of San Cristóbal, because then the country will say to us, 'Who named you as my spokesperson?' For this to happen there must be a larger movement ... and in order to create a democracy, the dialogue table must be bigger, encompassing the whole country."[22]

The EZLN never placed their hope for the creation of a national democratic government in the triumph of their struggle or in any single organization or group. They placed this hope in "the whole country," and especially in the multiple representatives of different places and peoples that make up civil society organizations and that might begin to articulate some form of collective decision-making. This proposal was made explicit in the "Second Declaration of the Lacandon Jungle," which calls on all independent political parties to form a transitional government and invites civil society to a "National Dialogue for Democracy, Freedom, and Justice for all Mexicans." This understanding of a transition to national democracy is consistent with the logic of the Revolutionary Laws: any sense of national collectivity and governance on a national level must arise through the coming together, dialogue, and mutual agreement of organized authorities from all the peoples and places of Mexico. The organized authorities of each locale, or their approximation in civil society organizations representing or at least arising from diverse peoples and places, are understood as the ultimate source of authority.

The Revolution Within the Revolution: Zapatista Women's Struggle

These aspirations might at first seem to point to an idealization of local decision-making or the naive assumption that anything local is by definition socially unified and harmonious. However, any such idealization could not survive the internal contradiction within Zapatista communities that produced what Subcomandante Marcos has called the "first uprising of the EZLN" in March 1993 during the process of approving the Revolutionary Laws and, in particular, during the passage of the Revolutionary Law of Women. In a letter to the newspaper *La Jornada* dated January 26, 1994, Subcomandante Marcos writes:

> [I]n March 1993, the compañeros debated what would later be the Revolutionary Laws. [Comandanta] Susana had been in charge of going around to dozens of communities to speak with groups of women and put together the Women's Law from their thoughts. When the CCRI got together to vote on the laws, each one of the commissions got up: Justice, Agrarian Reform, War Taxes, Rights and Obligations of the Peoples in Struggle, and Women. Susana had to read the proposals that she had gathered from the ideas of thousands of indigenous women. She started to read and, as she read on, the

assembly of the CCRI became more and more restless. You could hear rumors and comments. In Chol, Tzeltal, Tsotsil, Tojolabal, Mam, Zoque, and "Castillian," the comments jumped from one side to the other. Susana, undisturbed, kept charging forward against everything and everyone: "We don't want to be forced into marriage with someone we don't want. We want to have the number of children we want and can care for. We want to hold positions of authority in the community. We want the right to speak up and for our opinions to be respected. We want the right to study and even be drivers." And she kept going until she was done. At the end there was a weighty silence. The Women's Laws that Susana had just read meant a true revolution for the indigenous communities. The women authorities were still receiving the translation in their languages of what Susana had said. The men looked at each other, nervous, restless. All of a sudden almost at the same time, the translators finished, and in a single moment, the women authorities began to applaud and talk among themselves. Needless to say, the Women's Laws were approved unanimously. One of the Tzeltal men commented, "The good thing is that my wife doesn't understand Spanish, because otherwise…" A Tsotsil woman insurgent with the infantry rank of major interrupted him: "You're screwed, because we're going to translate it into all of the languages." The compañero lowered his eyes. The women authorities were singing, the men were scratching their heads. I, prudently, called a recess…. The EZLN's first uprising was March 1993 and was led by Zapatista women. There were no casualties, and they won.[23]

The internal revolution in the Zapatista organization asserted women's rights to participate in the process of creating and electing local democratic authorities and to be elected as local authorities,[24] to reach the highest ranks of the military and organizational structures of the EZLN,[25] and to participate in the struggle and possess all the rights outlined in the Revolutionary Laws.[26] Furthermore, it also sought to address the gendered structures of oppression in the indigenous communities of Chiapas that actively denied them the ability to exercise these rights. The majority of the rights in the Revolutionary Law of Women specifically target an aspect of gendered oppression in Zapatista communities that prevents women from participating in local democratic authorities and, ultimately, from having control over their own lives.

For example, point two of the Revolutionary Law of Women gives women the right to work for a just salary and directly confronts the economic dependence of women on their husbands that often traps indigenous women in the home and prevents them from participating in the public life of the community. This economic dependence severely limits women's ability to participate in a multicommunity political organization like the EZLN for two reasons: first, because it reinforces their social role as only existing in the home and facilitates a husband's ability to enforce this role, and second, for the pragmatic reason that without economic independence they cannot cover their own travel expenses to meetings of the organization and thus have to rely on the generosity of their husbands. Similarly, point six guarantees a women's right to education and implicitly attacks the idea that women don't need an education because their primary social purpose is domestic work. Point three of the Revolutionary Law of Women explicitly seeks to combat the huge amount of labor required in childcare by asserting a woman's right to decide the number of children she will have and care for. Lastly, the Revolutionary Law of Women recognizes that lack of autonomy for women not only prevents them from participating in public life, it can also trap them in situations of domestic violence. Point eight of the law states, "No women shall be beaten or mistreated physically by family members or strangers. The crimes of attempted rape or rape will be severely punished."[27] The EZLN had no utopian illusions about the internal divisions and forms of oppression within indigenous communities in Chiapas. Rather than promoting the blind assumption that these communities were already harmonious collectivities, the organization facilitated women's abilities to speak out about their experiences of oppression in their own communities and to take concrete steps to address them.

The Dangers of the EZLN's Military Hierarchy

In addition to attempting to remedy the internal gendered exclusions in the creation of local civilian authorities, the EZLN also saw the danger of its own hierarchical military structure preventing the free determination of these local authorities. The Revolutionary Laws attempt to address this issue by creating an explicit separation between the civilian authorities and the armed forces of the EZLN. The role assigned to the armed forces of the EZLN is to liberate territory from the forces of the oppressive government. They are explicitly prohibited from intervening in the new political forms of democratic governance that would begin to flourish in the newly liberated locales. The Law of Rights and Obligations of the Peoples in Struggle even circumscribes the EZLN's monopoly on the use of force. The law states that all peoples in struggle have the right:

c) To organize and exercise the armed defense of their collective and personal goods, as well as to organize and exercise means of insuring the security of the public order and good government according to the popular will.

d) To demand that the revolutionary armed forces guarantee the safety of persons, families, and personal and collective properties of residents or temporary residents as long as they are not enemies of the revolution.

e) The inhabitants of each place have the right to acquire and possess arms to defend their persons, families, and properties according to the laws of the expropriation of agricultural, commercial, financial, and industrial capital *against attacks or abuses planned or committed by the revolutionary armed forces or the oppressive government.*[28]

The deployment of armed military force, with all the power it implies, is not only vested in the EZLN but also in every civilian authority elected in liberated territory. This unsettles the most common definition of the armed forces of a governing body: the monopoly on the legitimate use of force. Control and governance of a nation state, and thus the implicit goal of many struggles for national liberation, is the consolidation and maintenance of a monopoly on the legitimate use of force. This was certainly the implicit definition of "victory" in the statutes of the FLN, which equated the triumph of the struggle for national liberation with the neutralization of all forces opposed to the revolutionary armed forces and the consolidation of a monopoly on the use of force in the hands of the revolutionary state. The FLN saw the consolidation of state power as the precondition for the appropriation and redistribution of resources. Although the EZLN is obligated to fight the bad government and protect the civilian authorities, they do not have a monopoly on the legitimate use of force. While there are no reported cases of civilian authorities in Zapatista territory violently resisting the EZLN, it is nonetheless significant that the collective aspirations of these communities explicitly define this as a right. Ultimately, the assumption of the Revolutionary Laws is that the local civilian authorities are the highest source of authority in their locale, both in their right to make decisions affecting the people, land, and resources of this locale and to defend their decisions by any means necessary. This authority should not only be defended from the forces of the oppressive government or from the "enemies of the revolution" who will not give up their large tracts of land and accumulated capital but also from the EZLN itself.

Conclusion

The difference between a single national authority and multiple local authorities points to more than just a difference in political actors, it points toward a fundamentally different understanding of politics. In the political aspirations of the FLN statutes, the most basic starting point for a dignified life for the Mexican nation is the redistribution of resources made possible through the force of national state power. In this model, seizing control of the national government is seen as both the action that liberates the nation and as the means of enacting redistribution. "National liberation" in this model liberates the nation from control of large capitalists and foreign imperialism so that "the people" will share equally in the resources of the nation. In the Revolutionary Laws, "national liberation" implies liberation from large capitalists, foreign imperialism, and from the controls of a national government. The liberation of territory from the oppressive national government is the precondition for the self-determination of the peoples that inhabit this liberated territory, who in turn enact redistribution according to their local forms of governance. And most importantly, these local authorities are not placed under the control of a national government or coalition of revolutionary armed forces that embodies the will of "the people." The hope of the Revolutionary Laws is that they will be truly autonomous democratic authorities with the power to make decisions and to defend the fruits of those decisions.

This is the fundamental difference between the goals of the FLN of 1980 and EZLN of 1993: the FLN believed that the creation of material equality through the seizure of state power would set in motion broad social processes on a national level that would create a dignified socialist life for all. The EZLN believed and continues to believe that the liberation of territory from the state is only the first step that provides the necessary space—both economically, in the form of land and resources, and politically, in the form of autonomy from state control—for the elaboration of local democratic authorities that can begin to organize social relations to create a dignified life. They did not believe that a dignified life would miraculously emerge from economic redistribution, nor from an idealized version of a unified indigenous community liberated from state control, but rather through the creation of locally determined democratic structures that would begin to overcome the internal oppressions within the community and set in motion the long task of building a government that in their words "governs by obeying."

What happened during these ten years of clandestine organizing that so fundamentally altered the form of politics and aspirations for liberation of the EZLN? Simply put, the organization changed from a relatively small group of mestizos from urban areas to a massive organization overwhelmingly composed of indigenous peoples from six different language groups living in peasant communities throughout Chiapas. As Nicholas Higgins has argued, the EZLN went through a process of "indianization" in which the original FLN cadre gave up their political presumptions and "learned to listen." Higgins writes, "They [the mestizo Zapatistas from the FLN] became aware that the Indian language had its own referents, its own cultural markers, which were different from theirs, and that if they hoped to have any further or successful contact with the indigenous communities, these were differences that had to be understood." It was this contact with a different set of cultural referents, a different history, and ultimately a whole different understanding of the world that gave rise to "the keystones upon which to build a new politics."[29]

But for the indigenous peoples that came to compose the EZLN this politics was very old as well as new. While the aspirations of the 1994 uprising were certainly a new expression of political forms, the common sense that gave rise to these forms was already present in their languages, in their everyday experiences of the world, and in their own lengthy histories of rebellion. In Tsotsil the word for "army" in the "Zapatista Army of National Liberation" is different than the word used for the "army" of the Mexican state. The "army" of the EZLN is called *jpojvanejetik*, which literally means defenders, or someone whose social role or profession is to defend a people or community, while the "army" of the Mexican state is called *jmilvanejetik*, which literally means killers, or someone whose social role or profession is to kill.[30] Furthermore, an education promoter from Caracol II Oventik who taught me Tsotsil said that "jpojvanejetik" does not just refer to the insurgents of the EZLN, but rather to the whole community once it joins the organization. It refers more to a people that is trained to defend itself rather than to a separate "army" that defends a people, a meaning that is entirely consistent with the Zapatista experience of participation of the whole community in resistance to military and paramilitary violence since 1994. This shows the roots of the political understanding of the EZLN as a force that liberates and defends the peoples in struggle, but which is not defined by the monopoly on the use of force, whose social role is not defined by the capacity to kill. In Tsotsil, a liberating "army" is not really an "army" in the sense of a body whose profession is the capacity to kill, but rather a people that has learned to defend itself. Thus, it would make no sense for the EZLN to be defined as a separate "army," a jmilvanejetik with a monopoly on the use of force, because it is not this type of "army" when it is described in the cultural referents of the Tsotsil language. The EZLN is a body that liberates and defends those communities that are unable to defend themselves, but the result of liberation is always that each community creates its own processes of self-defense to guarantee its right to self-determination as defined in the Revolutionary Laws. But is the right to self-determination a new political concept created by the Revolutionary Laws or can it also be traced to linguistic categories and local history, in other words, to the specific worldviews of the indigenous peoples that "indianized" the EZLN?

CHAPTER TWO

The Zapatista Clandestine Organization: The Creation of a Collective Heart (O'on) and Collective Potentiality (Ch'ulel)

The definition of self-determination for each people in struggle in the Revolutionary Laws warrants a deeper question: What defines a "people in struggle"? Or perhaps more precisely: How does a locale come to define itself as a people, a community, a collectivity and then decide to struggle for self-determination? This question is always complex, especially when we place it in terms of the Tsotsil word for struggle: pask'op, to make the word. In order to make the word, there must be a collective word that demands its own materialization in the world, and in order for the collective word to be born there must be a collective heart that can give rise to common thoughts and feelings in a certain place and people. To put it very concretely, imagine that the EZLN came to the place where you are reading this text and expelled the forces of the national government, the army, the police, and the large capitalists and landowners. Who would you seek out as your people, your community, your collectivity? Would they be prepared to democratically elect their own civilian authorities and take up the struggle, the endless task of creating your collective word? Would they be able to take the first step of administering economic redistribution or even day-to-day governance in your locale in a way that seemed fair and just to everyone that lives there? These questions may sound naively utopian, but they were nonetheless the questions posed by the Revolutionary Laws of the Zapatista uprising. They are based in the hope that every place and people can come to understand itself as a collectivity, and from this sense of collectivity create forms of democratic self-government.

The implicit aspiration of the Revolutionary Laws, the foundation that underlies all their political proposals, is the creation of an understanding and feeling of collectivity. What does this process look like for the Zapatistas? How do they describe it? How do they understand it? In a communiqué addressed to the Consejo Guerrerense 500 Años de Resistencia Indígena (Guerrerense Council on 500 Years of Indigenous Resistance [Guerrerense means from the state of Guerrero]) published February 1, 1994, they describe the feeling of their process of coming together as a collectivity in struggle:

> There was so much pain in our heart, our sadness and death were so much, that they no longer fit, brothers, in this world that our grand-parents gave us to continue living and struggling in. Our pain and sadness were so big that they no longer fit in the heart of a few, and it began overflowing and began filling other hearts with pain and sadness, and the hearts of the oldest and wisest of our peoples were filled, and the hearts of young men and women were filled, all of them brave, and the hearts of the children were filled, even the small-est, and the hearts of the animals and plants were filled with sadness and pain, and the heart of the stones was filled, and our whole world was filled with sadness and pain. Everything was sadness and pain, everything was silence. Then this pain that united us made us speak, and we recognized that there was truth in our words, we knew that not only sadness and pain inhabited our language, we knew that there was still hope in our breasts.[1]

At first reading this passage looks like a poetic description of what is commonly called the creation of political consciousness in contempo-rary political discourse: the naming of pain resulting from oppression, the realization that this oppression is shared by others, and the decision to speak out and take action, to create hope for a better future together with others. However, what at first appears metaphorical and sentimental in Spanish or English is, in fact, the result of a direct translation of very common expressions in Tsotsil and Tzeltal.[2]

The Tsotsil Understanding of Collective Heart (O'on) and Potentiality (Ch'ulel)

The heart is central to Tsotsil and Tzeltal ideas of knowledge, feelings, and understandings of what it means to live in the world. In these lan-guages all thoughts and feelings, or better "thoughts/feelings" since they are understood as one and the same, reside in the heart and are seen as the realizations of the inherent potentialities of the heart.[3] In Tsotsil and Tzeltal the name of this potentiality that gives rise to certain feelings is ch'ulel, often translated as soul or spirit, while the location of these potentialities is o'on in Tsotsil and o'tan in Tzeltal, which translate to heart.[4] O'on and o'tan are relatively easy to translate into English because our understanding of the heart as a location in the body where feelings reside is very similar in meaning, though certainly less linguistically and culturally important. However, ch'ulel does not align whatsoever with the English or Spanish understanding of soul, spirit, or heart and is much more difficult to translate. In an ethnography of the Tzeltal municipality of Cancuc, based on fieldwork conducted between 1989 and 1994, Pedro Pitarch lays out one possible translation of ch'ulel:

> In Cancuc, a person is composed of a body (bak'etal), made up of flesh and blood, and a group of "souls" (ch'ulel; plural ch'uleltik) residing within the heart of each individual. The term soul is used here for the sake of convenience. The conventional understanding of the words root (ch'ul) in both Tzeltal and Tsotsil is "holy" or "sacred." However, in a strict sense, ch'ul denotes a thing's radical "other." Thus, it is a purely relative concept, and when applied to the notion of personhood, ch'ulel may be defined as "the body's other."[5]

Toward the end of his book Pitarch further defines this translation of ch'ul:

> The ch'ul state is not so much another place but rather another sort of reality or form of existence—perhaps we could call it "virtual"—that develops in a time and space distinct from ordinary understandings of these dimensions.... This world must be carved out of the sacred dimensions, which constitutes the definitive underlying plan, the state on which existence is based.[6]

Although Pitarch does not make this connection explicit, given his extensive reliance on the work of Gilles Deleuze to frame his theoretical work, I believe he means "virtual" in the Deleuzian sense of a reality that is not separate or distinct from the world, but is rather a means of describing the inherent or immanent potentialities of an entity that may not be materially realized, but which nonetheless exist and define this entity's place in the world.[7] In both the Deleuzian virtual and in Pitarch's interpretation of the ch'ul aspect of reality, these potentialities constitute the "underlying plan" because they define the possible changes and developments in the world and thus the shape, form, and directions of the dynamic relationships that compose reality.

However, while Pitarch largely defines ch'ulel in terms of an individual body's "other," or its manifestation of virtual potentiality, every Tsotsil or Tzeltal person I have talked to about ch'ulel has framed it in terms of multiple relationships and the creation of a collective potentiality. As Xuno López Intzín, a contemporary Tzeltal intellectual and political activist, writes:

> [T]hat which all existing beings share is ch'ulel. From this understanding of the ch'ulel in everything, the human being establishes relations with all that exists, in other words the human being interacts with their environment and the environment with the human being on a material and immaterial plane. From this plane or universe of ch'ulel existence is ordered, and social relations are ordered with all that exists.[8]

For López, ch'ulel is inherently tied to interaction and the creation of relationships, a view that was echoed in my Tsotsil lessons from the Zapatista education promoters. In this understanding, every entity in the world has ch'ulel that defines its potentials and shapes its relationships with other entities. For example, fire's ch'ulel includes the potential to give warmth among its characteristics, human ch'ulel includes the capacity to cultivate the land, and the ch'ulel of land includes the capacity to nourish and give birth to plants. There are already relationships apparent even in these few potentials: the warmth of the fire sustains the ch'ulel of human beings through cold but relies on the capacity of their ch'ulel to care for and sustain fire, the capacity of the earth's ch'ulel to grow certain plants, for example, the corn plant, relies on the human ch'ulel's capacity for cultivation, while humans rely on the earth for cultivation and thus for sustenance. These capacities are entities or forces in and of themselves that inhabit the hearts of different entities such as humans, fires, and earth.

Keeping this idea of the potentiality (ch'ulel) that inhabits and arises from all hearts (o'on) we can come to a more precise and nuanced understanding of the Zapatistas' description of their coming together in collectivity through their process of organization. Most Tsotsil and Tzeltal phrases that describe anything involving human will, thought, feeling, emotion, or intention are formed either through reference to the heart as a container of potentiality or to some force that inhabits the heart. For example, a Zapatista education promoter told me that when a community consumes alcohol the Zapatistas say in Tsotsil: *Ch-cha'y ta yo'onik svokolik*, which literally translates as "their sadness (svokolik) mistakes itself (ch-cha'y) in their heart (yo'onik)," meaning that their sadness mistakes itself in the sense of being obscured or imperceptible, and thus they do not see the sadness that inhabits their heart.[9] There are two important insights that can be drawn from this sentence. First, heart is not pluralized; the phrase uses heart (o'on) rather than hearts (o'onetik), implying that there is a single shared collective heart.[10] Second, sadness is the subject that reflexively mistakes itself, it is an agent or force (an aspect of ch'ulel) that inhabits and acts in the heart rather than a characteristic of the heart. I interpret this phrase as illustrative of the close connection between shared emotions or potentialities and the creation of a collective heart. Again, ch'ulel and o'on are not easily separable concepts. Thus, when a shared ch'ulel aspect such as a specific sadness enters the hearts of many people this immediately ties them together in a shared ch'ulel and thus a shared or collective heart (o'on). Heart (o'on) is not an individual container but relative to the particular ch'ulel aspect being described. O'on describes the space inhabited by a certain ch'ulel. In this case, it is a ch'ulel that traverses an entire community, and thus brings them together into the shared space of a single heart.

We can now see the EZLN's description of their process of first coming together in a new light through this understanding of sadness as ch'ulel that inhabits the heart (o'on) and enlarges the heart through its growth and spreading to others. Thus, the passage is not a metaphorical description of individuals coming together. It is a mostly literal description of the ending of sadness (vokol) mistaking itself (cha'yel) and of the growth of a shared sadness and thus of a collective heart. The first sentence—"There was so much pain in our heart, our sadness and death were so much, that they no longer fit"—is significant both because it uses "heart" in the singular, implying a collective shared heart, and in its portrayal of sadness as a force (ch'ulel) that grows until it no longer "fits," until it can no longer be obscured (cha'yel) and thus begins to overflow. The second sentence describes how sadness overflowed the "heart of a few," again using heart in the singular collective sense, and filled the hearts not just of other people but of animals, plants, and stones until it filled the heart of every entity in the world. This is not a metaphorical description meant to emphasize the intensity of human sadness, it is the literal description of every entity's heart (o'on) being filled with the force (ch'ulel) of pain and sadness. Lastly, given the previous insight that shared sadness implies a shared heart, this process of the overflowing of sadness also implies the growth of a collective heart. This insight would be directly stated in a Tsotsil translation of the final phrase "we knew that there was still hope in our breasts." In Tsotsil *smuk'ul ko'ontik* means "we have hope,"[11] but it literally translates as our heart (ko'ontik) is big (muk').[12] Thus, this final arrival of hope in the heart is not a reversal or negation of shared sadness, but rather the direct result of sadness overflowing the heart of a few and thus bringing many entities together in a big (muk') heart.

In Tsotsil, expressions involving a heart (o'on) that is large or whole has several specific positive connotations, while a heart that is small or fragmented has several specific negative connotations. These expressions often apply equally to the heart of an individual and to the collective heart of a community or people and are central in Tsotsil understandings of emotion, happiness, and ultimately what it means to live a good and dignified life. The wholeness or fragmentation of the heart is a constant everyday concern in Tsotsil. For example, a very common way of saying "how are you?" is to ask *k'usi javo'on*, which literally means what is the state of (k'usi) your (the prefix jav-) heart (o'on). The two general responses to this question are *jun ko'on*, which literally means one (jun), my (the prefix k-) heart (o'on) or my heart is one and describes a positive state, and *chkat ko'on*, which literally means I am counting (first person transitive conjugation in present periphrastic of the verb *atel*, to count) my (the prefix k-) heart (o'on), giving the sense of a fragmented heart or a heart broken in pieces and communicating a negative state. These answers can both be used for an individual heart (my heart, ko'on) and a collective heart (our heart, ko'ontik). In Tsotsil the wholeness or fragmentation of the heart describes the positive or negative emotional, physical, and spiritual state of either a collective or an individual. Again, it is important to remember that heart (o'on) and potentiality (ch'ulel) are closely tied almost reciprocal concepts. Saying that the heart is one means that the ch'ulel is inhabiting the heart and is fully present, and saying that the heart is fragmented means that the ch'ulel is partially lost, hidden, or blocked in some way. Furthermore, ch'ulel, though it is a force and spirit in itself, is also closely tied to relationships that allow the realization of its potentiality as in the example of a community uncovering the potentiality (ch'ulel) of the earth to give food through cultivation. Thus, the wholeness of the heart implies both that the heart is big (muk'),[13] since it is inhabited by the full realization of its ch'ulel, and also that it is in relations that allow the full realization of ch'ulel. This is especially relevant in the case of a collective heart, where fragmentation directly equates to a splintering of the collectivity, a loss of relationship, an obscuring or loss of ch'ulel, and thus the loss of the potentialities that made the collective heart one. It is not that the fragmentation of the heart causes the loss of ch'ulel, or that the loss of ch'ulel causes the splintering of the heart, but rather that there is a single process of losing relationships, harmony, potentiality, and cohesion.

Thus, creating collectivity in Tsotsil is understood as the reciprocal process of the growth of the heart (o'on) and of potentiality (ch'ulel). The education promoters of Caracol II Oventik have described this process to me using the phrase *ichbail ta muk'*, which means to bring (ichil) one another (ba) to largeness or greatness (ta muk')[14] and implies the coming together of a big collective heart. I have also seen this phrase translated simply as "democracy."[15] Furthermore, this process of bringing one another to greatness (ichbail ta muk') is understood by the education promoters as the creation of *lekil kuxlejal*, which literally means the life that is good for everyone,[16] but which is usually translated as autonomy or dignified life. For the Zapatistas, dignity, autonomy, and democracy for each people, as well as the creation of this people as a collectivity, arises through the growth of the heart, through bringing one another into one collective heart, through ichbail ta muk'.

Clandestine Organizing: The Creation of the Collective Heart of the EZLN

However, the creation of ichbail ta muk' is not a spontaneous "mystical" process, it arises through concrete forms of political self-organization. Ways of thinking and feeling that might appear "mystical" often only appear as such because they employ different ways of understanding and describing the dynamic relationships that compose existence in the world, ways that may not conform to Western ideas of causality. The growth and strengthening of ch'ulel through the process of ichbail ta muk' encompasses multiple aspects of the everyday life of self-organization. One of the education promoters in Oventik told me that ch'ulel is not an eternal spirit or soul, rather it only exists in a person if she creates it. For example, this promoter told me that very young children do not have ch'ulel because they have no consciousness of the world or their place in it. A child creates her ch'ulel by learning how to create respectful relationships (ichbail ta muk') with her community and with all entities in her environment, just as a community creates their ch'ulel when they build respectful relationships (ichbail ta muk') in their process of self-organization.

The process of Zapatista self-organization described by the Zapatista responsables in the second-grade video is readily understood in terms of the growth of the heart (o'on, ch'ulel) or the creation of ichbail ta muk'. However, this understanding should not undermine the purpose of the second grade according to the responsables: to describe a certain "way" of organizing that is a "seed" capable of bearing fruit in numerous different social, cultural, and linguistic contexts. The purpose of using Tsotsil categories to understand Zapatista political aspirations is not to make these aspirations unintelligibly "other." On the contrary, the purpose is to provide a deeper and more nuanced understanding of these aspirations, to learn from them as much as possible, and to fully engage with them as a "seed."

How might the idea of the growth of the heart shape an understanding of the self-organization described by the responsables? The responsables describe the process of bringing people into the shared heart of the organization as a two-stage process. First, they describe the slow and careful clandestine recruitment into the collective. Second, they describe strengthening the cohesion and potentialities of this collective. Manuel, an elder responsable from a village in the zone of Caracol I La Realidad describes how he was recruited and how he went about recruiting others:

> I'm going to explain to you how we were recruited as elder responsables, how we were recruited, and how we went about recruiting the other compañeros. A compa from over there from another village recruited me.... There was a meeting in my village, and the compa arrived and asked me how I felt and how I see it and how we are doing right now in this situation. Well, I started asking questions. We didn't really know how we were doing. Then he started telling me that we work to grow and harvest our products, but we don't control the price. Well, that is how the compa started. Then he told me—once he had explained all that about exploitation, about the situation—then he told me that I could begin to recruit compas, and there I began thinking about how to go about recruiting the compas. Well, I pulled them in one by one, looking for compas who mostly

don't drink a lot, who understand a little more, and when there was a celebration or a political meeting there, I began pulling them in, the compas, one by one. When there were ten or fifteen, well, then we could have an assembly there in my village. We would find a place outside of the village. We would come together there. That is where security began. The comapañeros said that we are going to leave one by one—we wouldn't do it in twos or threes—and everyone knows the place where we will meet. And after ten or fifteen minutes some will be there, then others begin to arrive. There the compas began to meet up. Then later on the insurgents arrived who can give a clearer political orientation, how we will be in the situation and how we will organize our people more, how we are affected by the government, capitalism, monopolies. There we would pull the com-pañeros in a little more. Then little by little I began, when there was another area nearby, then I began going in there, again one by one. Then we were pulling in more compas. we went to another place, we went to recruit another compa, another little village. This is how our struggle went about embracing others. We had more security compañeros. As an elder responsable—I became a responsable in 1987—these are all my words compañeros.[17]

This slow careful process described by Manuel was repeated with striking similarity in most testimonies of the elder responsables in the second-grade video. Most were pulled aside by a responsable in the organization after some form of political meeting of a nonclandestine organization. In general they describe a conversation in which the person who recruited them talked about their experience in terms of a system of exploitation, and most describe recruiting others as a slow process of identifying potential recruits, talking to them one by one and, once there were between five and fifteen, organizing a secret assembly outside of their village.

The defining feature of recruitment is the realization that oppression is a common collective experience. Many second-grade testimonies described recruitment in these terms. César from a village in the region of Caracol I La Realidad said, "He/she explained to me all that about exploitation, he/she explained how we are exploited here in our country, Mexico. . . . Then he/she asked me if I would join our struggle. I joined because he/she told me that we are exploited."[18] Lucio, also from the region of La Realidad, used almost identical language: "Then they told us about how we are exploited, that here in our country Mexico there are two social classes, those that are exploited and those that exploit them. This was not very easy to learn. It took us a long time, it took several times before we learned from them, then once we had learned from them, they gave us other work."[19] The common feature of all these experiences is the realization of a shared experience of exploitation, really a shared sadness with a common cause that exists throughout Chiapas and all of Mexico. The responsables are describing the process of sadness overflowing the heart. The spreading of shared sadness, and thus of shared ch'ulel, does not happen spontaneously, rather it is the first step in a process of self-organization, what might be called "creating political consciousness" in English or Spanish.

According to Manuel's testimony, once someone has been brought into the organization, the second step is for this person to begin "pulling in" new recruits. In the original Spanish, Manuel uses the verb "*agarrar*," literally "to grab," which is a strange choice in both in English in Spanish and might be a direct translation from a Mayan language. Although Manuel is speaking in Spanish without a translator in the video, it is possible that he is at least influenced by Tsotsil forms of speech.[20] An education promoter from Oventik told me that the Tsotsil verb *tsakel*, meaning to grab or to touch, is commonly used to describe the activity of ch'ulel that creates the process of ichbail ta muk'. In particular, the phrase *tsakbail ta venta*,[21] literally to grab or touch each other in mutual recognition or to take one another into account, is the process that allows a people to carry one another to greatness (ichbail ta muk'). Similar to Manuel's use of the verb "agarrar," this phrase implies taking a person into a collectivity, organization, or collective heart that describes the first step of recruitment as described by the elder responsables.

However, the conversation in which a person is recruited, or the initial "grabbing" (tsakel) of a person, is only the first step toward mutual recognition (tsakbail ta venta). This mutual recognition is first fully practiced in the clandestine assembly where the first few people recruited into the organization begin to experience their common potential to understand their shared sadness, to make collective decisions, and to organize themselves. Once the whole village is recruited, the entire community begins to hold assemblies as part of the organization and participates in this process.

Women's Participation in the Organization of the Collective Heart

If the goal of these clandestine assemblies was really to include the entire community, then they had to include women. The EZLN's clandestine organization of collective decision-making cannot be understood without special attention to the complexities of women's participation and to the rights of women outlined in the Revolutionary Laws. Hilary Klein summarizes the deeper implication of the right to "participation" in the community, the organization, and the struggle outlined in the Revolutionary Law of Women:

> The word participar (to participate) has wide-ranging implications in this context. When Zapatista women say, "Now women participate," they are expressing that women have rights, that they have a voice. In addition to holding positions of public responsibility, they use it to mean any kind of involvement in community affairs or political activity. Women often talk about the right to participate in meetings and gatherings, for example. For the indigenous people of Chiapas, community assemblies have historically been an important institution for making collective decisions about anything impacting the whole community. These assemblies are held in any available communal space: the church, the school, or in an open-air structure with a thatched roof and wooden benches. Discussions are informal and can be long, because everyone has the right to speak until an agreement is reached. In the past, however, women rarely attended community assemblies. When women say they have the right to "participate" in these meetings, it means being physically present, as well as speaking up and voicing an opinion. It also implies that their opinion will be heard and respected.[22]

This right to participate rests on a strong commitment to a mutual recognition (tsakbail ta venta) that includes women. This inclusion is not an afterthought, it is central to the creation of ichbail ta muk'. How can you say that the heart of the community is one and great if the women of the community are not recognized and respected? The collective definition of dignified life as the process of ichbail ta muk' requires the participation all members of the community, including the women. However, the assertion of this principle does not miraculously dismantle the concrete structures of oppression that deny women the ability to participate. As Klein points out, one of the principal weaknesses of the FLN and the EZLN before 1994 was their belief that gendered forms of oppression would disappear if women simply joined the movement.[23] With the passage of the Revolutionary Law of Women, the EZLN took the first concrete step toward not only guaranteeing the right to participate but also fighting against those structures that deepen women's economic and social dependence on men and thus prevent their participation. As Subcomandante Galeano said:

> You all have heard or read the wonderful genealogy of the struggle of Zapatista women. . . . These rebellions and resistances could grow, develop, and extend... only once the material base existed that could make them tangible. It passed from theory to reality only once women began dismantling their economic dependence on men.[24]

The process of mutual recognition (tsakbail ta venta) and carrying one another to greatness (ichbail ta muk') cannot be spontaneous. It arises through concrete economic, social, and cultural processes that took particular forms in the case of women. The Revolutionary Law of Women allowed Zapatista women to begin developing economic and social independence from men, and this independence was the precondition for women's participation in the process of ichbail ta muk' contained in the aspirations of the Revolutionary Laws as a whole.

One Zapatista law that doesn't at first appear aimed at creating women's economic independence is the Zapatista ban on alcohol consumption in all their communities. However, beyond its immediate effect of reducing domestic violence, the ban has greatly increased the economic independence of women. Before alcohol was prohibited, men would spend a large portion of the household income on alcohol, leaving very little for their wives to buy enough food for themselves and the children. As Ernestina, a Zapatista women from Morelia, said in an interview with Hilary Klein:

> Before, when the men used to drink, there was no money. The men could always find money for alcohol, but they didn't worry about whether or not there was any food to eat in the house. It was the women who suffered. Our children didn't have anything to eat and we had to find a way to scrape together some money for food. All the men used to drink, not just some of them. You could say it was their custom.[25]

This aspect of the law opened up the space for women to begin to have more control over household resources.

But how did women take advantage of the space created by the Revolutionary Law of Women to create their own forms of income and self-determination outside the home? Subcomandante Galeano attributes this economic independence to the creation of women's cooperatives that allowed them to collectively build economic independence and political self-determination. In a group interview with women from the zone of Caracol IV Morelia conducted by Hilary Klein in 2001, the women shared a similar sentiment saying, "Organizing in the cooperatives is where women first began to understand that we have rights. Working together collectively is a way for us to support each other, and to help the community."[26] There are many different types of women's cooperatives. Some are organized around work that is historically assigned to women, such as weaving and embroidering to make products that can be sold to tourists or solidarity groups outside the community, baking bread in a collective bread oven, or selling food at Zapatista parties. Some are organized around work that has been historically assigned to men, for example, cultivating a collective cornfield or vegetable garden or opening a small cooperative store in the community.[27]

Many of these cooperatives were developed after the adoption of the Revolutionary Law of Women and the 1994 uprising; however, some of their roots can be traced to earlier forms of clandestine organizing. Araceli and Maribel from the zone of Caracol I La Realidad told Hilary Klein in an interview that before 1994, "[Women] organized to sew uniforms . . . for the insurgents as well as the milicianos. Those sewing collectives were one of the first ways that we began to organize as women."[28] Similarly, Estel, an elder responsable who appears in the second-grade video, emphasized the importance of women's collective work: "We compañeras really needed our work. When the war began in 1993 it was good for the compañeras, because there was a lot of work. How did we begin the war? We made the clothes of the militia."[29] All these women emphasize that women coming together in collective work both provided the means by which they participated in the struggle and preparation for war, as well as empowering them to create their own processes of organization and mutual recognition. Women have their own forms of shared sadness, shared ch'ulel, and thus their path to creating the potentiality of a unified heart must walk a path that often intersects with that of Zapatista men, but which also has its own route and its own obstacles. Although there are many forms of collective work developed with men or by men alone, the women's cooperatives are particularly important in truly creating a process of ichbail ta muk' that weaves together all the potentialities (ch'ulel) of a community.

Strengthening the Collective Heart of the Organization between Communities

Whenever I have visited a Zapatista community, whether as a student of the escuelita or as a human rights observer, I have been struck by the immense distances covered by the Zapatista organization. When the elder responsables describe walking to new villages to recruit new members of the organization, these are often journeys that take hours if not days. Walking was and continues to be an indispensable activity in the Zapatista organization, so much so that one student of the escuelita summed up his experience by saying, "I learned that I do not know how to walk."[30] So far, we have seen how members of Zapatista communities, both women and men, came to organize their communities and began to develop a collective heart in their communities. But how did these communities pull each other together (tsakbail ta venta) and carry each other to a collective heart (ichbail ta muk') over great distances and across five different languages? Rocias, an elder responsable from the zone of Caracol III La Garrucha addressed this question in the second-grade video:

> How did we come to know each other from village to village? We started to meet each other when the . . . regional [responsables] organized meetings by region. There we arrived and we saw that there are many compañeros and compañeras already participating in the organization, but we returned to our villages, and we arrived to share with them, and some didn't believe us. That is how it went, but as a responsable I returned one day with the regional [responsable] and I told him, "Compa, there are some in our villages who don't believe that there really are compañeros and compañeras." He told me not to worry, that one day we are going to organize a party to commemorate the anniversary of the organization and then we are going to invite the compañeros and compañeras, so they will come to the party, and that is how it was done. The time arrived and the compañeros went to the party, and when they came back, well, they

also brought with them the happiness and the strength that yes it is true that there are compañeros and compañeras participating in the Zapatista organization. But since everyone doesn't go, there are always doubts for some young compañeros, so they don't believe it. They think that it's not true, but later on, days pass and again the message arrives with the regional [responsable]. I tell him again that this is how it is, and again he told me not to worry one day we will organize a training for the militia and base communities. We are going to invite several villages so that they all arrive and become stronger. And that is how it is done, how it was done, and at that time everyone became stronger, because they saw that it's true that the organization is strong and also that there are military compañeros that arrive to give the training. That is how it is compañeros, that is how we lived it in the beginning.[31]

The role of a regional responsable was not just to relay information or directions to the EZLN communities, it was to actively organize ways for different villages, often spanning a very large geographical area, to come together and build a sense of collectivity. It is especially significant that a common way of creating this sense of collectivity was first with parties, and then through military training.

There is a close relationship in Tsotsil between parties or festivals and the bringing of the heart to greatness (ichbail ta muk'). An education promoter from Oventik told me that when a village or several villages organize a party or festival (k'in in Tsotsil)[32] it is understood as the manifestation of three Tsotsil verbs: *tajbail*, which means to encounter one another, *tso'mbail*, which means to come together, to organize, to unify, or even to recruit, and, lastly, *kuxo'onil*, which means to give life to the heart, or to strengthen, rejuvenate, and recharge the heart. The combination of these three verbs define a party in terms of coming together and organizing reciprocally so that life can be given to the collective heart. Although the elder responsable Rocias comes from a Tzeltal-speaking region, even in Spanish his language has a similar connotation. For example, he says that when the compas returned from the party they brought "happiness and the strength" back with them. Treating happiness and strength as a potentiality or a force that can be brought back may sound strange in English or Spanish, but it is entirely accurate if we understand happiness and strength as forces (ch'ulel) that reside in the heart (o'on, or o'tan in

44

Tzeltal). Lastly, Rocias describes how military trainings did the same thing as parties, bringing different communities into a collective heart and creating the Zapatista organization as a collectivity. This is the same creation of collectivity but with a more explicit potentiality: to be ready for the uprising and the armed struggle for liberation that began on January 1, 1994.

Conclusion

The process of change from the FLN's political aspirations for a socialist state to the EZLN's call for the formation of local democratic authorities in which all members of the community participate equally could rightfully be called a process of "indianization." However, this characterization does not begin to address the heart of what happened. To "indianize" an organization means to rearticulate the political understandings, aspirations, and practices of this organization. This rearticulation relies on specific complex conceptual framings that spring from a long cultural memory, but which are interpreted and given meaning by those who live in the present. When the EZLN says that they struggle for democracy, justice, freedom, autonomy, and a dignified life, these terms are spoken and interpreted in the contemporary words and voices of Tsotsil, Tzeltal, Tojolabal, Chol, Mam, Zoque, and a form of Spanish that has been deeply influenced by the cultural referents of these languages.

The struggle for Zapatista autonomy is not just for the creation of a democratic process independent from the Mexican state. It is the struggle for the right of every place and people to define the meaning of democracy and to create forms of government that embody that definition. It is a struggle for the right to a new politics in which every people defines its own particular forms of governance and social relationships. A Tsotsil definition of this struggle for democracy would be ichbail ta muk', a form of relations among all existing people and peoples and all of the beings with ch'ulel based in mutual respect and recognition. It is this mutual respect that defines the dignified life, or *lekil kuxlejal*, that is the ultimate aspiration of Zapatista autonomy. The proposal of the second grade of the escuelita is that others learn from the Zapatista creation of autonomous democratic governance (ichbail ta muk') when beginning their organization and take this lesson back to their own calendars and geographies. The definition of Zapatista ichbail ta muk' is not a model, it is not even really a definition, it is a certain direction or orientation toward mutual respect, in other words, a seed. The particular forms of governance and politics that emerge from this seed when it is planted in new places can take many forms. As Subcomandante Galeano has pointed out, the course Freedom According to the Zapatistas has a final exam with only one question, "What is freedom according to you?"[33]

Even in Zapatista territory this seed has yet to fully grow and flower. Neither the process of clandestine organizing before 1994 nor the development of the Zapatista struggle up to the present have realized the full reach and depth of the EZLN's political aspirations for ichbail ta muk' and lekil kuxlejal in their own communities, let alone for all the peoples of Mexico. They have been unable to realize the hope expressed in the "First Declaration of the Lacandon Jungle" that the Zapatista troops could "advance to the capitol of the country defeating the Mexican Federal Army, protecting the civilian population in their liberating advance, and permitting the peoples to elect their own administrative authorities freely and democratically."[34] However, as a result of the Zapatista uprising the organization reclaimed up to 250,000 hectares (617,763 acres) from the large landowners of Chiapas, which was redistributed by local Zapatista Agrarian Commissions, while other indigenous organizations took advantage of the political opening to reclaim at least another 250,000 hectares.[35] And although the EZLN was at first hemmed in by a massive military offensive, on December 19, 1994, they sneaked past the military blockade into 38 of the 119 official municipalities of Chiapas and without firing a single shot announced the formation of thirty autonomous self-governing municipalities following the structures laid out by the Revolutionary Laws.[36] At the inauguration of the autonomous municipality San Pedro de Michoacán in the jungle town of Guadalupe Tepeyac, Comandante Tacho said:

> Today, taking into account what is said in the First Declaration of the Lacandon Jungle . . . and in fulfillment of that which is outlined in the Law of Rights and Obligations of the Peoples in Struggle, in all the Zapatista Revolutionary Laws of 1993. . . . In the name of the CCRI-CG of the EZLN, I formally hand over civilian authority in this territory to the freely and democratically elected municipal authorities chosen to preside over the local government of the new Zapatista municipality San Pedro de Michoacán.[37]

The forms of autonomous governance in this municipality and in every other place in Zapatista territory have continued to function into the present. This process of self-determination or the creation of ichbail ta muk' has not stopped, and its continuation has been the result of constant struggle by thousands of Zapatistas.

CHAPTER THREE

The Creation of the Caracoles: Relationships of Difference in the Collective Heart (Ko'ontik, Ko'onkutik)

The democratic structures laid out in the Revolutionary Laws describe the collective aspirations of the organized Zapatista communities on the eve of their uprising. They are their collective word calling for the creation of ichbail ta muk' and lekil kuxlejal. With the creation of the thirty autonomous municipalities in December 1994, the EZLN took the next step in bringing that collective word into reality. They took another step in their process of pask'op. It was the first of many steps they would take in the course of their twenty-five-year struggle (pask'op) to bring a form of autonomous government based in ichbail ta muk' into the world. The Revolutionary Laws continue to govern Zapatista territory, but the local democratic authorities that they name have taken on multiple different forms. These forms were at the center of the first grade of the escuelita. The first grade was a message to the world, an articulation of the relationship between civil society and the Zapatistas based in a politics of listening, but there was also a great deal to be listened to during the one week we were invited to spend in Zapatista territory. The students who arrived for the first grade of the escuelita were given four textbooks and two videos. The textbooks were titled *Autonomous Government I*, *Autonomous Government II*, *The Participation of Women in Autonomous Government*, and *Autonomous Resistance*. As these titles indicate, the reality and practice of autonomous government was at the center of the lesson being taught in the first grade of Freedom According to the Zapatistas.

Based on these titles, it might seem reasonable to assume that the majority of the first grade would be spent in one or several of the Caracoles. Since these were built to be centers for autonomous government and house the offices of the Good Government Councils, they could be thought of as the places where students could receive a tour of the intricacies of Zapatista governing practices. However, the escuelita only consisted of two days in one of the Caracoles (students were sent to all five). The real heart of the lesson was in the time spent in one of the thousands of Zapatista communities, and this was framed as the most important lesson. As Subcomandante Marcos wrote:

> In what we have prepared for you, the "classroom" is not a closed space with a big blackboard and professor at the front giving knowledge to the students, who he or she will evaluate and grade (that is to say, classify: good and bad students), but rather the open space of a community. And not a sectarian community (Zapatistas live with non-Zapatistas and, in some cases, with anti-Zapatistas), nor hegemonic, nor homogenous, nor closed (people from different calendars and geographies visit throughout the whole year), nor dogmatic (here we also learn from others).[1] Therefore, you are not coming to a school with a normal schedule. You will be in school every hour of every day of your stay. The most important part of being in the Zapatista escuelita is living with the family that receives you. You will go with them for firewood, to the cornfield, and to the canyon river spring. You will cook and eat with them.... You will rest with them, and, above all, you will get tired together with them.[2]

This choice of "classroom" was a poetic statement that the heart of the Zapatista movement can only be seen in the organized communities that compose it, but it was also a concrete lesson on Zapatista forms of autonomous governance. A consistent thread running throughout all the escuelita textbooks, my own experience in the Zapatista "classroom," and the experiences I have heard about from others is that the center of Zapatista autonomous governance is not in the Caracol; it is in every Zapatista community, and these communities are not homogeneous or closed but are widely varied and in a state of constant conversation and change.

To understand Zapatista practices of autonomous government one must develop a framework that encompasses the tensions between different local forms of governance that nonetheless exist in a framework of shared aspirations born from a collective heart. In many ways, this has been the same problem faced by the pask'op of the organized Zapatista communities over the past twenty-two years. How can the right of every people to create its own form of governance described in the Revolutionary Laws be realized in a way that brings numerous people together in a unified Zapatista organization? How can this unity be created in such a way that it does not subsume the right of every community to democratically decide its own form of government? These questions cannot have a single answer, rather they can only be answered through the multiple voices of numerous different communities. Valentín, a former member of one of the municipal councils in Caracol V Roberto Barrios, provides a good summary of the nature of these multiple community voices in the *Autonomous Resistance* textbook:

> Our idea with the structure of the autonomous government takes this form: the people are those with the power to decide their form of political, economic, ideological, and social organization, starting from below, and then going up.[3]

Valentín is not describing a certain form of democracy, he is describing a democracy of democratic forms. Zapatista democracy does not just consist of the right to elect their own authorities, it consists of the right to define and constantly redefine the form of democracy practiced by each community. This process of definition always proceeds "from below, and then going up," from the community, through the different layers of autonomous government, until it defines the entire Zapatista organization. Just as the Revolutionary Laws only became the guiding principles of the Zapatista organization after every community had debated and agreed on their content, the voices of the Zapatista communities are at the center of every decision in the Zapatista organization. As Valentín makes clear, the different levels of authority, such as the autonomous municipalities or Caracoles, can only exist insofar as they represent the communities that compose them. They can only exist once all of these communities have reached a collective agreement defining their responsibilities and how they will function, and if the communities decide that their authorities are not functioning in the way they imagined, then they can change them. There is no Zapatista "constitution" describing their rules of self-government, there are only those principles laid out through collective agreement, such as the seven principles of autonomous government or the rights in the Revolutionary Law of Women. There is only a constant process of creation and re-creation of various governance structures that have developed and changed throughout the past decades of Zapatista autonomy.

How would it be possible to describe such a government? It depends on how one does the describing. If you try to lay out a single model composed of set rules and regulations, if you try to argue that the Zapatistas govern themselves through consensus, majority rule, direct democracy, checks and balances, you will not get very far. The single most important commonality in Zapatista autonomous government is that every community, autonomous municipality, and Caracol does things differently and has the right to do things differently. The only commonality is their adherence to the seven principles of autonomous government and the rights collectively ratified in the Revolutionary Laws. The diverse voices of the communities materialize these principles and rights in multiple ways. This was the form of description employed in the escuelita "classroom" and the escuelita textbooks. The textbooks themselves do not lay out a model of government. Rather each textbook consists of numerous testimonies from different Zapatista authorities from each Caracol addressing its own particular forms of autonomous government and responding to questions from the other authorities. It is a transcribed assembly to which each Caracol sent some of their authorities and former authorities to share their different experiences of autonomous government with each other, as well as with the visiting students of the escuelita.

There are some commonalities among the experiences shared in the textbooks, but there are just as many differences. And in general, the more one attempts to find the commonalities, the more differences emerge. For example, one would expect that each Caracol would share a basic common structure, and at first this might appear to be the case: one could say that each of the five Caracoles is made up of several autonomous municipalities that are in turn made up of several communities, and that each of these three levels have their own autonomous authorities with defined sets of responsibilities. However; as one reads the escuelita textbooks all the exceptions to this model begin to emerge. For example, the communities in Caracol IV Morelia decided to reorganize their seven original autonomous municipalities into three larger municipalities made up of several regions of various communities that now function as a different level of authority between the autonomous municipality and the community, and in Caracol II Oventik and Caracol V Roberto Barrios there are some communities that are organized in regions that are not part of any autonomous municipality. Furthermore, although every Caracol is made up of autonomous municipalities, there are many differences in how these municipalities govern their territories. Although they may share the same name, the autonomous municipalities of each Caracol have their own ways of doing things that are constantly defined and redefined by the communities. But if there is no single decision-making structure in Zapatista autonomous government, how are they able to define themselves as a collectivity? If a collective heart is made through concrete practices of self-organization, how can this collective heart be sustained when there are differences or even disagreement over how to continue the process of self-organization? The answer lies in the Zapatista way of working through disagreement. If there is one commonality throughout all the different levels of Zapatista autonomous government, it is the process of coming into agreement in an inclusive assembly where all have the right to speak and be heard. A nuanced understanding of the Zapatista practice of the assembly can be found by returning to the idea of collectivity found in the Tsotsil language.

The Double Sense of Collectivity in Tsotsil

The previous chapter discussed the complex meanings of heart and the potentialities of the heart (o'on and ch'ulel) in Tstotsil. However, this on its own does not completely describe the nature of the heart in the Tsotsil language. In Tsotsil grammar, "o'on" and "ch'ulel" cannot exist in isolation. They belong to a certain class of words that must always be accompanied by an affix that marks their relationships in the world. If the speaker does not know the relationships of the particular heart or is speaking of heart in a general or abstract sense, she must use a suffix marking that the heart is in relation somehow even though the speaker doesn't know what the relationship is or does not think it is relevant to what she is saying.[4] For example, all nouns describing family relations belong to this same class of words. To say "older sister" (vix) in Tsotsil, you must always say whose older sister it is (for example: jvix, i.e., my older sister). If you were to refer to the idea of an older sister you would have to add the suffix -il (vixil), signifying that the older sister is in relationship somehow even if the specific relation is irrelevant or unknown.[5] In English or Spanish grammar we would say that o'on and ch'ulel are nouns that must always have a "possessor," they cannot exist in the abstract and only sound right to a native speaker if it is clear that it is his, her, their, or our heart.

"Possessive" affixes are very common in Tsotsil and very important for the grammar of the language. However, in my Tsotsil lessons with the Zapatista education promoters they always insisted that possession is not really the best way to describe this part of Tsotsil grammar, because possession implies a very unidirectional relationship of one possessing subject relating to a possessed object. In Tsotsil it is more a matter of marking a subject's place in the world and its relationships with other subjects. According to the education promoters, "relational affixes" would be a more accurate description of their function in Tsotsil grammar. In general, anytime something is in a relationship with anything else, this relationship will be marked by a relational affix. "O'on" and "ch'ulel" belong to a class of Tsotsil words where being in relationship is understood as integral to the meaning of the word itself. Thus, the collectivity of the heart, the fact that it is "our heart," is an integral part of understanding the concept of the heart (o'on or ch'ulel) in Tsotsil.

At this point the translation becomes more difficult, because in Tsotsil there are two different forms of the first person plural, two different forms of "we," and two different senses of collectivity. There are two different ways of saying "our heart" in Tsotsil, *ko'onkutik* and *ko'ontik*, and each has a distinct meaning. The first "our heart" (ko'onkutik) uses what linguists term the exclusive "we" and the second "our heart" (ko'ontik) uses what linguists term the "inclusive" we. However, these are descriptions aimed at understanding similar grammatical structures across languages and do not get at the particular significance of these two different forms of we in relation to the Tsotsil Zapatista political understandings of collectivity.

An education promoter from the Oventik language school used the example of an assembly in the Zapatista autonomous governance system to describe the difference between the two Tsotsil forms of we. He said that when multiple communities come together in an assembly, for example, in an autonomous municipality in one of the Caracoles, each community will use the "exclusive" we when speaking from its own perspective. For example, if someone from a certain community wanted to say "our heart (of my community) is hopeful," she would use the "exclusive" form of "our heart" (smuk'ul ko'onkutik) to make clear that she is referring to the collective heart of her particular community not the collective heart of all the communities in the assembly. If the assembly comes to an agreement and someone in the assembly wants to describe that agreement, then she would use the inclusive "we" to make clear that everyone present has come to a collective decision. For example, if she wanted to say that "our heart (of the assembly) is hopeful," then she would use the "inclusive" form of "our heart" (smuk'ul ko'ontik). In both these examples, the meaning is the same in English and Tsotsil, however, the Tsotsil sentences do not require the same amount of context in order to be meaningful. Even absent any other context, "smuk'ul ko'onkutik" means that we who are a collective that is part of a larger collectivity have hope in our hearts. For example, if a speaker were to use the exclusive form of "our heart" (ko'onkutik) in an assembly of several communities she would describe a collectivity that looks something like this:

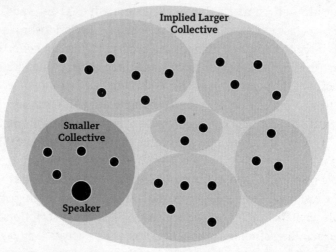

Figure 1: The Exclusive We

The dark grey area represents her primary emphasis on the perspective of her own community. However, her use of the exclusive "we" (ko'onkutik) necessarily implies that her community is part of a larger collective, in this case the assembly as a whole represented by the light grey shading. Similarly, one of the education promoters in Oventik told me that the inclusive "we" often implies that there are other smaller collectives that make up the larger "we." For example, smuk'ul ko'ontik, especially when used in the context of an assembly, can often imply that there are many collectives that at this moment are in agreement, that there is hope in their hearts. In this case the inclusive form of "our heart" (ko'ontik) would look something like Figure 2 below.

The primary emphasis of the inclusive we, represented by the dark grey shading, is on a perspective shared by the assembly as a whole. However, this emphasis does not subsume the existence of the smaller collectives represented by the light grey shading, it merely conveys that all these smaller collectives happen to share the same perspective. The

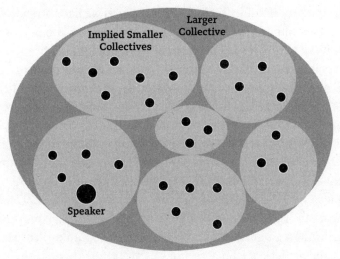

Figure 2: The Inclusive We

two Tsotsil forms of "we" define two reciprocal forms of collectivity that
are mutually dependent concepts. The exclusive "we" implies that the
speaker's collective is different than a larger collective, while still being
a part of it. Similarly, the inclusive "we" implies a collective made up of
other smaller collectives that are in agreement.

Although the inclusive and exclusive Tsotsil forms of "we" have a
wide variety of conceptual meanings and are present in all possessives
and verb conjugations in the language, they nonetheless are very useful
in understanding the particularities of political collectivity in a Zapatista
context. To say "our heart" in Tsotsil one must either use the exclusive
"we" (ko'onkutik) implying a smaller collective that is part of a larger collective heart even though it is different or even in disagreement with
this collective heart, or the inclusive "we" (ko'ontik) that in the context
of political collectivity often implies the presence of multiple other collective hearts that have become one through mutual agreement. The two
Tsotsil forms of "we" speak to a form of collectivity that is born through
the mutual agreement of different collectives and that can remain as a
collective while still allowing for differences and disagreements. This
double sense of collectivity is central to understanding decision-making
in the Zapatista system of autonomous government. The heart of Zapatista
governance is the "agreement" that is reached between several communities or individuals and that only lasts as long as those communities or
individuals remain in agreement. The communities reach an agreement

through the process of ichbail ta muk', which as we have already seen in Chapter Two implies mutual respect and the democratic process of an assembly, but which literally means "carrying one another to greatness or largeness in size" and implies the creation of a big collective heart. Ichbail ta muk' describes the process of reaching an agreement, of multiple collectives coming together in assembly to bring their hearts to greatness through their unity in organization. However, this big collective heart never implies homogeneity. In a Zapatista context it implies the "our collective heart" of the inclusive we (ko'ontik) that does not subsume the different exclusive "our hearts" (ko'onkutik) that compose it. As we saw in Chapter Two, the clandestine military organization of the EZLN was the first Zapatista organizational structure to be born through this process of coming into agreement or the passage from many ko'onkutik to a ko'ontik through the process of ichbail ta muk'.

The history of Zapatista autonomous government described in the escuelita textbooks can be understood as a process of multiple collectives coming into agreement, in other words, as the passage from the exclusive to the inclusive form of collective heart (from ko'onkutik to ko'ontik). Again, this process did not occur mystically or spontaneously, but rather was the result of a long process of self-organization shaped by historical circumstance and fraught with challenges and setbacks. A form of governance that functions according to the logic of ichbail ta muk' does not create governing authorities who can impose their will on the people. Rather, it creates authorities who work according to the Zapatista principle of governing by obeying. In other words, authorities that obey the agreement of the Zapatista communities and that only act to implement the decisions that have already been made by the communities, never acting on their own personal judgment.

The autonomous municipalities were created to put the Zapatista principle of governing by obeying into practice. They were one of many steps of the Zapatista pask'op, their struggle to bring their collective word into the everyday life of the communities. However, the process of pask'op is never simple. The Zapatistas' attempts to practice their collective word over the past decades have been replete with difficulties and mistakes. But these mistakes and problems have not destroyed the Zapatista organization. On the contrary, they have given rise to new solutions, new agreements, and ultimately to the system of the five Caracoles that make up the autonomous government system in the present. When problems arise in the Zapatista collective heart (ko'ontik), they are most often solved in an assembly of the smaller collective hearts (ko'onkutik) coming together to create a new agreement and ultimately a new collective heart (ko'ontik) that reflects the necessities of the given moment. But what are the problems that have led to the agreements forming the current system of autonomous government? What caused the autonomous municipalities to come together to form the five Caracoles and Good Government Councils?

Governing by Obeying: The Creation of the Autonomous Government

One of the most significant obstacles to the creation of Zapatista autonomous government has been the EZLN itself. Despite the promise of the Revolutionary Laws to maintain a strict separation between the EZLN military and the local democratic authorities, the strength and legitimacy of the EZLN military organization in the communities has always threatened to subsume the independence of Zapatista democratic authorities. Although the political-military organization of the EZLN was made through the mutual agreement of all the Zapatista communities during the clandestine period, once it was organized it remained a military structure. Although the high command received directions on important decisions like the declaration of war or the content of the Revolutionary Laws from the democratic decision of the communities, the day-to-day decision-making structure was still that of a military organization: the commanding officer always had the final say. As Subcomandante Marcos wrote in 2003 in the announcement of the formation of the Caracoles:

> [S]elf-government . . . is not an invention or contribution of the EZLN. It comes from further back, and when the EZLN was born it had already been functioning for quite some time, although only at the level of each community. As a result of the explosive growth of the EZLN . . . this practice passed from the local to the regional level. It functioned with responsables at the local (those with responsibility in each community), regional (a group of communities), and zonal (a group of regions) levels. . . . Although here, given that it was a political-military organization, the commanding officer made the final decision. What I want to say with this is that the military structure of the EZLN in some way "contaminated" a tradition of democracy and self-government. The EZLN was, so to speak, one of

the "antidemocratic" elements in a relationship of direct communitarian democracy.[6]

Although the EZLN grew in the indigenous communities of Chiapas through the process of ichbil ta muk', the resulting organization had antidemocratic tendencies imposed by the necessity of fast wartime decision-making through a set chain of command. Despite the promises of the Revolutionary Laws, the political context after 1994 gave the EZLN's military structure even more influence over civilian government in the communities. Many of the clandestine forms of organization that existed in the communities before 1994 were weakened with the outbreak of war. The organization confronted a new social reality after 1994 with new problems and new possibilities, such as the continuous counterinsurgency violence perpetrated by the government, the interaction with national and international civil society, and the difficulties involved in transforming from a clandestine military organization to the form of democracy outlined by the Revolutionary Laws. All of these issues tended to shift power to the EZLN command structure and away from the local democratic authorities of the Zapatista communities.[7]

The declaration of the autonomous municipalities was a first step toward addressing these problems. For example, Lorena, a promoter of herbalism, midwifery, and bone medicine[8] from the autonomous municipality of San Pedro de Michoacán in the zone of Caracol I La Realidad described the creation of the autonomous municipalities in her zone:

> Before 1994, in the clandestine period, some compañeros and compañeras who had been doing the work were also already participating in trabajos colectivos since that time,[9] in different trabajos that we were doing, but at that time no one thought that was autonomy. . . .
> [W]hen we declared war in 1994, we kept doing the trabajos, we gave them more effort to be able to continue working, to continue participating in the different spaces where we were organized. . . . [B]ut because we were at war, we were losing the authorities in the community, we were losing the local authorities, the agents of the community. It was as if they were becoming uncontrolled in the communities.
>
> The commanders also realized how we were working at this time, that we were losing that structure we had before the war. They saw that we could not continue like this. They took on the work of

controlling those from civil society who were arriving, because we didn't have any idea how to control them in each community, in each community where we are.... [B]ut, they saw that they were not the ones who needed to do this work, so that was when they told us that we had to prepare ourselves to be more able to see for ourselves how we need to work.

They found other compañeros to analyze this problem. It was not the role of the commanders. They called the people together and spoke about all the tasks that they were doing that it was not their role to do.... These compañeros had a discussion. They saw that we had to form groups, to organize ourselves, and that is when the creation of the thirty-eight autonomous municipalities was declared in December 1994. Then the local and municipal authorities began seeing to the work. They had a responsibility to attend to the people, to organize more, to continue working better, to control in what form we are going to continue.[10]

The new realities after the 1994 uprising weakened the internal organization of the communities and put a previously clandestine organization into contact with national and international civil society, not to mention global media and the counterinsurgency strategies of the Mexican government. The EZLN command was more prepared to deal with these issues and as a result had increasing control over general political decision-making, as well as some aspects of economic reality in the communities. The EZLN command's responsibility for relating with national and international civil society gave them disproportionate power to define the political relationships and messages of the movement. It also gave them control over solidarity funding that would impact many aspects of daily life in the communities, ranging from access to electricity and drinking water to the initial development of the Zapatista health and education systems. These projects should be controlled solely by the communities in keeping with the principle of governing by obeying and the tenets of the Revolutionary Laws. With the declaration of the autonomous municipalities, the EZLN attempted to remedy this problem and allow the autonomous municipalities to directly control solidarity funding and develop their own relationships with civil society.

However, according to Lorena, the autonomous municipalities were not formed through a unilateral decision by the EZLN command but through a process of several groups of Zapatista communities coming together and reaching an agreement. This agreement was made in democratic assemblies organized by the EZLN command, but in which they had no voice. Although breaking out of the military blockade would not have been possible without the coordination of the EZLN military structure, the decision to form an autonomous municipality was ultimately in the hands of the communities. Thus, there were three processes that brought about the formation of the autonomous municipalities: an organizational structure, in this case the EZLN, saw a problem with how the agreements of the organization were functioning and made a proposal to the Zapatista communities; the Zapatista communities then agreed on a new form of organization that would address the problem in a democratic assembly free from coercion by the larger organizational structure of the EZLN; finally the organizational structure of the EZLN coordinated the implementation of the communities' agreement, in this case by coordinating the nonviolent military offensive that founded the autonomous municipalities.

However, the creation of the autonomous municipalities did not completely solve the problem and gave rise to new problems that would eventually be addressed through the formation of the Caracoles and the Good Government Councils. The autonomous municipalities are distributed throughout the state of Chiapas. Some are in areas closer to major cities or near highways, and some are very remote and include communities that can only be reached by walking for many hours. These geographical factors, combined with the limited capacity of many civil society groups, led to an unequal distribution of resources and ultimately an unequal process of development among the autonomous municipalities.[11] Furthermore, there were also problems between the autonomous municipalities and civil society groups. In some cases this relationship looked more like charity and less like solidarity. Some groups would do projects in the communities regardless of whether this was what the community actually wanted or needed. As Subcomandante Marcos writes:

> [S]ome NGO's and international organizations . . . decided what the communities needed and without even consulting them not only imposed particular projects but also the time frames and forms of their implementation. Imagine the despair of a community that needs potable water and ends up with a library, that requests a school for children and they give them a course on herbal medicine.[12]

This was not only useless for the communities, it was also contrary to the core of the Zapatista struggle, which always places autonomy, self-government, and dignity above material development. As Marcos points out, "If the Zapatista communities wanted it, they would have the highest standard of living in all of Latin America. Imagine how much the government would be willing to invest to secure our surrender and take a lot of photos ... while the country falls apart in their hands."[13] The Zapatistas have never struggled for handouts, they fought and died for dignity and democracy, for lekil kuxlejal and ichbail ta muk' for all the peoples of Mexico.

The second problem was one of internal coordination among the autonomous municipalities. In the beginning of 1996, the EZLN created five centers called "Aguascalientes" in honor of the place where the radical forces of Emiliano Zapata and Pancho Villa formed an alliance during the 1910 Mexican Revolution. Although these physical spaces would later become the Caracoles, they were not initially intended to be centers of autonomous government, but were rather spaces for gatherings of civil society in Zapatista territory.[14] There was no civilian government structure that coordinated between autonomous municipalities, and as a result the EZLN military structure fulfilled this need. This coordination on a larger geographic scale was central in combating the government's counterinsurgency strategy of military intimidation and the formation of indigenous paramilitary groups in Zapatista territory. The EZLN command took on the role of mediating between human rights groups committed to stopping the counterinsurgency violence, the autonomous municipalities, and official municipal authorities aligned with the government.[15]

This lack of coordination also produced a different form of unequal development among the municipalities, with some organizing a functioning autonomous municipal government quickly, while others did so more slowly. Gerónimo, a former member of the Good Government Council from the autonomous municipality Lucio Cabañas in the zone of Caracol IV Morelia, described the experience of creating autonomous municipal authorities in his zone:

> When the autonomous municipalities were declared many of us didn't have experience with how to be an authority, some did have it but others didn't, some had been authorities of official communities

but others hadn't. When it was said that we needed to work on autonomy, what did we do? What was done was to call a meeting of all the communities so that they could discuss it, first the name, what to name the municipality, and afterward, so that they could name authorities, the different roles of the authorities, the committee.... Each municipality called an assembly of all the base, then they directly chose this group of compañeros to do the work of autonomy.

What work would these compañeros do? Because we practically didn't know how—maybe some did, but the majority didn't know, what are we going to do? We are going to work on autonomy. We are going to govern ourselves. The how is the question that arose. What is it that we are going to do? Since no one knew the answer but time was still passing, once these authorities were there, then the problems came up. Really, there were problems in every one of our communities, in our municipalities...

In that time the principal problems that were confronted were alcoholism, familial problems, problems between neighbors, and some agrarian problems.... [I]n around 1997, there were municipalities that were the first to be declared, that had already advanced, one of those is the municipality 17 de Noviembre, which is a municipality that had already started to do more work when the other municipalities were still lagging behind.[16]

Although there is a long tradition of community democracy in the indigenous communities of Chiapas, this knowledge did not necessarily mean that members of Zapatista communities were prepared to address all the problems that can arise in a municipality made up of scores of different communities with different histories and customs, sometimes even speaking different indigenous languages, and which are also in the process of defending and redistributing vast tracts of land reclaimed in the 1994 uprising. Although everyone in each autonomous municipality participated in the creation of the municipality, local circumstances allowed some to better organize a functioning municipal government structure able to address the many problems in their territory.

In answer to all these problems the Zapatistas announced the transformation of the Aguascalientes into the Caracoles and the creation of the five Good Government Councils on August 8, 2003. However, just as with the formation of the autonomous municipalities, the EZLN did not make this decision unilaterally. Subcomandante Marcos made clear in his announcement of the Caracoles and Good Government Councils that their formation was not a decision of the EZLN command, but that he had been chosen by the communities to communicate their agreement to the rest of the world.[17] The EZLN command identified many of the problems with the autonomous municipalities, but they did not make the decision about how to address them. In fact, the testimonies from Caracol IV Morelia, Caracol I La Realidad, and Caracol III La Garrucha in the escuelita textbooks describe processes that were already being developed in these zones to fulfill the need for more coordination between their municipalities. Gerónimo states that in 1997, when they began to recognize that some of the municipalities had not advanced very far in developing their systems of autonomous government, all the municipal authorities in the zone of Caracol IV Morelia started having regular meetings to coordinate their efforts. As a result, Gerónimo tells us,

> all the municipalities were strengthened, all the municipalities formally named their authorities, named their autonomous *consejos*.[18] Once all the municipalities had their autonomous consejos and the whole body that makes up the consejo, then there started to be other work, then they started to work more in other commissions, then they didn't just dedicate themselves to addressing problems, but rather worked more for the development of the municipalities.[19]

Gerónimo makes clear that this process of coming together to coordinate their work not only helped advance those municipalities that were still having trouble governing well but also allowed all the municipalities in the zone to better organize their development. Lorena describes a similar process of organization in the zone of Caracol I La Realidad:

> [T]he compañeros of the political and military command realized that there was an imbalance among the communities, that things weren't equal. They realized that both [solidarity] support as well as the trabajos colectivos that were being organized in every municipality were not equal. This was why they initiated a meeting of the municipal consejos. They started to have their assemblies to begin to see how each municipality was doing, what [solidarity] support they had, what trabajos they are doing, what trabajos they were organizing to reinforce their resistance.

They started to have a lot of meetings, and around 1997, after several meetings, they named the assembly of municipal councils the Association of Autonomous Municipalities. This is what they called the meetings the municipal councils were having. Months and years passed, and this is how they were working and organizing. During this time of the association of municipalities they started to look at the tasks, the trabajos of health, education, and commerce....

Arriving in 2002, the compañeros of the association of municipalities decided to name a group of compañeros who would be responsible for coordinating these trabajos of health, education, and commerce. They named seven compañeros and one compañera.... They called this group of compañeros the Administration of the Association of Autonomous Municipalities....

We continued working until we arrived in 2003, with the formation of the Good Government Councils.... But in our zone we didn't know if the members of the administration of the association of municipalities would someday be authorities and government. In 2003, when the Good Government Councils were created, the people and the association of municipalities decided that these eight compañeros, the members of the administration of the association of municipalities, would become the authorities of the Good Government Council.[20]

Coordination among autonomous municipalities also began as early as 1997 in the zone of La Realidad and was directly transformed into the work of the Good Government Council in 2003. Both the formation of the Association of Autonomous Municipalities and the decision that the administration would take on the role of Good Government Council were made in assemblies of the Zapatista communities convened by the EZLN command, but with the decision remaining in the hands of the communities. Similarly, Artemio, a former member of the autonomous municipal consejo of Ricardo Flores Magón in the zone of Caracol III La Garrucha, says that before the formation of the Good Government Council they had periodic assemblies of the four autonomous municipalities in their zone to coordinate projects involving all of the municipalities, although he doesn't mention when these assemblies were first organized and doesn't discuss what these projects were or how they were coordinated.[21]

The seeds that would eventually mature into the Caracoles were already being developed in three of the five zones of Zapatista territory. The growth of these seeds was encouraged by the EZLN command, for example, by calling on the municipalities of Caracol I La Realidad to address the problem of inequality among municipalities, but every decision and organizational agreement was made in assemblies of the Zapatista communities. Although the testimonies in the escuelita textbooks from Caracol II Oventik and Caracol V Roberto Barrios do not mention any governing structures that foreshadowed the creation of the Caracoles, they also make clear that the communities in their zones decided to form their Good Government Councils and determined how they would function without coercion from the EZLN command.[22] Even though it remained a hierarchical military structure, the EZLN military organization has always sought to follow the tenets of the Revolutionary Laws that place all authority in the democratic decisions of the communities. Throughout more than twenty years of creating autonomous government, the Zapatista communities have sought to develop structures that function according to the principle of governing by obeying, the principle that any decision must be made through the mutual and reciprocal agreement (ichbail ta muk') of the communities.

Conclusion

The commitment to obeying the agreement of the communities defines the history of the creation of Zapatista autonomous government. After the outbreak of the war the EZLN command saw that the agreements of the communities outlined in the Revolutionary Laws were not functioning, but rather than alter them on their own, they called the communities together, and the communities came up with their own agreement, giving birth to the first autonomous government structures, the autonomous municipalities organized in fulfillment of the Revolutionary Laws. And again, when the autonomous municipalities began to encounter problems, the EZLN command together with municipal authorities in Caracol I, III, and IV convened the communities and called on them to develop governance structures that would allow for coordination between autonomous municipalities. These structures took several different forms before finally coalescing into the Caracoles and Good Government Councils formed through the agreement of all five zones of Zapatista territory in 2003.

During the first ten years of Zapatista autonomous government the EZLN military organization, the autonomous municipal councils, and above all the organized Zapatista communities constantly worked toward the creation of a government that governed by obeying. Did they find the solution in the creation of the Caracoles and Good Government Councils? If so, why did these provide a solution? What were the new forms of governance that could coordinate vast geographical areas and many communities, while still obeying the collective decisions of all the communities reached through the democratic process of the assembly? As with the organization of the autonomous municipalities, the Good Government Councils did not take a single form; they developed numerous different structures that were constantly reorganized and changed by the communities. Every change was an attempt to bring into practice the aspiration of governing by obeying. The Caracoles and all levels of autonomous government follow the seven principles that guide them toward always obeying the agreements of the people. As Doroteo, a former member of the Good Government Council of Caracol I La Realidad, puts it:

> [In autonomous government] [w]e always do our work with attention toward fulfilling the seven principles of governing by obeying in what we are doing: 1) to serve others not oneself; 2) to represent not supplant; 3) to build not destroy; 4) to obey not command; 5) to propose not impose; 6) to convince not defeat; 7) to go below not above. We think that we have to do it like this, that it is an obligation so that we won't commit the same mistakes that the levels of the bad government commit. So that we won't take on the same ways as them, the seven principles are what will direct us.[23]

Even though every Caracol and Good Government Council has developed different methods and forms of governance, all of them are different attempts to bring these seven principles into practice. Although the particular forms of pask'op are different in each Caracol, the collective word that they are seeking to create is the same. It is this collective word that, as Doroteo says, guides them down a path that is fundamentally different than that of the official Mexican government and that might begin to construct a dignified life (lekil kuxlejal) and democracy of mutual respect (ichbail ta muk').

PART TWO

The Practice of Autonomous Government

CHAPTER FOUR

"The Community Has the Final Say": The Assembly and the Collective Work of Governance (A'mtel)

By the time the Zapatistas announced the escuelita in 2013, the Good Government Councils had ten years of experience of self-government in their zones. The escuelita textbooks describe all the problems, setbacks, and advances that occurred in each zone over these ten years. They tell a story in the multiple voices of numerous current and former authorities from all five zones. It is a story defined by constant setbacks, reexaminations, and reinventions of governing systems and practices in each zone. However, even though there are many differences between the five zones, there is a common commitment to the seven principles of governing by obeying that create a general shared form of governance present throughout the ten years since the announcement of the Caracoles. It is the same form that created the Caracoles themselves: an assembly where the communities of the zone come together to reach an agreement, where their different collective hearts (ko'onkutik) agree upon a unified collective heart (ko'ontik).

The assembly is the heart of the Zapatista form of autonomous government. It is the process by which collective decisions are made and, more importantly, by which the functioning of the autonomous government itself is constantly defined and redefined. The Zapatista form of autonomous government is not a rigid model, rather it is a commitment to the multiple diverse voices of the communities that aims to produce numerous governing structures where these voices can speak, be heard, and come into agreement. This chapter describes the practice of this assembly form of government, as well as the work of Zapatista governing authorities within this system. The Zapatistas understand governance as a particular form of work in service to the community, rather than as the exercise of power through administration or rule. Zapatista authorities make proposals to the communities, they do not make decisions. This circumscribed role further emphasizes the importance of the assembly as the central mechanism of autonomous government.

In practice, the assembly form of governance does not require that every single decision be made with the participation of every individual Zapatista. Rather, the principle of governing by obeying guides the decisions of those who are chosen by the communities to carry out and sustain their collective agreement. This principle dictates that those who are chosen as authorities by the communities must always obey the agreement of the communities. If any problems develop that undermine or complicate the agreement, the authorities cannot alter the agreement based on their own judgment, rather they must convene the communities, which then can decide on a new agreement. In other words, they must always be aware of the multiple smaller collectives (ko'onkutik) that make up their collective heart (ko'ontik), and when these collectives (ko'onkutik) come into disagreement and imbalance, the answer is never to force them back into the existing agreement (ko'ontik). In such a case, the government would really be imposing its own perspective on all the collectives that granted it its responsibility, which would mean the breaking of mutual respect, and ultimately the fragmentation of the collective heart (ko'ontik). When there is disagreement, the only possible answer is to call for a new agreement, to convene all the smaller collectives (ko'onkutik) in an assembly so that each can speak and be heard until all can create a new agreement (ko'ontik) through mutual recognition and respect (ichbail ta muk'). Despite the many differences between the histories and contemporary practices of autonomous government in the five zones of Zapatista territory, they are united by their shared goal of creating a system where all aspects of governance are created through the collective agreement of every Zapatista community in the zone.

In the gathering of intellectuals from civil society convoked by the Zapatistas in May 2015 called "Critical Thought Confronting the Capitalist Hydra," Subcomandante Moisés described how this system of governance functions in practice:

> [W]hat our authorities do is they call a meeting, for example, an Autonomous Rebellious Municipality, which can be fifteen, twenty

compañeros and compañeras, they are there with the [compañeros and compañeras from the] areas of trabajo, health, education, agriculture, commerce, and these things, then this compañero, compañera, the one that has the *cargo* has to say, "I have this problem," she says to the collective of authorities, or it might be that the others that have cargos in the areas tell them, "I have this problem."[1] Then they start to have a discussion among authorities. For this reason we say that it is government in collective. This is where they come up with ideas, proposals, but then they don't just apply them according to the perspective reached by the compañeros. They can't. They have to go to the municipal assembly of authorities, which is made up of [local authorities] the *comisariadas*, *agentas*, *comisariados*, and *agentes*. Then these compañeros throw out a proposal to address a problem. Then the authorities, the assembly, the authorities of the communities, they are guided by our Zapatista law . . . because there they will see "if this has already been discussed, we already know that this is permitted, our communities already are permitting us, and therefore we can say here that yes we will go forward with this proposal." That is when the compañeros comisariados, comisariadas give approval. The authorities know we can't say here if we are in agreement, we have to go consult with our compañeros and compañeras in the communities.[2]

The core of the practice of autonomous government is an assembly of all the local authorities ("comisariadas" and "agentas" are the titles of Zapatista authorities at the local level) from each community in the zone. The responsibility of the authorities of the autonomous municipalities and of the zone are to watch over the initiatives and agreements that are currently functioning in their territory, and if they see a problem to bring it to this assembly of local authorities. Then, the assembly as a whole discusses whether the already existing agreements of the Zapatista communities, or the "Zapatsta law," permits them to do what needs to be done to solve the problem or if the communities must reach a new agreement to address the problem. If a new agreement must be reached, then all the local authorities in the assembly go back to their communities and discuss the problem and come back with proposals until all the communities can agree on how best to solve the problem. As Moisés makes clear, "[T]he autonomous authorities aren't alone in what they do. Their work . . . is laid out by the compas from the communities. They don't make their own policy ... rather, it must be approved by the people."[3]

The process of direct community approval of all decisions requires constant movement to and from assemblies at the different levels of autonomous government. The practice of autonomous government requires numerous hours-long car rides over dirt roads and long strenuous hikes on mountain paths to remote communities, all to ensure that all voices are heard and respected. I saw some of the activity of autonomous government firsthand when I was in Caracol II Oventik while the Zapatistas were organizing the escuelita. During the week I spent there, cars full of Zapatistas were constantly coming and going from the Caracol, and every time I walked past the big assembly hall it was full of people listening as a compañera or compañero spoke their word. This incessant movement connects the multiple communities of the Zapatista organization, it is the thread that weaves their multiple collective hearts (ko'onkutik) into one (ko'ontik).

If the principle of governing by obeying calls all authorities to follow the agreements of the communities rather than their personal judgment, then what do these authorities do when they see a problem with how an agreement is functioning? Having the responsibility to coordinate and administer the agreements of the communities, they should do something, but their actions must take the form of a proposal to the communities, which is then decided upon in assembly, rather than an imposition that is determined by the authorities alone. The principle "to propose not impose" guides the processes of proposing and creating new agreements, projects, and initiatives in each of the five Caracoles. The assembly of all the communities of the zone should be the final authority for all decisions of the autonomous government. All new agreements, projects, and governing structures that affect the entire zone must emerge from this assembly.

A'mtel: Government as Work for Collective Survival

A sense of responsibility to watch over and serve the agreements of the communities defines the role of all Zapatista autonomous authorities. The work of autonomous government is not to make decisions, although they do still participate and give their perspective in the assemblies. Their work always serves the collective agreement of the communities. This conception of work can best be understood through another concept in the Tsotsil language. In the predominantly Tsotsil-speaking Caracol II

Figure 3: Office of the Good Government Council of Oventik

Oventik, the Good Government Council's Office is painted with a mural in both Tsotsil and Spanish (see Figure 3 above). Part of the Tsotsil text of the mural reads "*Snail tzobombail yu'un lekil j'amteletik*," which is translated in Spanish as "*Casa de la Junta de Buen Gobierno*" (House of the Good Government Council). While this translation is correct, the exact connotations of the Tsotsil phrase are very different than those of the Spanish. The first word is the noun "na" meaning "house," with the third person relational or "possessive" prefix s- and the suffix -il, which in this case means that the house is not in relation with a single person or individual. In this case the house is in relation with the tzobombail, a construction of the verb "tzobel" meaning to come together or to meet,[4] the affix -ba- that, as we have already seen in translating "ichbail ta muk," denotes a process that is mutual and reciprocal in the world and the suffix -il that gives the verb a general infinitive sense. "Tzobombail" can be fairly directly translated as "junta" in Spanish or "council" in English. However, the use of the suffix -ba- in the Tsotsil places special emphasis on the reciprocity and mutuality of this coming together to form a collective body or council. So far "snail tzobombail" has essentially the same connotations as "*casa de la junta*" or "house of the council," with the additional connotations of the suffix -ba- that communicates that this council is defined by and works according to reciprocity and mutuality.

However, the translation becomes much more complicated with the rest of the phrase, "yu'un lekil j'amteletik," which has a much broader meaning than that communicated by "de buen gobierno" and "of good government." "Yu'un" translates directly as "de" or "of," but a literal translation that communicates the full meaning of "lekil j'amteletik" would be something like the following: *"la ocupación de hacer trabajos que son buenos para todos,"* or "the occupation of doing works that are good for everyone." As we have already seen in the translation of "lekil kuxlejal" (literally the life that is good for everyone, or dignified life), "lek" means "good" but when modified by the suffix -il it means something that is good for everyone. "J'amteletik" is a construction of the verb "a'mtel," meaning to work, the prefix j- that in this case transforms a verb into a noun meaning the occupation or activity of doing that verb, and the pluralizing suffix -etik.

However, a'mtel is a very particular understanding of work specific to the indigenous communities of Chiapas. A'mtel was one of the central concepts in my Tsotsil lessons with the Zapatista education promoters in Oventik, and it is fundamental in understanding the lesson of the escuelita. One of the education promoters in Oventik told me that a'mtel means work that one does to live, to survive, and to thrive in the world. However, "a'mtel" does not have the individualistic connotation that "work for one's survival" often has in English. On the contrary, in the Zapatista context being able to live in the world necessarily implies collective work. A'mtel describes all the different forms of Zapatista trabajos colectivos or collective works, all those activities that my guardian in the escuelita pointed out by saying, "This is our work." A'mtel encompasses the work of the education promoters who teach the next generation of Zapatistas, the health promoters who work to heal the sick and prevent the spread of diseases, the daily labor of every Zapatista who goes out to work with others in their collective cornfields, and the work of every Zapatista authority charged with watching over the agreements of the communities.

Thus, the "government" of the Good Government Councils has a very different set of connotations than the usual understanding of the English word "government." The primary role of this form of government is not to exercise authority or make decisions, it is the occupation of a'mtel: to work for the survival of the collective and to fulfill certain responsibilities that are defined by the communities, so that every Zapatista community can live and thrive in the world. Furthermore, it shows that there is not a strict separation between the work of the Zapatista trabajos colectivos, for example, in health and education, and the work of the autonomous government. It is not entirely true to say that the good government council "administers" or even "coordinates" the trabajos colectivos in the sense of controlling how they function or exercising unilateral authority over them. Rather, both are different forms of a'mtel, one that is more focused on working in a particular trabajo colectivo and the other that is more focused on coordinating among trabajos colectivos and watching over them to make sure they have the resources and support they need in order to function.

The Tsotsil idea of a'mtel, together with the idea of the assembly understood through the two forms of collective heart in Tsotsil (ko'onkutik and ko'ontik), provides a useful framework for understanding the contemporary practices of autonomous government in the Caracoles. These ideas are the two threads that weave together the current structures of autonomous government as well as the aspirations to improve these structures in each Caracol. Again, these ideas are meaningless without their realization in the practices of the communities. I will now turn to these practices in the five Caracoles as they are described in the escuelita textbooks.

Creation and Re-creation of a Collective Heart: The Assembly of the Zone

The constant creation and re-creation of a collective heart, or the passage from ko'onkutik to ko'ontik, defines decision-making processes in the five Caracoles. This process is practiced in the assemblies and consultation processes that exist in each zone. Fanny, a member of the Good Government Council of Caracol I La Realidad, gives an overview of the process of creating new agreements that is currently in place in her zone:

> The initiatives, in many cases, come up within the Good Government Council where they see necessities arising from the different areas of trabajo. If there is a necessity to make an agreement or a trabajo collectively as a zone or any trabajo colectivo in a municipality that isn't moving forward or to make an agreement on how the *trabajos* can best function, what is done is that they convene regular assemblies, which we normally do every three months in the zone, where the municipal consejos and all the authorities and also all the areas of trabajo plan, analyze, discuss, and propose how the trabajos can best function.
>
> These assemblies are where everyone reaches agreements on how they will work. Often everything can't be decided there in the

assembly itself because the communities, the bases, are there behind us. So proposals are created and brought for consultations with the communities, and in the next assembly the answer will arrive, if it is good or if the communities propose something else. This is how everything gets determined, whether they are regulations or plans for work that needs to be done in the zone. This relationship is also present when there is, for example, a trabajo or a project in a municipality. There the relationship is with the [municipal] consejo who see how the trabajo is going, the reports on how the trabajo is working, if it is working or isn't working.... When there are cases of emergency the Good Government Council also convenes special assemblies. When there is something urgent to do, an agreement or a work plan, they convene special assemblies.[5]

Every three months Caracol I La Realidad holds an assembly of all the local, municipal, and zonal authorities that have been chosen to represent every Zapatista community in their territory. This assembly is the only governing body that can create proposals for new agreements and projects or for modifications of existing ones. However, this assembly does not decide whether to approve these proposals. Once they have developed a proposal in detail, each authority goes back to the community and discusses the proposal with all the Zapatistas who live there. They can either approve the proposal or propose modifications. If all of the communities in the zone approve the proposal, then there is another assembly, and whichever authority is responsible for coordinating the agreement begins to work on implementing it. However, if some communities make modifications to the proposal, then when the authorities come back to the assembly of the zone they have to work to synthesize these proposals and then take the new proposal back to their communities that can again either agree or propose new modifications.

But what if no proposal satisfies all of the communities? Can a proposal move forward if a majority of the communities approve it, even if there is still a dissenting minority? The escuelita textbooks do not explicitly answer this question, and when I asked my guardian during the escuelita he thought for a long time and then only answered, "It depends." Nowhere in the escuelita textbooks does anyone mention the exact procedure for voting on a proposal. The only place I have found an answer to this question is in Rafael Sandoval's summary of his experience attending the escuelita remotely via video conference in August 2013. Discussing one of the question and answer sessions, he summarizes the Zapatista teachers' statements on this subject:[6]

> Often it is necessary to have a prolonged assembly until we arrive at a consensus that is practically unanimous. On issues of autonomy, education, health, and much more, there is a unanimous consensus. There is a majority consensus concerning decisions on immediate issues (secondary, minor things) that must be resolved quickly.[7]

The answer is, as my guardian told me, "It depends." In fact, the lack of a precise description of voting procedures in the escuelita textbooks is more significant than the answer itself. Questions regarding majority rule or consensus voting procedures are premised on a Western understanding of democracy as procedural decision-making in a congress or parliament. In Zapatista autonomous governance, the emphasis is on coming into agreement through the principle "to convince not defeat," through the process of ichbail ta muk', not on the procedural intricacies of making a decision. The initiatives of the Good Government Council only exist insofar as they manifest the aspirations of a shared collective heart (ko'ontik). The exact procedure for voting on a proposal never seems important to the Zapatistas, because every proposal is made through the participation of every municipality, community, and individual Zapatista. The only way a proposed initiative is created in the first place is by all the communities agreeing on its contents.

The authorities from Caracoles III, IV, and V describe a similar process of the communities coming into agreement through an assembly of the zone. However, the particularities of how the assembly functions are slightly different in each of these three Caracoles. Ceferino, a former member of the Good Government Council from Caracol III La Garrucha, says that his Caracol has a regular assembly of all local and municipal authorities every six months and additional assemblies whenever the Good Government Council sees a problem that requires a new agreement. He also makes clear that the communities have the final say. For example, he said that during his time as an authority whenever there was a land dispute that needed solving, "[I]t was always done with the people, who helped us a lot in providing a solution, because they were the ones doing the analysis. We simply made proposals, and they would discuss them, analyze them, and come back to put them together in the zone, and then the plan of how we were going to do the work would come together."[8] Similarly, Johana and Fermín, former members of the Good Government Council of Caracol IV Morelia, say that their Caracol holds regular assemblies of all municipal, regional (Caracol IV has the additional regional level of autonomous government between municipal and local), and local authorities every two months, and that they also convoke additional special assemblies of the zone when there is an urgent problem or initiative. Again, Johana makes clear that the role of the authorities is to make proposals not decisions:

> The communities have to know about any plan or agreement of the zone. The regional and municipal consejos are responsible for bringing it to the communities, but the community has the final say. Here the people decide and the government obeys. As Good Government Council, municipal, and regional authorities we can't make any plan or agreement if the people don't agree. This is why we first ask the communities before making any plan or agreement.[9]

Caracol V Roberto Barrios also makes decisions through an assembly of the zone convoked every month. However, while all the other Caracoles hold their zonal assemblies in the Caracol itself, Roberto Barrios alternates every month between holding it in the Caracol (located in the eastern part of the zone) and in the autonomous municipality of Acabalná (located to the west, near the border with the state of Tabasco) to make it easier for the authorities in the western part of the zone to attend. An unnamed authority from Roberto Barrios underlines the purpose of these monthly assemblies: "[W]e know well that the Council can't decide for itself. As we say, if we want to do a trabajo we always have to consult with the communities, among the men and women."[10] All four of these Caracoles have developed their own particular ways of convening assemblies of the zone. They all share relatively similar decision-making structures that bring the principle of governing by obeying into practice.

However, in the Zapatista practice of autonomy every commonality usually has an exception. In this case, the exception is Caracol II Oventik. Abraham, a member of the Good Government Council of Oventik in 2013 at the time of the escuelita, states:

> One of our duties as Good Government Council is to organize meetings and assemblies, but we haven't carried it out. The only thing

we have done are gatherings of base communities throughout the zone when there is an anniversary, where we have cultural events, sports, and where we give our [political] message. We have not convoked a general assembly with the bases to address special issues. On the other hand, the municipal authorities do convoke general assemblies of the base communities of their municipalities, where they give their reports, where they choose new authorities, and there are times when they convoke assemblies through the autonomous agentes [local authorities] when they see the necessity for urgent work. . . . The communities and regions that haven't been able to form their autonomous municipalities have their gatherings when, by internal agreement, some communities have named their autonomous agente, autonomous comisariado, or autonomous judge. These authorities convoke assemblies of the base communities, together with the regional and local [responsables of the EZLN], and they are the ones who intervene to solve the problems in these communities.[11]

As of 2013, the Good Government Council of Oventik had not been able to convene an assembly of all the authorities of their zone. The process of assembly decision-making where the autonomous authorities make proposals and take them to the communities for approval was only operating at the municipal level. However, as Abraham makes clear, organizing an assembly of the zone is a defined goal of the Good Government Council, and it is possible that they have been able to organize one during the years since the first grade of the escuelita.

A brief look at the map of Zapatista autonomous government might begin to explain why organizing an assembly of the zone is so difficult in Oventik. It covers a large geographical area that includes some of the most populous areas of Chiapas and many regions with Zapatista communities that have not been able to organize themselves into autonomous municipalities. Most of the southwestern half of Oventik's zone has only a very few Zapatistas dispersed among a non-Zapatista majority. Furthermore, Zapatista organizing arrived relatively late to the highland region covered by Oventik. The clandestine organization began in the mid-1980s in the jungle and canyon region in the Caracols of La Realidad, La Garrucha, and Morelia but did not reach the highlands until the early 1990s.[12] However, Oventik's failure to organize zonal assemblies does not mean that the autonomous authorities in the zone have unilateral authority over initiatives such as the education or health systems. These are still controlled by assemblies at the municipal level, and initiatives at the level of the zone, for example, the secondary school or central hospital, are still run by promoters who are assigned their cargo by the communities and who are accountable to them.

Although it is not true that every Caracol makes decisions through an assembly of the whole zone, all the authorities in the escuelita textbooks agree that the organization and coordination of this decision-making process is one of the central responsibilities of the Good Government Councils. Furthermore, the numerous differences in how this responsibility is realized point to a foundational aspect of Zapatista governance: there is no single model or blueprint, rather every governing structure is determined by the communities that compose that structure. It is up to the communities in each zone to create a form of democratic decision-making in an assembly that works in their own contexts. The communities have the sole power and responsibility to create their governing structures.

The Assembly of the Zone and the Creation of Trabajos Colectivos: An Example from La Realidad

How are concrete issues addressed through the assembly of the zone? In particular, how have the assemblies of each zone worked to create trabajos colectivos in their territory? There are too many examples mentioned in the escuelita textbooks to give a full description of every case. I have selected one example from Caracol I La Realidad that provides a good illustration of the difficulties that arise in the process of creating and implementing agreements through an assembly of the zone. The testimonies of the authorities from Caracol I La Realidad give some of the most detailed examples of the decision-making process of their assembly of the zone. They describe how this process has given rise to several collective initiatives, including an autonomous health system with a central hospital near the Caracol and a clinic in each autonomous municipality,[13] an autonomous education system with promoters in each community who teach in their own indigenous languages[14] and who received their training in the Caracol,[15] a system of autonomous community radio stations,[16] an autonomous bank called the People's Autonomous Zapatista Bank (Banco Popular Autónomo Zapatista, or BANPAZ) that gives loans to cover health expenses for serious illnesses requiring treatment in the government health system,[17] and another autonomous bank called the Autonomous Bank of Women Zapatista Authorities (Banco Autónomo de Mujeres Autoridades Zapatistas, or BANAMAZ) that gives loans so that women can start their own trabajos colectivos.[18] The story of the creation of the People's Autonomous Zapatista Bank provides a good illustration of the Zapatista decision-making process in practice. Roel, a former member of the Good Government Council, tells this story:

> BANPAZ, which is the People's Autonomous Zapatista Bank ... [w]as created as an initiative, because we saw that a problem came up in our zone. At this time, there were many compañeros who came to the [Good Government] Council to ask for a loan, but the communities hadn't authorized us to give these loans. It happened that in a community in our zone there was a child that was receiving support because he was sick. When this came up in an assembly of authorities, men and women, agentas and comisariadas, they started to say: Why does only this child get to be supported if there are many children in the zone? This was where the idea of the bank was born, also thanks to the idea that the first compañeros had, for example, from the CCRI, from the command of our zone, who already had this idea when they were in control of health, of commerce. But since the trabajos passed into the hands of the [municipal] councils the bank remained as an idea ... so we proposed what they were thinking of doing, it was proposed in the assembly. The compañeros took what we were thinking about doing back for discussion, then once they had brought it back for consultation the answer came. In our zone we are accustomed to having regular assemblies every three months. ... Then when an initiative is born from an authority, for example, from the [Good Government] Council, this is very helpful in making it known and in bringing the proposal down to the communities.[19]

As with most Zapatista initiatives at the level of the zone, the original idea of creating the BANPAZ grew out of a problem confronted by the Good Government Council: they had to attend to many compañeros who were asking for loans, presumably many of them for good reasons, as in the case of the child who was receiving support for his medical expenses, but there was no agreement among the communities that gave them the power to give loans. The Council brought this problem to the assembly, where they also heard the idea of creating a Zapatista bank from the CCRI. This assembly eventually decided to go forward with the idea of creating a BANPAZ.

All the authorities brought the proposal to their communities, where it was unanimously approved. The Good Government Council then started gathering the funds to start the bank. They took twenty thousand pesos that had been generated by the public transportation route of the small bus, "el solidario," that had been created through a previous initiative of the zone, another twenty thousand pesos that had previously gone toward the medical expenses of the child, and the CCRI provided an additional fifty thousand pesos for a total of ninety thousand pesos. They then went back to the assembly to further develop the initiative. As Roel explains:

> [W]e then had an agreement of the zone that we would move forward.... We pulled out the ninety thousand pesos, and the same assembly now had to see what we were going to do, because now we had it. Now we had to make a regulation for how it is going to work and that is the most difficult. How it is going to work, because we were starting to put everything together. The idea is good, but what problems are we going to confront? We had to continue in the assemblies that are convoked to make an internal regulation so that it could work and to see what things will work for us and what things won't, so that the next authority can go on improving these regulations. By agreement of everyone at the assembly, it ended up that we would charge the minimum interest, 2 percent of the loan that we gave. When we began the assembly we discussed it. We brought it to the communities, and they returned their proposals. Then in an assembly of authorities, men as well as women, we thought that the loans should only be for health care, this is one of the rules that we made. So that we could give a loan to a compa, so that we could confirm that is was actually going to be for health care, the compas have to bring a sealed paper signed by the authority so that they can be authorized for the loan and aren't lying, that they aren't going to use it for other things.[20]

By coming up with ideas about how the BANPAZ would function in the assembly, then taking these proposals to the communities, which would send their responses back to the assembly for synthesis and more deliberation, they eventually reached an agreement that included all the communities of the zone: the BANPAZ would give loans at 2 percent interest to cover medical expenses. The bank would be a form of mutual aid and could not be used for an individual's personal profit. Presumably these loans are for medical costs in the government health care system. I can attest from my own personal experience that care in the autonomous system is free to anyone, Zapatista and non-Zapatista alike. It was also possible to use the loans to cover the cost of pharmaceutical medicines from the autonomous system, since Zapatista pharmacies do charge a small fee for those medicines that must be bought from outside the Zapatista organization.

However, almost as soon as the communities agreed on how the BANPAZ would function, they started having problems. Roel continues:

> We had a problem because it was only the authority who was signing the paper that confirmed that the compa needed the loan for health care. Then what happened is the authority conspired with the compañeros. We had one case in the municipality General Emiliano Zapata, a compa arrived to ask for a loan with his paper signed by the authority, and we trusted this authority from the community. The loan was given to the compañero, but it turned out that this compañero didn't have anyone who was sick, he used it for other things, to do business, he was buying other things.
>
> When it was seen that this was happening and that the authorities of the communities were giving loans for these types of things that they shouldn't be giving loans for, then we returned again to the assembly to make it so that not only the authority of the community had to sign. They have to go to their health promoter who will see they are really getting the money for an illness. Things got adjusted as we confronted different types of problems.
>
> Also within the regulation of the BANPAZ it says that ... the money loaned to the compañero would be returned within six months.... But we saw that this gave the compañeros very little time, six months—there are illness that take more time. All these things showed us how to continue improving the internal agreements.
>
> Now the compañeros can take out their loan for up to a year. Also, if the compañero or compañera hasn't gotten better during this year, then the compañero has the right to speak with the authority of the [Good Government] Council to extend the time on their loan and explain why they need more time. There are also compañeros who,

confident that they have the loan, seem to forget about paying. The authority starts to think that this compañero doesn't want to pay, because he doesn't even show up to explain why he hasn't paid. But the authority does understand those who go and explain, and they give them more time, because they explain their reasons. We see that the BANPAZ is working well.[21]

After its creation, the BANPAZ encountered problems both with individuals not following the collective agreement of all the communities and with this agreement itself not taking into account the legitimate needs of individuals. Zapatista authorities are not immune to temptations that might cause them to break the agreements of the communities for their own personal gain. Some local authorities took advantage of the BANPAZ and did not follow the agreement that loans would only be used as a form of mutual aid to help someone who is sick. But the democratic decisions of the communities are also sometimes fraught with mistakes. Their agreement was not responsive to the needs of families who took out loans to care for sick relatives. It imposed an arbitrary time limit on repayment that was unrealistic in many cases, causing the Good Government Council to think that families were being dishonest, when in reality they simply couldn't pay back the loan that quickly. The Good Government Council saw that the BANPAZ was departing from the original intention of the communities to create a form of mutual aid. They brought these problems to the assembly, where proposals to remedy them were developed and brought to the communities for approval. As a result, they ended up with a better functioning BANPAZ that had a way of insuring that the loans were really being used for health care and were responsive to the individual situations of those who needed them.

Roel also goes on to mention several other agreements that improved the functioning of the BANPAZ. The communities agreed that if the mother or father in a family that receives a BANPAZ loan dies from their illness the family doesn't have to repay the loan, and if it is a child who dies the family automatically has more time to pay back the loan. They also agreed that if someone fails to repay their loan, then no one else from their community can receive a loan from the BANPAZ. This is meant to encourage the other people in the community to convince the compañero to do their best to pay back their loan. However, if the compañero really doesn't have the means of paying, then the assembly agreed that they can pay back the loan by working for a period of time in one of the trabajos colectivos that supports the zone.

The BANPAZ had been functioning well for a year when the Zapatistas collected 300 thousand pesos from the 10 percent tax each Caracol charges all outside companies that do roadwork or any other public works project in their territory. They went to the assembly of the zone to decide what to do with this money and they agreed to invest 200 thousand in the BANPAZ and to give the remaining 100 thousand to the women of the zone who had decided to create their own autonomous bank called the Autonomous Bank of Women Zapatista Authorities (BANAMAZ). They created this initiative through an assembly of all the women authorities in the zone in consultation with the women in the communities. The bank would only give loans to communities and regions made up of several communities so that the women could start their own trabajos colectivos. Eloísa, a former member of the Good Government Council, explains why the women decided on this initiative:

> We did this because in the communities and in the regions sometimes they want to make colectivos, but there is no way of getting a fund of money to support us in starting the colectivo. It was said that it is going to be exclusively for colectivos of compañeras, either from a community or a region. It was said that in small communities they are going to give three thousand pesos, in the large ones they are going to give five thousand, and in a region they are going to give ten thousand pesos, with a payment of 2 percent interest.[22]

The creation of the BANAMAZ both recognized the concrete barriers to women's participation in the collective work—the a'mtel—of the Zapatista struggle and took steps to overcome these barriers. Thanks to BANAMAZ loans, women who don't control any of their household income and whose husbands or fathers won't give them resources to help start a collective can still access funds to create trabajos colectivos.

Although some of the other Caracoles have created similar autonomous banks, the BANAMAZ of La Realidad is the only initiative specifically created to fund the creation of women's trabajos colectivos. Caracol III La Garrucha created a bank called the Zapatista Autonomous Bank (Banco Autónomo Zapatista, or BAZ) that would give loans of up to three thousand pesos at 2 percent interest for health care costs and up to five thousand pesos at 5 percent interest for other necessities, such as purchasing a donkey or cow, but at the time of the escuelita the bank was faltering because only around half of the money loaned out had been paid back.[23] Similarly, Caracol IV also has a BAZ that gives loans of between three and five thousand pesos at 2 percent interest for health care costs or loans of five thousand pesos at 3 percent interest for other necessities. Despite some early setbacks, the BAZ in Caracol IV was doing well at the time of the escuelita and had also inspired another smaller bank at the municipal level in the autonomous municipality Lucio Cabañas.[24] Although all these banks in La Garrucha and Morelia give loans to anyone who wants to start a small cooperative, including women, they are not specifically targeted at the creation of women's cooperatives like the BANAMAZ in La Realidad.

The case of the creation of the BANPAZ and BANAMAZ provides a good illustration of the core responsibility of the Good Government Council: to administer and watch over the agreements of the communities and propose possible solutions in the assembly of the zone that can then be decided upon by the communities. In practice, this responsibility requires attending to anyone who comes to the Good Government Council with a problem that needs resolution, coming up with proposals for the communities that address broad needs of the whole zone, and making sure that the resulting agreements are functioning as they should. The role of the Good Government Council is to serve and obey the communities not to make decisions for them. It is just one of many forms of a'mtel, the collective work that is divided into different sets of responsibilities at the multiple levels of the Zapatista organization.

Zapatista Justice

The day-to-day work of the Good Government Council involves watching over the trabajos colectivos and coming up with proposals for new initiatives that can then be submitted to the communities for approval. However, they are also responsible for attending to anyone who brings them an issue that needs to be addressed. As Doroteo, a former member of the Good Government Council from La Realidad, explains:

> We consider one of the obligations of the autonomous government to be to attend to anyone who comes to the office with different issues, it doesn't matter if they receive or don't receive a solution to their issue but they must be listened to. Whoever it may be, Zapatista or non-Zapatista, they are attended to. As long as they aren't people

from the government or sent by the government, they could be from any social organization, they are attended to.[25]

In many cases the issues brought to the autonomous government are questions of justice. In other words, they are issues that require the autonomous government to address violations of Zapatista law or to resolve disputes between people or communities in their territory. The different levels of autonomous government in the five Caracoles attend to many different people and address all sorts of issues from petty theft through cases of murder and rape to paramilitary attacks and land disputes. In general, the Good Government Councils are responsible for resolving more difficult problems that involve more people in the zone. As Doroteo makes clear, this includes anyone, Zapatistas as well as non-Zapatistas, who arrives at their office with a problem. Although only Zapatistas can participate in assemblies or serve as authorities in the autonomous government, they often live in villages that are split between Zapatistas, non-Zapatistas sympathetic to the movement who remain outside the organization, and sometimes even anti-Zapatistas who are hostile to the movement. Any of these groups can bring an issue of justice to the Good Government Councils for resolution. Gerónimo, a former member of the first period of the Good Government Council of Caracol IV Morelia, gives examples of some of the problems that have been addressed by the Good Government Council in his zone:

> One experience that we had as members of the Good Government Council was to resolve serious agrarian problems. Our [non-Zapatista] brothers from San Fernando, official municipality of Huixtán, came to the Council to submit a complaint regarding agrarian problems that were so bad that serious things were about to happen. There was even going to be killing. When the brothers came to us, they told us all their problems. As the Council we know what our responsibility is. It is to resolve anyone's problems, without distinction, coming from wherever they come from, so we called the other party who are [non-Zapatista] brothers from Chanal, we called them and we had a dialogue. We listened to what these brothers said and afterward we went to the place in question. Then we analyzed who was in the right and who was in the wrong. In this case, thanks to the intervention of the Council, this problem received a satisfactory

solution. We avoided any bloody incidents. We feel that it was an important accomplishment for the Council.

The same happened with other organizations. We do it this way— when a group arrives to submit a complaint we call the other party, we dialogue. We as the Council never impose the solution. Instead, they have to find the solution, they have to be convinced. With the mediation of the Good Government Council other land problems were satisfactorily solved, and in the end they remained peaceful. This is how we resolve various kinds of problems, like family problems. Although resolving family problems wasn't our responsibility as the Good Government Council, but when we were asked we resolved them, and if not, we sent them to the municipality, because the municipality also has to do their work. When a problem is not the responsibility of the Council it must be sent to the municipality. This is how we work in questions of justice.

In these two problems, as Good Government Council, we believe we were successful, because we avoided bigger problems. We have also resolved problems between councils, for example, if there is some problem that is happening in our zone, but the compañero that has the complaint is from [the territory of] another Council. What we do in these cases is we meet with the compañeros from the other Council, we do the investigations. . . . One example is an agrarian problem that happened, I believe it was in 2003. It was an agrarian problem with one Gerónimo de Meza. As Good Government Councils of Morelia and Garrucha we had a meeting and formed the agreement, and in the end we solved this problem. We did it so there wouldn't be any misunderstandings between us.[26]

The Good Government Council resolves problems according to the principle of "to convince not defeat" and "to propose not impose." They do not reach a decision and issue a judgment as to which party in a dispute is in the right, rather they act as a mediator between the two parties, investigate the facts involved in the dispute, and convince both parties to come together to create a peaceful solution that everyone can agree to. Although they propose possible solutions to the problem, the ultimate solution is up to the communities or persons involved in the dispute. In general, the Good Government Council is supposed to deal with very serious issues like the tense agrarian disputes described by Gerónimo, while smaller disputes like problems in a family are the primary responsibility of the municipal consejos.[27] Gerónimo also mentions that the consejos use the same process as the junta: they listen to both parties, investigate facts, and propose some solutions, but the ultimate resolution of the problem has to be agreed to and created by the people involved in the dispute. Furthermore, the autonomous government works to resolve disputes regardless of whether they involve Zapatista communities or not. They act as mediators for anyone within their territory, even if they are not part of the Zapatista organization.

The commitment to mediate a just solution to any problem brought before them is both an ethical commitment to justice for all the peoples of Chiapas who are denied a fair hearing by the government and a practical antiparamilitary strategy. When non-Zapatistas seek and find justice with the Good Government Councils they are more likely to value their work. Even if this does not cause them to join the organization, it nonetheless builds respect for the autonomous government among non-Zapatistas. In fact, many non-Zapatistas remain outside of the organization not because they oppose it, but because, as one education promoter told me in Oventik, "It is a lot of work being a Zapatista." Joining the organization requires abiding by Zapatista law, including the prohibition on alcohol, a great deal of organizational work, and the refusal of all contact with the government, including all government aid. By opening their doors to these sympathetic non-Zapatistas, the Good Government Councils pull them away from the side of the government and toward the collective heart of the organization.

Violations of the agreements of the communities, from consuming alcohol to serious crimes, such as murder or rape, are generally punished by assigning work for the collective or by paying a fine. For example, Doroteo says that during his period serving on the Good Government Council there was a case of murder that was resolved because the families of the perpetrator and the victim agreed on a sum of money that would be paid in compensation to the victim's family.[28] However, the Zapatistas promote collective work over payments as a form of punishment, so that "justice does not become a business."[29] Violations of Zapatista law are also handled according to the principle "to convince not defeat." The resolution aims to come up with a solution that is agreeable to everyone who was affected by the violation in order to move forward and prevent the fragmentation of the community. As the escuelita teachers said:

In Zapatista justice there are no lawyers, procedures, paperwork, or hearings. There are a hell of a lot of people who come and participate so that there will be a solution for those involved in the problem. There are no police who come for the accused, instead lots of people tell them and insist that they present themselves and confront the accusation, people who convince them.[30]

This practice of community justice applies even to non-Zapatistas who violate Zapatista law in their territory. For example, trafficking of migrants across the Guatemalan border is prohibited by Zapatista law, not because they want to prohibit the migrants from passing, but rather because they know that these migrants are often overcharged, robbed, or otherwise exploited by the traffickers, called *polleros* in Spanish, who guide them across the border. Doroteo describes one case where they caught a group of polleros during his period on the Good Government Council:

[N]ine polleros were detained during our period, including a Guatemalan who stayed here six months to pay his punishment. This Guatemalan pollero worked on the construction of the bridge to the San José del Río hospital.... The funniest thing for us was that, since the polleros we detained remained six months doing their work, we were punishing them. For us it is a punishment so that they will correct themselves, to go and work. In the end one of these *cabrones* thanked us for punishing him. He thanked us because he said that for him it wasn't a punishment. They put me in school—this is what he told us—because he said that now he is a master builder and he never thought he would be one, and now I can go build houses, and now I can go build whatever I want. This is the punishment we give them, that is, instead of putting them in jail, we put them to work. Of course, he left the product of his work in the community, but he left with something good. This is what we think. This is how we do justice. I don't know if it is good or bad, but this is how it is. This has happened with everyone. They always come away with something.[31]

As Doroteo points out, the goal of Zapatisa justice is not primarily to assign punishments, it is to try to make the person who committed the crime change their habits and ways of thinking, while also compensating the community in some way. Even in questions of justice the Zapatista government proceeds according to the logic of a'mtel. It aims to serve the will of the community, first, by ensuring their agreements are respected by punishing those who violate them. But it also punishes by assigning a'mtel, by assigning work that benefits the community. This ensures that punishments strengthen the cohesion of the community, rather than dividing it. It brings those who committed the crime back into the way of life defined by the community's agreements and ensures that punishment gives back to the community and to those who were wronged.

Conclusion

The assembly is at the center of the Zapatista autonomous government. It is the means by which all decisions are made and all problems are addressed. This form of governance is the concrete manifestation of the creation of the collective heart, of the passage from ko'onkutik to ko'ontik. It is a form of governance that aims to ensure that all voices are heard and that their words have equal weight. Decision-making in Zapatista autonomous government proceeds by dialogue, consultation, and mutual agreement. It functions according to the logic of the seven principles of governing by obeying. Although the assembly is the core of the autonomous government system, the principles that are manifested in the assembly inform numerous aspects of Zapatista governance. These principles guide multiple different aspects of the government system, from the creation of initiatives like the BANPAZ in La Realidad to the redress of grievances in the practice of Zapatista justice.

CHAPTER FIVE

Decolonizing Work:
Zapatista Collective Work (A'mtel) and the Struggle against Systems of Desperation-Dependence-Displacement (Kanal)

One of the primary tasks of the Good Government Council is to coordinate the implementation of trabajos colectivos in its zone. However, once a project has been approved by the communities, where does each Good Government Council get the funding and resources to implement the project? There are three main sources of funding: donations from solidarity groups, a 10 percent tax that the Good Government Council charges on all infrastructure projects undertaken by any private or government company in their territory, such as building and repaving roads, and the resources that are generated by their own trabajos colectivos.[1] Although the Zapatistas gather resources from diverse sources, how they go about gathering them reflects a common commitment to the principles of a'mtel. This form of work not only describes the work of autonomous government, it describes a general form of work that encompasses many activities in Zapatista communities and the autonomous government system. "A'mtel" can describe collectively working in a cornfield or serving the community as an education promoter. All these activities share a common form: they are collective forms of work that are democratically defined and administered by the community. This form of work is understood in opposition to capitalist forms of wage labor and any general organization of work in a community that is not collectively controlled by the community. In fact, this undemocratic organization of work cannot be described by the word "a'mtel." There is a different Tsotsil word for this form of work: *kanal*, or work that is done for a boss in order to earn money.

   The distinction between a'mtel and kanal goes beyond just a distinction between unpaid subsistence and paid wage labor. When an education promoter from Oventik explained the distinction to me he focused more on how each form of work affects the collective capacities of a community—in other words, how each form either strengthens or weakens their collective ch'ulel. The ch'ulel of communities is made up of their capacities to live in the world, to take each other into account (tsakbail ta venta), and through this taking into account carry one another to greatness (ichbail ta muk'). The organization of work in terms of money and work for a boss (kanal) undermines these capacities in several ways. First, the organization of work as kanal creates a whole social system that undermines a community's ability to sustain itself through its own labor and makes them dependent on external sources of capital. This was the predominant organization of labor in the indigenous communities of Chiapas before the 1994 uprising, where lack of sufficient agricultural land to sustain their communities forced them to survive by working in virtual slavery for the Chiapan landowners or for the upper classes in the cities. It was a social system where indigenous communities were maintained in a state of perpetual economic dependence. Their dependence destroyed their capacity to autonomously control their own sustenance and perpetuated their enslavement to the landed elites.

In order to understand the deeper implications of the distinction between kanal and the Zapatistas' commitment to a'mtel, it is necessary to understand the nature of the system of exploitation by the large landowners as well as the rearticulations of this system in the present. The kanal form of work was forged in the finca system that existed before 1994 and has been perpetuated in the intertwined economic development and counterinsurgency strategies of the contemporary Mexican state.[2] These systems reveal the centrality of the Zapatista trabajos colectivos and the creation of a'mtel not just in the day-to-day functioning of the organization but also as a struggle for decolonization: to undo the reproduction of colonial forms of exploitation and domination and to build a different world and way of life. There are many challenges facing the Zapatistas' creation of a'mtel, both from external forms of state repression and from internal organizational problems. The organization of trabajos colectivos in the five Caracoles is fraught with numerous challenges and setbacks and has not had equal success throughout the Caracoles. However, the Caracoles have remained steadfast in their creativity. The struggle to create trabajos colectivos is central to the Zapatista struggle as a whole, to their process of decolonization, and to the construction of a new way of life defined by the democratic relationships of a'mtel.

Cycles of Desperation-Dependence-Displacement: The Kanal of the Finca and Its Contemporary Reproduction

Although the literal meaning of "kanal" is wage labor, the history of wage labor in Chiapas gives it a particular set of connotations. For indigenous communities in Chiapas, engaging in the kanal form of work was rarely a choice, it was a necessity imposed by various concrete mechanisms, including land scarcity, indebtedness, and outright violence and intimidation by the landed elite. Work on the fincas was an almost universal experience for the rural indigenous population for most of the twentieth century. This experience took one of two forms: that of seasonal migrant labor and that of the peons who lived on the finca permanently.

Migrant laborers lived primarily in the highland region of Chiapas in what now comprises most of the zone of Caracol II Oventik. The harvest time for the cash crops grown on the fincas, including sugarcane, coffee, and cacao, corresponded to the unproductive period for subsistence crops in the highlands. This five-month period from November to March was a time of hunger and desperation in the highlands. Acute land scarcity, created by a long history of dispossession and illegal land invasions by the large landowners and exacerbated by population growth, made it impossible for most families to store enough corn and beans to sustain themselves through these months. They were often faced with the choice between going hungry or going to work in the lowlands on the fincas. The landowners took advantage of this desperation to further exploit the migrant labor force. Migrants would be paid in advance by a local labor contractor, or *enganche*, and would then work off their loan on the finca. However, once they were there all their food, purchases at the landowner's company store, and alcohol added to their debt. It was often possible to end the harvest with more debt than when they began. Indebted workers were either thrown in jail or had to continue to work on the fincas in future harvests. As Andres Aubrey writes, "The connections between *ejido* and finca, between debt-payment-enganche-prison-alcohol-company store,[3] are the diabolical chains that transform the labor force into prisoners."[4]

This imprisonment was even more acute for the peons who lived on the fincas themselves. While the migrant laborers could survive on their own lands for a portion of the year, the peons were completely dependent on the landowner for their survival. Although they had some very small plots for corn, they were of such poor quality that they never came close to providing enough for their subsistence.[5] These resident peons formed the permanent year-round labor force on the fincas. They worked in the fields, took care of the cattle, and served the landowner in his home. Their complete dependence perpetuated their entrapment in a pervasive system of domination. The landowners would whip or even hang those who disobeyed them. The physical abuse was especially acute for women, who were also subject to sexual violence. Hilary Klein quotes Amina, a Tzeltal elder from the zone of La Garrucha, who, at the Comandanta Ramona Women's gathering in 2007, described her experience growing up on the Las Delicias finca:

> There was another finca called Porvenir. [The landowner] Don Javier Albores, he also had children with his servants. The fathers couldn't say anything because they had already seen that if they didn't hand over their daughters, they would be hanged. They couldn't do anything, but they knew the young women were being raped. All the young women! Not just one or two, it was all the young women. The women he had already raped, they could walk by the patrón [boss]. It didn't matter if he saw them because he didn't care about them anymore. That's why Don Javier Albores had so many children on his finca. That was what life was like when we lived on the fincas. It was all large coffee plantations and sugarcane plantations, all owned by the patrones. They had us under complete control. We had to work all the time, and we had to do whatever they told us to do. What one patrón did the rest of them did as well. El Rosario, Las Delicias, Porvenir, those were the fincas I saw with my own eyes, and all the landowners were the same.[6]

The institution of the finca in Chiapas was not just a system of labor exploitation, it was system of domination that encompassed all spheres of social life. As Amina states, this was a system of "complete control" that not only provided the landowners with an exploitable labor force but also exposed the indigenous communities, and especially indigenous women, to multiple forms of violence. This is the full connotation of the word "kanal" in the context of Chiapas. While it certainly implies wage exploitation and economic dependence, it carries the larger significance of a social system of domination and violence. The social system implied by the word "kanal" was hegemonic in Chiapas until the 1980s when radical campesino organizations, including the clandestine EZLN, began eroding the power of the fincas.[7] This process ultimately culminated in the 1994 uprising and land reclamations that virtually abolished the finca system. The end of this system forms the backdrop to the subsequent struggle to create autonomous and collective forms of labor, or a'mtel.

However, the struggle against a social system defined by kanal did not stop with the 1994 revolution. Since the revolution, the Mexican government has undertaken a counterinsurgency strategy that uses social programs to buy the loyalty of members of non-Zapatista communities and encourage the formation of paramilitary groups. These paramilitary groups attempt to displace Zapatista communities from their land and attack their means of subsistence, for example, by destroying crops or houses.[8] Paramilitary violence serves a dual purpose: it seeks to destroy the means of subsistence that allows Zapatista communities to sustain their autonomy while also attempting to provoke the EZLN into breaking its ceasefire agreement with the government to justify further military repression. This strategy is itself a continuation of the prerevolutionary system of local caciques, or indigenous bosses, who would receive power and resources from the ruling Partido Revolucionario Institucional (PRI) in exchange for controlling their communities and maintaining their dependence on work in the fincas.[9] Although the counterinsurgency strategy is very different than the finca system, it nonetheless functions according to a similar logic: it aims to create economic dependence in order to control the indigenous communities, with the ultimate aim of displacing them and using their lands for resource extraction and other economic development projects. Just as economic dependence forced the indigenous population to obey and work for the patrones on the fincas, dependence on government aid forces non-Zapatista communities to obey and work for the Mexican government and its counterinsurgency strategy. Once a community has become dependent on government aid, it can be threatened with the withdrawal of this aid and the disappearance of its means of survival if it does not comply with the wishes of the government.

Government social programs create economic dependence not only by encouraging campesinos to rely on government money rather than the product of their own labor on their land but also by imposing conditions that actively seek to destroy the ability of campesinos to survive without government aid. In a communiqué released in February 2016,

Subcomandantes Moisés and Galeano describe the reality of government programs in *partidista* communities (communities that receive aid in exchange for loyalty to a political party). The cases they describe were brought to them by the partidista communities themselves after they realized the real intentions of the government programs. The first case involves a partidista community near Caracol I La Realidad that received cattle as part of a government program. Each family received its own cows, horse, corral, salt, and free vaccinations. Everyone was very happy until a government inspector arrived in their community:

> [T]he damned inspector . . . called all the ejidatarios together and there he told everyone, he got out a bunch of papers and showed them to the people, said to them, "All these papers are the lists, receipts, and invoices for everything you have received from the government. This is why this land is no longer yours. You will have to leave, and it would be better if you went voluntarily, because if you don't you will be forced to go. If you go willingly, the place where you will go to live is ready for you: it will be in Escárcega, state of Campeche, or else you will go to Los Chimalapas." This whole time that the people were feeling happy with the support of the bad government, in reality they had been taking care of cattle that weren't even theirs, like peons. And all the papers they signed, with their ejidal accords and voter credentials, sold off their lands for a pittance without them knowing it. Right there the smiles stopped and the shame, sadness, pain, and rage started.[10]

The cattle from the government program weren't actually free, they were a loan. Now the ejido was in debt to the government and their only means of payment was their land. They could either sell it willingly or be removed by force. Their ejido was unfortunate enough to be near some beautiful islands in the middle of the Jataté River that were slated to be transformed into an ecotourism resort. The government's offer of moving to Escárcega or Chimalapas would not provide any real solution. Both of these regions are riddled with conflict among campesinos due to land scarcity.[11]

This communiqué tells many other similar stories. A community in the northern zone of Chiapas received coffee, corn, a school, clinic, church, and road improvements, all with the help of government social programs. Then a government functionary came to tell them that these had all been given on credit and that they had actually sold their land to the government. The community is located on top of a uranium deposit, and in order to extract the uranium the community must leave. The communiqué also mentions two other communities that inadvertently sold their land by receiving government programs. One used to mine amber on their lands and now the amber is being extracted by a Chinese company, the other ended up selling all their land to someone from Japan.

Moisés and Galeano also relate how three other communities near Caracol III La Garrucha received the government program ProÁrbol. This program is described on the REDD desk website:

> ProÁrbol is a comprehensive programme promoting actions for the conservation, restoration and sustainable use of Mexico's forests.... ProÁrbol works on the premise that sustainable forest management is best achieved by allocating the rights to exploit forest resources to forest owning *ejidos* and communities. Each programme under ProÁrbol therefore favors projects in *ejidos* and communities, and in Mexico's highly marginalised regions.[12]

The communiqué describes a very different reality in the three partidista communities. Once they became part of ProÁrbol the communities were prohibited from cutting any trees for firewood, to clear land for their fields, or to repair their houses. They were forced to buy wood from lumber companies that were given the rights to cut trees in the forest previously used by the communities. But where could these communities get the resources to buy the firewood they burn every day to cook their food? From other government programs that provide cash assistance. But these programs also come with a price. To receive the aid, the campesinos must have all the correct identification and land title papers. And, as Subcomandantes Moisés and Galeano write, "And why does the bad government want these papers? Well, to demonstrate that the campesinos sold their lands legally, to be able to drive them out them legally, and to legally displace them to other lands that were invaded illegally."[13]

And where might the government send these communities once they are displaced? They could offer them land far away, as in the case of the community that received the cattle program, or they could pit them against a Zapatista community in Chiapas, for example, by giving them "legal" title to reclaimed lands controlled by the Zapatistas. Although this particular communiqué doesn't give examples of this practice, it is a common strategy employed by the Mexican state in Chiapas. For example,

Hilary Klein quotes an interview she conducted with Heriberto, a member of an Agrarian Commission in La Garrucha, in 2001:

> In 1995 and 1996, many organizations collaborated with the government's Agrarian Commission . . . and the government began to give out title to the land where the [Zapatista] support base had settled. The government comes here to fool people, telling them that they have title to this land. That created all the problems that now we have to try and solve. But it's the government that started the problem. [The government] gives out documents to the land so they'll go fight with the Zapatistas.[14]

The government aims to produce a cycle of displacement. They take advantage of the needs and poverty of the indigenous communities and trick them into to giving up their lands. Then this displacement makes the community even more desperate and even more susceptible to government manipulation. Their desperation for land allows them to be used as a means of attacking and undermining the Zapatista organization. The engine that drives the government's counterinsurgency strategy is the desperation of the indigenous campesinos. Their so-called "social programs" rarely aim at producing long-term social security, stability, and well-being, but rather provide short-term benefits that exploit the desperation of the indigenous communities to create dependence, trick them into giving up their lands, and in turn create more desperation and dependence.

Just as with the finca system, dependence allows for exploitation and domination. Moisés and Galeano write that even the old system of sexual violence from the fincas is being reintroduced through government programs:

> In two communities . . . the women went out to get their projects, but the government told them that the girls should also go, and the meeting place is in Tuxtla Gutiérrez, which is the capital of the Mexican state of Chiapas, where the governor lives with his functionaries. It turned out that when they arrived in Tuxtla, they took the girls over to one side and the older women to the other. But it so happened that an older woman went along with the girls by mistake. She was the one who called her husband and told him that they were locked up in a house for three hours. And the girls tell how they

were made to have sexual relations.... The bad government is again
imposing the right of the first night (when a girl was going to get
married, the finquero or hacendado had the right to rape her) in
the partidista communities. They govern and look just like the old
finqueros and hacendados.[15]

The contemporary counterinsurgency strategy of the Mexican government displays many of the same characteristics as the previous finca
system. It relies on the poverty of indigenous communities to create
dependence on government programs, not to alleviate their poverty but
rather to perpetuate it through tricks and indebtedness. The difference
is that now the goal is not to force the indigenous to work on the fincas,
rather it is to displace them from their lands to build mines, ecotourism
resorts, highways, military bases, or to arm them as paramilitaries to
invade Zapatista lands. In the context of Chiapas, "kanal" describes this
cyclical system of desperation-dependence-displacement undertaken in
the name of economic development and the elimination of the Zapatista
insurgency.

The Zapatistas resist this cycle through the creation of a'mtel. The
organization of work as a'mtel in Zapatista communities is a commitment
to autonomy, to never again allow their capacity to sustain themselves
to be controlled by others, whether they are the old landowners or the
current government. While this is certainly a commitment to economic
autonomy, it implies a much more significant commitment to political
autonomy. Control over how a community sustains itself implies the
capacity to make collective decisions regarding the way of life and forms
of organization that define the day-to-day activities of sustaining the life
of a community, from working to harvest corn to making a decision in an
assembly. An education promoter from Oventik told me that when the
compañeros and compañeras in his zone talk about struggling to create
autonomy they say: tsk'an ta julestik jch'uleltik, or "it is necessary that we
(inclusive) bring back our (inclusive) ch'ulel." What they mean is that
they need to re-create their capacity to live in the world, to sustain themselves autonomously, and to make decisions together. They say that these
capacities have been denied by the colonization of their lands and their
forced economic dependence and enslavement to the landed elite. They
understand the work of autonomy as bringing back the capacities that
were taken from them by these systems of oppression.

When the testimonies in the escuelita textbooks talk about sustaining themselves through trabajos colectivos, they are not just talking about a source of resources and funding. They are speaking to one of the core aspects of the Zapatista struggle: the struggle to sustain themselves through a'mtel. However, this struggle has experienced its share of complications and setbacks. The massive land reclamations during the revolution greatly improved the situation of countless indigenous communities throughout Chiapas, but they were still very poor and had many necessities that were very difficult to meet on their own, such as building basic infrastructure like potable water systems. In the mid-1990s, many solidarity organizations and NGOs started to fulfill these needs, but in doing so they brought new problems and the danger of a new form of dependency. The creation of a'mtel has not only had to resist the government counterinsurgency strategy, it has also had to grapple with many issues created by well-meaning solidarity from national and international political organizations and NGOs.

The Contradictions of NGO Aid

The understanding of autonomy as a'mtel has often been at odds with reliance on solidarity funding from outside NGOs. In his study of NGOs doing solidarity work in Zapatista communities conducted between 1996 and 2000, Niels Barmeyer observes that the NGOs tended to reproduce some of the same problems that arise from government programs. Although they certainly never aim to displace the community or use them as paramilitaries, solidarity NGOs often relied on individual contacts in Zapatista communities who coordinate between the NGO and the Zapatista organization and, as a result, can receive special benefits for themselves or their family. For example, Barmeyer describes one case where the NGO SHOXEL did a project to build dry compost latrines in a Zapatista community. Dry latrines separate urine from feces to prevent water contamination and to produce sanitary organic fertilizer. The area's municipal consejo chose this particular Zapatista community because they had high incidences of waterborne parasite infections. The project was coordinated by one member of the community who had previously worked with SHOXEL. The local contact received a salary from SHOXEL in 2000 and 2001 that made him the richest man in the village, and the project ended up only building dry compost latrines at his relatives' houses. His salary was discontinued after the project as part of the restructuring of Zapatista-NGO relationships during the organization of the Good Government Councils.[16]

NGO involvement in Zapatista territory made many important infrastructure improvements but also generated many local inequalities. Often these inequalities were the result of special clientelistic relationships that an NGO would develop with a single person or a few people from a community who would coordinate the project. As a result, these communities and individuals had unequal access to resources and power. NGO clientelism created an undemocratic power structure in the Zapatista organization, whereby access to resources and decisions regarding projects could be made by the community members who happened to have contact with an NGO, rather than community members who were democratically chosen by their community, municipality, or zone to coordinate NGO projects. This problem was one of the main reasons for the formation of the Caracoles. One of the central roles of the Good Government Councils was to reorganize the relationship with NGOs so that they could be controlled by the democratic processes of the communities, in other words so that their work could function according to the principles of a'mtel, rather than kanal. They sought to replace the kanal relationship that allowed certain communities and individuals related to NGOs a source of personal gain with an a'mtel relationship where all monetary relationships remain under the democratic control of the communities.

Each of the five Good Government Councils has developed its own methods to begin to create this a'mtel relationship and has tried out several methods before arriving at one that worked. For example, when the Good Government Council was created in Caracol IV Morelia they attempted to address the problem of NGO clientelism by dividing funding for projects equally among the autonomous municipalities. However, they soon realized that this did not actually result in an equal distribution of resources. As Fermín, a former member of the Good Government Council of Caracol IV points out:

> Before, the NGOs gave more support to the municipalities that they knew better. Because of this, now, so that there won't be this problem, the Good Government Council has to make the proposals. . . . The Council has to report in an assembly of the zone how many donations arrived at the Good Government Council and what they are going to spend these donations on, but this would already be an

agreement of the zone, how this money is spent is an agreement of the municipalities. But it wasn't always like this. In the period from 2004 to 2008, the resources were divided by municipality and there were municipalities that had fewer members. These were receiving the same as the municipalities with higher populations, so we realized that this is not equality. Afterward, thanks to our realization, this changed. Now we do focus on equality, and it is done by population. For example, if a municipality has six hundred we have to calculate how much they should receive, and those that have less will also receive less.[17]

The first solution to the problem of unequal NGO development did not work well in practice, so they had to go back through the assembly process and reach another agreement for the zone. The Good Government Council of Caracol III La Garrucha went through a similar process to that of Caracol IV and now also divides all funding from solidarity donations and from the 10 percent tax on government projects among its municipalities based on population.[18]

However, the process described by Fermín reflects a significant change from the practice in the pre–Good Government Councils period. Now the distribution of NGO funding in Caracol IV Morelia is being controlled by the assembly of the zone, rather than the NGOs. Furthermore, democratic control also extends to the elaboration of the projects themselves. With the creation of the Good Government Councils, each community can now decide what project they need and then ask the Good Government Council to search out an NGO that will fund it. An unnamed authority from Caracol IV describes how this works in practice:

It is the [Good Government] Council's obligation to create projects if a community is lacking development, but in order to create the project the Council has to convoke a meeting with the municipal consejos and their commissions in different areas, like health, education, and production. They have a meeting, and the Council tells the commissions that they have to go out for a visit to ask the communities what they need. The commissions go to the municipalities, bring together their local commissions, and ask what their community lacks. When they have the list of necessities in their communities they return again to meet and write up the project, depending on the need of each community. Once the project is written, the Good Government Council has to find an NGO that can support them to make this project work.[19]

The creation of Caracol IV placed the work of administering solidarity projects in the hands of the Good Government Council. The communities now have the power to decide what projects they need and want. This is not a perfect system. The same authority quoted above describes some projects that the Good Government Council accepted, for example, building efficient woodstoves and dry latrines, that ended up not being useful for some communities. However, overall it is a far better system that can meet the real needs of the communities.

I can attest from my personal experience attending the escuelita in the very small community of Nueva Esperanza (it is made up of only three households) in Caracol IV Morelia that they had several projects created through the Good Government Council that were directly addressing their needs and a few that fell somewhat short. The family that hosted me had a dry latrine that they seemed happy with and that doubled as a way to naturally fertilize the cornfield that surrounded their house. They used their efficient woodstove to make some of their tortillas but still used an open fire to do most cooking, because the stovepipe clogged frequently. I also got the sense that the light and warmth from the fire (they did not have electricity) provided an important social space, since most evenings all three families would gather around the fire in the house with the largest kitchen to eat and talk into the evening. They also had a rainwater collection system and tank provided by a project designed by the Good Government Council that provided more reliable access to potable water. However, it wasn't enough to meet their needs, so they had received an electric filtration system and were waiting on the Zapatista electric lines from the regional center to reach their community to start using it. They also had a communal medicine cabinet with herbal medicine and basic antibiotics that was taken care of by the community's health promoter, and they were in the process of building a small one-room primary school so their three education promoters would have a space to teach the five young children from the community. The two older children studied at the secondary school in the Caracol. I did not ask at the time whether the medicine and the school were supported by resources from the Good Government Council or by the collective resources of their own community. It was most likely a mixture of the two. For example, the school was clearly being built by the people of the community, though they may have received some help with obtaining building materials. Similarly, the antibiotics in the medicine cabinet most likely came through their municipality or the Caracol, while some of the herbal remedies could have been gathered in the community.

However, by far the most important trabajos colectivos in the community were sustained through the collective work of the community itself. The heart that sustained the community was its collective cornfields, bean-fields, and vegetable garden. These trabajos colectivos created the tortillas, tostadas, beans, vegetables, and chilis that sustained the everyday life of the community, fed the children who were attending secondary school in the Caracol, and supported the members of the community who fulfilled all the various cargos of promoters or local authorities in the Zapatista organization. Every day that I was there all the men, women, and children went together to work in their fields, with all tasks being shared equally between men and women. It was harvest time, and everyone spent the day husking corn and beans and cutting and carrying firewood. In the kitchen, everyone also worked together, with men and women both participating in making the meal. Although there were some differences in men's and women's work—for example, the women did the more skilled tasks in the kitchen, like making the salsa and beans, while the men carried a little more firewood and would do more of the heavier agricultural labor like clearing fallow fields—overall the distribution of labor in the community was very gender equal.

By far the most important source of resources in a Zapatista community is that community's own trabajos colectivos. The core of the Zapatista organization is the collective heart of the community, where decisions are made and work is carried out democratically and collectively. Although funds provided through solidarity projects and the 10 percent tax are important for certain things, for example, for potable water projects like the previously mentioned electric water filtration system, the majority of the numerous initiatives in Caracol IV Morelia are funded through their own trabajos colectivos. An unnamed authority from Caracol IV states that the creation of collective initiatives throughout the zone "is really done through the efforts of the people. For example, there are com-pañeras who have a store of forty thousand pesos, but it is from their own efforts; they don't need a project. There are some communities that do have projects, but the majority work thanks purely to the strength of the people."[20]

This reality runs contrary to the claims of some authors, including Barmeyer, who argue that the Zapatista struggle is dependent, at least to a certain degree, on outside NGO funding. Barmeyer even goes so far as to claim that one of the principal reasons the Zapatistas have developed relationships with international political organizations is

> to brighten the prospects for economic independence of its base communities by keeping international aid on the flow. The input of goods, money, and people into the remoter parts of Chiapas has enabled many Zapatista base communities to come closer to their aim of a life in dignity by raising the living standards in their villages. However, independence from the Mexican State has been achieved only at the cost of new dependencies on outsiders with regard to assistance, funding, and volunteers.[21]

Barmeyer's argument is accurate to a certain extent. Many basic infrastructural developments in Zapatista communities would not have been possible without NGO aid, but to claim that this relationship "enabled" the creation of a dignified life completely misunderstands what the Zapatistas mean by dignity. An understanding of dignified life as lekil kuxlejal and ichbail ta muk' places self-determination and democracy above "raising living standards." In fact, the Zapatistas have been very explicit both in the announcement of the Caracoles and their public initiatives since then that the flow of international aid into the communities is often detrimental to their processes of self-determination and the creation of dignified life. Furthermore, both my own experience in the escuelita and the testimonies in the escuelita textbooks make clear that NGO funding is not the principal means of sustaining the organization. The lifeblood of the Zapatista organization is their own a'mtel, their own trabajos colectivos that feed them every day, sustain their system of governance, and are completely under the democratic control of the communities. However, although NGO funding is not the principal economic means of survival for most Zapatista communities, it is still a very significant source of income for the organization. If it were to suddenly disappear it could be difficult for the Zapatista organization. However, this reality has not resulted in the Zapatistas attempting to keep "international aid on the flow," rather it has deepened their commitment to become completely independent from international aid. It has deepened their commitment to their own a'mtel, to the creation of trabajos colectivos.

The A'mtel of the Trabajos Colectivos

One of the central topics in the escuelita textbooks is the creation of trabajos colectivos. Although the Zapatistas have tried to bring solidarity projects under democratic control, to make them function according to the logic of a'mtel, they are still administered by an external organization, and there will always be aspects of their work, for example, how they raise funds or make internal decisions, that will be outside the direct control of the communities. One of the principal struggles of the Zapatista organization is to create trabajos colectivos that can be completely under the control of the communities. The creation of trabajos colectivos is not just important for a community's subsistence or for small initiatives at the local level. It is also the most important source of funding for the projects and initiatives at the level of the zone or municipality. The creation of trabajos colectivos at these levels are important because they can provide a reliable source of funding that is completely controlled by the Zapatista organization and can sustain their struggle into the future. Johnny, a member of the Good Government Council from Caracol I La Realidad at the time of escuelita underlines this importance:

> As a government . . . we think, we analyze, we discuss how to create trabajos colectivos as a zone so that later there will be a way to sustain the work, so that the different tasks that we have to do as a government will function. We have to discuss what we will do when we no longer get support from other compañeros, we have to focus on trabajos colectivos.[22]

Unlike the resources generated at the local level by projects like collective cornfields, these trabajos colectivos at the level of the zone do not go toward sustaining individual Zapatista families or creating projects in any one community. Rather, they sustain the collective projects and initiatives of the organization that affect large areas of Zapatista territory at the level of the municipality and zone. As Doroteo, a former member of the Good Government Council of Caracol I La Realidad, makes clear:

> [W]e are organizing ourselves from the communities, from the families, the communities, regions, municipalities, and zone. All these

trabajos colectivos, cooperatives, aren't made with the goal of dividing the profits. We have to begin from the family. This is to sustain
our own family, and then the trabajos colectivos and cooperatives at
each level have their own purpose at each level of government. This
is how we are trying to organize ourselves.[23]

Each level of autonomous government, from the zone to the community, has its own trabajos colectivos that sustain the work of the organization at that level. Just as local trabajos collectivos go toward meeting
the needs of one community, trabajos collectivos of the zone go toward
addressing the needs of the whole zone. For example, the "el solidario"
bus route is a trabajo colectivo that belongs to the zone of La Realidad,
meaning that the resources that it generates go toward initiatives that
affect the whole zone. Thus, the Good Government Council was able to use
money generated by the bus to help with the formation of the BANPAZ.
The Good Government Council of La Realidad also has several other trabajos colectivos, including three small stores, a cornfield, and a herd of cattle.
Focusing on these examples can allow us to see the purpose of trabajos
colectivos at the level of the zone, as well as illustrate how these trabajos
colectivos are administrated through the same democratic process of the
assembly of the zone that creates the initiatives and projects that they are
intended to fund. They will allow us to see how the practical reality of the
trabajos colectivos functions according to the logic of a'mtel.

The small stores in La Realidad were created both to generate funds
for initiatives in the zone and to provide access to store-bought products so people in the communities would not have to travel all the way
to Las Margaritas, the nearest city, when they needed to buy something.
The first store to be created is in the autonomous municipality San Pedro
de Michoacán, the second is in Libertad de los Pueblos Mayas but also
serves and is administered in collaboration with the neighboring autonomous municipality General Emiliano Zapata, and the final store is in
Tierra y Libertad. These stores are administered collectively by the Good
Government Council of La Realidad and the authorities of the autonomous
municipalities that they serve, but each also has its own *directiva* (governing board) made up of people from the communities. This directiva
was at first made up of everyone in the communities who used the store
and who would take turns working in the store. But they immediately
encountered problems with this model because many of the people from

the communities were not adequately prepared to do the accounting work necessary for running the store, and as a result they were losing money. The assembly of the zone together with the communities had to make a change so that only those authorities in the communities who had a basic knowledge of accounting would work in the directivas of the stores in fifteen-day cycles.[24] Now the stores are functioning and generating income. The decisions that determine how the stores function are not made by a single community or proprietor but are collectively controlled by all the communities in the zone. While only those with some accounting knowledge do the day-to-day work of administration, the overall operation of the stores is decided collectively and democratically. Work in the stores is just another cargo in the Zapatista organization, another form of a'mtel. Furthermore, the funds generated by the store also have a specific function in the Zapatista organization in La Realidad. Roel describes the purpose of these funds:

> Right now, the agreement for our stores, the goal of the [Good Government] Council, is that what they generate in profit will be used when there is a mobilization of the zone. This is where the resources will come from, this is the final goal, that it will help us as a zone. Then the communities won't pitch in if we all need something, instead the Council will already have a trabajo as a zone that will help us. For example, if we need thirty thousand pesos we can get together with the [municipal] consejo and start taking out probably ten thousand from each store.[25]

The stores generate a fund that can cover the cost of mobilizations in the zone that defend Zapatista communities from government or paramilitary aggressions. For example, in August of 1999, the Mexican military occupied the ejido Amador Hernández in the Municipality General Emiliano Zapata and planned to displace the community and build a military base on the land. In response, all the communities in the zone of La Realidad organized to occupy the land, they cooperated and took turns sustaining the occupation with the support of solidarity groups until the military finally withdrew over two years later, in December 2001.[26] Mobilizations of this scale require funding, for food, transportation, and other necessities. The purpose of the funds produced by the stores is to have a permanent pool of resources in the hands of the Good Government Council so that they can easily support a mobilization of all the communities in the zone without having to drain the resources of the communities. Although a visitor from outside the community might mistake one of La Realidad's collective stores for a proprietary small business, in reality they are a manifestation of the collective labor of the whole municipality, and their proceeds are not destined for the pockets of an individual owner, but rather to the collective survival and defense of the entire zone.

The other trabajos colectivos of the zone are intended to support other initiatives that involve all the Zapatista communities in some way. For example, they have a collective cornfield of twelve hectares (just under thirty acres) that is worked in turns by all the Zapatista communities from each municipality. Roel tells us:

> The authority, the [Good Government] Council, has its plan so that the corn we can harvest in this cornfield of the zone will be to support our permanent workers that we have in the zone, for example, those in the hospital. Part of what is harvested will be given to these compañeros in the hospital so they can sustain themselves and the other part will probably be sold for other trabajos that the zone has planned.[27]

Just as with the collective stores, the products of collective labor in the zone's cornfield go toward a specific purpose: the corn feeds the health promoters working for the benefit of the whole zone, and the surplus harvest is sold to generate a fund that can be invested to create more trabajos colectivos for the zone. The Good Government Council plans to eventually convert these twelve hectares into a pasture for the twelve cows in the zone's cattle herd that, at the time of the escuelita, were divided among the pastures of the zone's four autonomous municipalities and mixed in with their own collective cattle herds. Raising cows is much less labor-intensive than growing corn, and the Good Government Council was in the process of converting its cornfield to pasture so that they could continue growing its herd to generate more resources for the future trabajos colectivos in the zone and to support its current initiatives like the central hospital. In general, the purpose of trabajos colectivos at the different levels of the Zapatista organization is to generate a fund with a specific purpose at each respective level. For example, a trabajo colectivo at the level of the zone might provide a sustainable source of funding for a hospital, while a trabajo colectivo at the municipal level might fund that municipality's clinic.

The Progress of Trabajos Colectivos in the Five Caracoles and the Importance of Autonomous Cows

The Zapatista organization has direct democratic control over all aspects of work in the trabajos colectivos; however, they do not exist in complete isolation and are still subject to outside forces. For example, fluctuations in the price of products sold at the collective stores directly affects the ability of those stores to continue generating resources. Many trabajos colectivos are still exposed to the pressures of local and global markets, but they are significantly different than a privately owned business. They exist to sustain the autonomy of the communities through a'mtel, not as a source of personal profit through kanal. If something is not working for whatever reason, they have processes in place that allow them to adapt and make changes. All changes are made democratically and for the benefit of the collective initiatives of the organization, rather than for private personal gain.

However, the national and global market beyond Zapatista territory does exert pressure on the development of trabajos colectivos. As John Holloway has argued, one of the foundational contradictions generated by capitalism is between the capitalist world, which "appears as an immense collection of commodities," and the larger world of human production that resists commodification.[28] Many trabajos colectivos exist in the midst of this contradiction. Although most of the local trabajos colectivos exist outside of it, since they only produce agricultural products for consumption, any trabajo colectivo that deals with making money or spending it must constantly resist the pressures of the world of capitalist commodity exchange. There is a fundamental struggle for these trabajos colectivos. While they represent a collective mode of production, or a'mtel, they must interact with an external market where the organization sells its commodities to survive. Even if individual Zapatistas do not engage in kanal for their own survival, some of the trabajos colectivos of the larger organization are in danger of being caught in a kanal relationship with the national and global capitalist market that they depend on to sell their products so that the Zapatista organization can survive.

The Zapatistas' goal is to create enough self-sustaining trabajos colectivos at the different levels of autonomous government to fund all the various Zapatista initiatives, including health and education systems, autonomous banks, mobilizations in defense of reclaimed land, or expenses involved in the operation of autonomous government, such as travel costs for transportation to attend meetings or fulfill cargos. The goal is to sustain these initiatives as they are now, provide funding for new projects that might be needed in the future, and eventually replace outside funding from solidarity NGOs. How feasible is this goal? Part of the argument for the Zapatistas' necessary dependence on NGO funding advanced by authors like Barmeyer is skepticism about the Zapatistas' ability to survive on the resources of their own trabajos colectivos. How successful have the Good Government Councils been at creating trabajos colectivos in each zone since their formation in 2003? The tensions created by the capitalist market are fundamental in understanding the relative development of trabajos colectivos throughout the Zapatista organization. These tensions interact with local conditions in the five Caracoles to deeply influence the successes and failures of their respective trabajos colectivos.

The creation of trabajos colectivos at all levels of autonomous government, from the community up to the zone, is one of the central roles of every authority in all five Caracoles. It is one of their most important responsibilities because the work of trabajos colectivos is the only way the Zapatista organization will be able to sustain itself into the future, from the sustenance of each family in every community all the way up to funding the autonomous health and education systems at the level of the zone. Most of the autonomous governments of the Caracoles have been fairly successful in fulfilling this responsibility. As we have already seen, Caracol I La Realidad has three collective stores, a collective cornfield in the process of being converted to pasture for its twelve cows, and the "el solidario" bus route as trabajos colectivos at the level of the zone. Furthermore, each of the four municipalities in the zone has a collective cattle herd and receives some resources from the collective stores. The municipality General Emiliano Zapata has a herd of fifty cows and a collective rice husker that had functioned for a time but wasn't being used in 2013, because the municipalities rice cultivation project had fallen apart and had yet to be reorganized. The municipality Tierra y Libertad has a herd of twenty cows and a collective blacksmithing forge that had not been functioning for a while but had recently started to work again in 2013. This forge manufactured a type of efficient woodstoves called "Lorena" stoves, as well as doing other general blacksmithing jobs. The municipality Libertad de los Pueblos Mayas has a herd of thirty-five cows and a shoemaking collective that also had ceased to function and was being reorganized in 2013.

The municipality San Pedro de Michoacán has a herd of thirty-six cows, but no other trabajos colectivos in that municipality are mentioned in the escuelita textbooks.[29] However, they do mention that when all four municipalities received the money that they invested in their cattle herds, the authorities of San Pedro de Michoacán decided to buy a small bus for a transportation route on their own without consulting with the communities. The bus broke down after its first trip. They wasted 200 thousand pesos buying and trying to repair the bus, and in the end they were only able to salvage ten thousand by selling it to a junkyard.[30] Finally, the zone of La Realidad has numerous community-level trabajos colectivos. Doroteo, a former member of the Good Government Council of La Realidad, talks about the local trabajos colectivos in the zone:

> Eighty percent of the communities have a trabajo colectivo. There are communities that have two, and there are communities that have three trabajos colectivos or four and up to five. It depends on how they are organized and the number of compañeros that are in the community. In the communities there are collective fields for beans, corn, there are cattle collectives, collective stores, chicken collectives, there are small businesses. It's not that they are permanent businesses that are there all the time. Sometimes they have small events and the compañeros go there with their small business. A compañera told us that in one community in her region they started with a chicken farm, free-range chickens, and every so often they would kill one or two chickens and make tamales. They would sell these tamales, and little by little they collected a fund, and with this fund they had they were able to buy a corn grinder. This is how they would create their trabajos.[31]

This is the daily work of the Zapatista struggle to slowly generate resources, despite constant mistakes and setbacks, at every level of Zapatista autonomous government in order to sustain the organization into the future.

Overall, the most successful trabajos colectivos at the municipal and zonal level in La Realidad are the collective cattle herds—at the local level most trabajos colectivos are based in some form of agricultural production. The primary reason for their success is that most Zapatistas are already very knowledgeable and experienced in agricultural production. The least successful trabajos colectivos are those that involve specialized training and equipment that must be purchased from markets outside the organization. Rice huskers, blacksmithing, shoemaking, and buses require specialized training and involve equipment that must be purchased and, if broken, repaired or replaced. However, most Zapatistas already know how to raise a cow and grow corn, and the Zapatista's reclaimed land doesn't need to be purchased and never breaks. The collective cattle herds are most successful because they are least dependent on the capitalist market. While they may require the purchase of fencing, salt, or vaccinations, their primary means of production is the Zapatista's own land.

In fact, autonomous cattle herds are the most common trabajo colectivo at the municipal and zonal level throughout the five Caracoles. Caracol V Roberto Barrios has a similar collective cattle project at the level of the zone. The collective is working on a 150-hectare piece of land (over 370 acres) that was reclaimed from a finca in 1994.[32] At first the authorities of Caracol V proposed that this land be used for collective cornfields and beanfields that would generate resources for the whole zone. This proposal was taken to the communities, which approved it and sent it back to the assembly of the zone to be implemented. They cultivated corn and beans for two years, with teams of ten compañeros from each of the zone's nine municipalities taking turns doing the work. They had two successful harvests and sold the corn and beans for a little money, but the third harvest was a complete failure and did not produce anything.[33] At this point, an unnamed authority from Caracol V Roberto Barrios says:

> A general assembly was called again. We came back to think about how we are going to continue with our collective. Each authority gave their point of view, what they thought about the collective that we had been doing with beans and corn, because there we had seen that we hadn't harvested anything. We again came up with a proposal to take up what had been proposed in a general assembly where the authorities had been thinking about making a cattle collective, because we saw that the land was no longer viable for cultivating corn and beans.
>
> We again brought the proposal to the municipalities, to the communities, with the authorities explaining that the collective that we had been doing wasn't working well. We returned to another special meeting, where we again collected the word of the people, where the authorities came and we saw that we were going to create this cattle

collective. They started to coordinate the work, what we are going
to do first, the agreement for how many municipalities are going to
go back to sending compañeros to now really start doing the work.[34]

At the time of the escuelita the cattle collective had been functioning
for a year without any major setbacks, with teams of twenty-three compañeros from communities in each municipality doing the work in one-
week cycles.[35] At that time, the zone had invested 700 thousand pesos they
had slowly accumulated from small solidarity donations that arrived in
the Caracol. They were able to buy and care for a herd of 101 cows.[36] The
experiences of Roberto Barrios illustrate an additional reason for the
prevalence of autonomous cattle herds in the Caracoles. While collective
cornfields and beanfields provide sustenance at the local level, initiatives
at the level of the zone primarily require monetary resources. Cattle are
a more reliable source of funding for the zone, because they exist as a
constant reserve of potential monetary resources that is more reliable
than the yearly corn and bean harvest.

The escuelita textbooks do not give a detailed description of the trabajos colectivos of the nine municipalities in Caracol V Roberto Barrios.
They mention that some have small collective stores that sell food and
sometimes clothing, some have collective cattle herds, cornfields, and
beanfields, and some have beehives and collectively produce honey.[37]
There is also a coffee collective that is run by Zapatista coffee producers in the municipalities of Acabalná, Benito Juárez, La Paz, La Dignidad,
and Rubén Jaramillo that sells coffee to organizations in Italy, Germany,
France, and Greece.[38] Besides cattle, coffee collectives seem to be the most
successful municipal trabajo colectivo for the Zapatistas. There are likely
two reason for this. First, just as with cattle, there is a long tradition of
coffee cultivation in Chiapas, and its primary means of production is the
land. Second, the commitment of international solidarity groups to buy
their coffee at a fair price mitigates the competitive pressures and price
fluctuations of the market.

The testimonies in the escuelita textbooks are clear that not every
community in Caracol V Roberto Barrios has trabajos colectivos. However,
they also give the general sense that most communities have been able to
at least organize agricultural trabajos colectivos, for example, collective
cultivation of corn, beans, and vegetables, and that some have been able to
save enough from selling their surplus product or from solidarity funding

to start larger trabajos colectivos, including small stores, cattle herds, bakeries, and other projects. Nazario, a member of the municipal consejo of Rubén Jaramillo, said that in one community in their municipality the compañeras started out with a collective beanfield and vegetable garden and were able to save enough resources to start raising pigs and chickens and open a small collective store and a collective bakery. Then, with the funds from these projects they started buying cows one by one until they had a small herd. At the time of the escuelita they had just bought butchering equipment for forty thousand pesos to start their own butcher shop. They accomplished all this without receiving any NGO funding through the municipality or Good Government Council, and despite some of the original women leaving the Zapatista organization.[39]

The zone of Caracol III La Garrucha also has a collective cattle herd that is kept in various pastures in their four autonomous municipalities. They also have a small collective store that is run completely by members of the Good Government Council and the CCRI, rather than by teams of compañeros from the communities or municipalities. Each municipality also has its own cattle collective, as well as a collective cornfield, beanfield, and small collective store. Additionally, the municipality of Francisco Gómez has a coffee collective that sells its coffee through a Zapatista solidarity collective in Mexico City.[40] Felipe, a former member of the Good Government Council from the autonomous municipality of San Manuel, said that the collective cattle herd of San Manuel had been started even before the formation of the Caracoles, and that they were able to grow their herd to a total of 120 cows. However, a large portion of the herd had to be sold off when the government funded paramilitary organization the Organización Regional de Cafetaleros de Ocosingo (Regional Organization of Ocosingo Coffee Growers, or ORCAO) invaded some of the reclaimed land in the zone in 2009. They had to mobilize teams of between 100 and 150 compañeros to defend the land, with groups rotating every five days. This resistance lasted for a year before ORCAO finally withdrew.[41] This illustrates a further advantage of autonomous cattle herds. Not only must the zone's source of funding be reliable, it also needs to be flexible so that the zone can raise large amounts of money quickly to fund resistance in times of crisis. Cattle are best suited to this need for flexibility. The testimonies from La Garrucha don't give any specific examples of trabajos colectivos at the local level in the zone, although they say that in general the communities have collectives that produce corn and beans, and that there are some collectives that raise chickens or cows and produce bananas and sugarcane.

In Caracol IV, the struggle to promote trabajos colectivos throughout the zone has resulted in a collective cattle herd, a small collective store, and most recently a coffee collective and a cacao collective. All these trabajos colectivos generate resources to support initiatives at the level of the zone. Furthermore, each of the three autonomous municipalities in the zone have their own small collective stores that support initiatives in their territories. The municipality 17 de Noviembre also has its own collective cattle herd, and the women are in the process of organizing an additional cattle-raising project for the women of the municipality. The municipality Olga Isabel also has its own coffee production collective.[42] Floribel, a former member of the municipal consejo of the autonomous municipality Lucio Cabañas, says that at the local level the majority of the communities have slowly developed their own trabajos colectivos on the reclaimed land in the zone:

> After 1994, we reclaimed the land. So then we organized ourselves in the communities to create the different trabajos colectivos. They could be poultry, vegetable gardens, stores, and also other things that can be done in the communities. So we have been here mostly going forward up to the present. We don't say it's much, but we have mostly advanced. For example, the majority of the communities in the zone have trabajos colectivos, but there are communities that don't have trabajos colectivos due to a lack of compañeros, because there aren't many in these communities. Because of this we can't say that all the communities have collectives, but the majority do have these trabajos.[43]

Overall, the testimonies from La Realidad, La Garrucha, Morelia, and Roberto Barrios give the impression that the work of creating trabajos colectivos has advanced significantly over the years of Zapatista organization, and in particular during the past decade since the creation of the Good Government Councils. Although many of these trabajos colectivos were started with the help of outside funding, most are now functioning independently, and there are even some that were created only using the resources generated by the communities. In all four Caracoles, autonomous cattle herds have been the most successful trabajos colectivos at the level of the municipality and the zone, because their primary means of production is the land, and they can act as reliable resource reserves to fund initiatives and mobilizations. Although solidarity funding has been important for development in Zapatista communities, any claims that the Zapatistas are somehow "dependent" on international donors is not borne out by reality in these Caracoles.

Inequality in the Development of Trabajos Colectivos and the Struggle of Caracol II Oventik

The creation of trabajos colectivos at the different levels of autonomous government promotes a much more equal form of development than the unequal distribution of solidarity projects that existed before the creation of the Good Government Councils. However, they still have the potential to generate local inequalities. Caracol IV Morelia offers a few examples. There was a community that had a small collective gravel mine on their land, another that collectively sold salvaged wood, and two communities that were located near beautiful rivers and ran small collective ecotourism parks. All these are relatively lucrative trabajos colectivos that only particular communities can create and benefit from. Jacobo, a former member of one of the municipal consejos in Caracol IV Morelia, describes what the Good Government Council did to address this issue in their zone:

> Before, in the three levels of government, there was income, there were resources, for example, if a little salvaged wood was sold. But the zone is big, and sometimes there was a percentage for the municipality, for the community, and for the [Good Government] Council. We saw that this money was not being used for everyone. It only went to the community that had this trabajo, to the municipality and the zone, but there are many communities that didn't receive anything. Because of this now all the resources that come in go directly to the Council…
>
> If sand or gravel gets sold, the money goes directly to the Good Government Council, and … the benefits help the whole zone, the three municipalities, and their communities, even though it's only a little. … Each municipality or each region that receives this small payment will agree whether they create a local cattle trabajo, create a cornfield trabajo colectivo, for example. … Also, they see if there is a group of compañeras that needs to create their collective.[44]

In these cases, the Good Government Council of Morelia was given control over all the resources from these trabajos colectivos so that they could be distributed equally throughout the zone and create more trabajos colectivos, rather than only being spent on the individual sustenance or development of one community. The zone collectively decided that it was not fair to let a single community reap all the benefits of a very lucrative trabajo colectivo, because they are lucky enough to be located near a beautiful river, gravel mine, or source of salvaged wood. This case is a good illustration of one of the central roles of the Good Government Councils in all the Caracoles: they are not only responsible for dividing resources equally among municipalities and communities but also for insuring that the resources of trabajos colectivos in the zone are being used to create more trabajos colectivos at the level of the zone and the municipalities.

However, the primary cause of unequal development of trabajos colectivos is not gravel mines or ecotourism, it is unequal access to agricultural land. As we have seen, the primary factor in determining the success of the trabajos colectivos is access to a means of production that is not dependent on the outside market; in other words, the primary factor is access to land. This is even the case on the local level. For example, if a community has access to more land for collective agriculture it might be able to sell its surplus and generate funds to start a small collective store or cattle herd that could then generate more funds. A community without enough land might harvest a smaller surplus or no surplus at all and would thus have a harder time creating trabajos colectivos. The unequal development of trabajos colectivos due to inequalities in access to land are most striking in the case of Caracol II Oventik. This Caracol faces different challenges in the creation of trabajos colectivos than the other Caracoles. An unnamed authority from Caracol II gives an overview of the severe difficulties involved in creating trabajos colectivos throughout the zone:

> Here in our zone in the highlands we barely have any trabajos colectivos at the level of the zone. In fact, we have discussed this, we have analyzed this, but it is very difficult because here in our zone we barely have any land, so there isn't anywhere where we can create a trabajo colectivo.
>
> Although we want to create trabajos colectivos like cattle herds, cornfields, cultivated land, whatever type of cultivation, we see that it is difficult. So we don't have trabajos colectivoes for our zone, because when you create a trabajo colectivo of the zone you need a little stretch of land. This is the problem that we have seen in our

zone. In the communities, they have started very little, very, very little, like only vegetable garden trabajos, at the municipal level there mostly aren't trabajos colectivos, and it is worse at the level of the zone.

What we do here with the projects is not like the other Caracoles explained, which have many collectives. In this zone we don't have collectives for lack of land, we only have land for our subsistence, so we can't have collectives of the zone. What we do with projects are construction projects. We just finished building a project to have potable water. In this project we were supported by the Basque government.[45]

There is very little surplus land in the highland region of Oventik, with almost all available land being used directly for the daily sustenance of the people who live there. They cannot afford to set aside land to create the same large-scale agricultural initiatives that can generate monetary resources for the zone without impacting the subsistence of the communities. This reality has led the Good Government Council of Oventik to search out other ways of creating funds at the zonal level. For example, by making an agreement between all the areas of trabajo to pool their resources and create a small savings fund that can support mobilizations in the zone and potentially be invested in some way in the future.[46] Furthermore, some of the projects that exist at the level of the zone are supported by their own trabajos colectivos. A case in point is the secondary school, which is supported by the language school where I studied Spanish and Tsotsil, as well as by a small collective store, cornfield, and some chickens. However, the health promoters in Oventik's central hospital only receive a little monetary support from the Good Government Council and must support themselves with small donations from the communities and their own individual and collective resources.[47] The escuelita textbooks do not give a complete list of all the trabajos colectivos in the municipalities of Caracol II Oventik. However, they do mention several examples, such as the women's artisan cooperatives Mujeres por La Dignidad and Mujeres de la Resistencia, which sell clothing, weaving, and embroidery, and the coffee collectives Yaxil Xojobal and Mut Vitz, the latter of which is no longer functioning.[48] They also say that the municipality of San Juan Apóstol Cancuc has been able to organize twelve trabajos collectivos, including collective cultivation of avocado, corn, pineapple, and beans and a small collective store. They organized all of this using their own resources, with no support from the Good Government Council.[49]

The difficulties with creating trabajos colectivos in Caracol II Oventik point to a significant problem that has yet to be fully addressed by the Zapatista autonomous government: an inequality between Oventik and the other four Caracoles caused by unequal access to agricultural land. Unlike the communities of the other Caracoles, Subcomandante Moisés says, "The compañeros of the highlands buy corn throughout their lives, they cultivate very little, and they mostly have to buy."[50] The highland region of Caracol II Oventik is much more populated than the four other Caracoles, and there often isn't enough land to support all the people in a given community. Perhaps the biggest cause of land scarcity has to do with the different social realities in the highlands that preexist the 1994 uprising. The other four zones are largely made up of land that was predominantly controlled by large landowners who generally used their fincas for cattle ranching. They also include the Lacandon Jungle of southeastern Chiapas, which was populated and opened for cultivation by migrants from the highland region or the fincas who founded new communities in the hope of escaping the exploitation and hardships of their previous homes. The communities in the highlands did not have enough land to support themselves and were forced to work as seasonal migrant workers on the fincas, while the communities in the fincas worked year-round as peons for the landowners.[51] As a result, in 1994, the communities of the other four Caracoles reclaimed huge tracts of land from the fincas where they had previously lived as peons, while the highland communities of Oventik could reclaim very little and in many cases still confronted the same land shortages that drove them to migrate to the fincas before the revolution.[52]

At the time of the escuelita, the Good Government Councils were just beginning to organize among the Caracoles to address this issue. The first example of this coordination is the case of the refugee camp of displaced peoples in the community of San Pedro Polhó. This camp has existed since 1997, when thousands of people throughout the municipality of San Pedro Polhó were driven out of their communities by government supported paramilitary violence. These people came together to live in the town of San Pedro Polhó and survived on Red Cross aid. However, the autonomous municipal consejo saw that this aid was giving the Red Cross too much power and influence in the community and asked the Red Cross to let them administer aid funding. In response, the Red Cross left the community with nothing. The consejo managed to get some support from other organizations to start a few small trabajos colectivos and to open a small gravel mine. However, it was still very difficult to get by, and they started to look for other options in the reclaimed land of other Caracoles. As an unnamed authority from Oventik put it:

> What the [municipal] consejo did was to start to organize a little better, they started to ask the people if they could endure more and how many compañeros could organize themselves, they asked other Caracoles where there is reclaimed land. They found out how many compañeros were willing to go and live on reclaimed lands, because they weren't going to let them go back and forth constantly, because then they had . . . an agreement about how to work the reclaimed land. This is what they proposed. I don't remember how many families decided to leave and go there, but it was only for a time. Little by little they started returning to their own homes. That was the problem that happened then. . . . The resistance was very hard, because no one could go back to their home, because the paramilitaries were waiting . . .
>
> [W]ork on reclaimed lands was again proposed, they asked who was willing to go and work. . . . But this is an agreement of the two [Good Government] Councils. The compañeros of La Garrucha have gone to the Council of Oventik. They have discussed whether there is still land where the compañeros can work even if they couldn't live there, but now there is an agreement. Now a path is being opened. There are compañéros that are in Benito Juárez, en Río Naranjo [in the territory of Caracol III La Garrucha], which is more or less where the land is. They are arriving there but we don't know how long they can endure, because we don't know if they can continue going and returning. This still has to be seen, but it is already an agreement of the two [Good Government] Councils, now not only for San Pedro Polhó but also for other municipalities where they are going to ask if they are willing to work on these lands.[53]

Although this might begin to address the problem of land scarcity in some communities, it is probably not a viable solution for every community in the zone. Another partial solution came from an agreement between La Realidad and Oventik shortly after the formation of the

Caracoles in 2003. Since most communities in the zone of Oventik must buy corn to survive, the Good Government Councils decided that it would be best if they bought it at a fair price from a Caracol like La Realidad that produces a corn surplus, so that the resources would stay within the organization instead of going to a government or privately owned store. However, at the time of the escuelita they still had not succeeded in organizing this exchange. During the first attempt some of the compañeros from La Realidad provided spoiled corn, and the Good Government Council did not check the corn before sending it to Oventik. The agreement fell apart as a result.[54] But the Good Government Councils still went forward with their idea and eventually crafted a new agreement. In a February 2016 communiqué detailing the progress of trabajos colectivos in the Zapatista communities since the time of the escuelita, Subcomandantes Moisés and Galeano write:

> In the Caracol of Oventik they now have an autonomous tortilla store. We don't know how much a kilo of tortillas is in your geographies, but in Oventik it is ten pesos a kilo. And they are made of corn, not *maseca* [processed GMO corn flour]. Even public transportation makes special trips to buy their tortillas there. In the zone of the highlands of Chiapas, where the Caracol of Oventik is located, they don't produce corn. The corn is produced in the jungle regions and it is exchanged between collectives of the zone so that the Zapatista families will have corn at a good price and without intermediaries. To do this they use trucks that were donated to the Good Government Councils by good people whose names we won't say, but they know who they are, as do we.[55]

By coordinating between Caracoles, the Good Government Councils were able to begin to address the problem of land scarcity in Oventik. Their agreement resulted in the first trabajo colectivo at the level of the zone. Although this is only a partial solution, it is still a first step that shows the potential benefits of increasing coordination between Caracoles. In May 2015, during the Seminar on Critical Thought versus the Capitalist Hydra, Subcomandante Moisés said that the Good Government Councils are starting to work on creating another level of autonomous government that would coordinate between the five Caracoles.[56] Although the Zapatistas have yet to fully organize this new coordinating body, the example of creating the *tortillería* in Oventik in coordination with the other Caracoles may be the first seeds that will develop into this new level of autonomous government.

Conclusion

The heart that sustains Zapatista autonomy is the creation of a new form of work in Zapatista territory, a form of work that is done by and for the collective, which can best be understood as a'mtel. The creation of this new form of work throughout the different levels of autonomous government is one of the most pressing responsibilities of those who fulfill cargos in the autonomous government system. It is a concrete necessity that will allow the organization to become independent from solidarity donations and projects. But it is also its own political project that aims to create a new world defined by different economic relationships, where work is *lekil a'mtel*, or the work that is done by everyone and that is good for everyone. Furthermore, the creation of this new world defined by the work of a'mtel is itself a process of decolonization. It necessitates the deconstruction of the colonial ordering of work (kanal), the cycle of desperation-dependence-displacement that sustained the fincas and continues to define the economic development and counterinsurgency strategies of the Mexican state.

The distinction between kanal and a'mtel is not just a distinction between wage and subsistence labor, or even between individual and collective labor. It is a distinction between a form of work that creates a system of control and domination and a form of work that strengthens the community's collective potential (ch'ulel) to decide together how they want to live, work, and sustain themselves and their organization. A'mtel, the work of Zapatista trabajos colectivos, does not aspire to a world where property and work are exclusively collective. As Subcomandante Moisés pointed out during the Critical Thought versus the Capitalist Hydra seminar, at first some Zapatista communities owned and worked the land they reclaimed in 1994 entirely collectively, but then problems started to emerge. For example, some compañeros wanted to pick the corn when it had just ripened, because they really like fresh corn (called *elote* in Spanish), but then there wouldn't be much corn left for the families that wanted to wait for the corn to dry, so they could store it to make tortillas. As Moisés says, this happened because the compañeros had not reached an agreement on how they wanted to cultivate the corn, and so, Moisés tells us, they started to work to find a solution: "So what the compas do is that we have to come to an agreement. We will do collective work for a certain number of days and a certain number of days we will have for ourselves."[57] Zapatista trabajos colectivos, or a'mtel, is not defined by one set form of collective work, rather a'mtel is a form of work in which everything is determined democratically by the collective. A'mtel does not imply that everyone does everything, but it does imply that everyone has democratic control over how everything gets done. It is yet another concrete manifestation of ichbail ta muk', where all aspects of governance and work are constantly defined and redefined through the agreements of the Zapatista communities.

CHAPTER SIX

Challenges in the Work of Collective Governance (A'mtel): Circumscribing Power, Creating Accountability, and Women's Participation

It is one thing to aspire to create a system of government where the work of governing authorities functions according to the logic of a'mtel and quite another to come up with concrete structures that ensure this aspiration is realized in practice. Governing according to a'mtel means always placing the voices of the communities above one's individual voice and their desires above one's individual desires. Zapatista authorities should always serve these voices and desires and never seek to accumulate wealth, power, or prestige. However, Zapatista authorities are far from perfect, and wealth, power, and prestige are all very powerful temptations. Thus, the challenge of autonomous government is to create concrete practices that mitigate these temptations and ensure that Zapatista authorities remain closely bound by the agreements of the communities. The Zapatista autonomous government has had to develop structures and practices that actively prevent the concentration of economic, political, and gendered forms of power. The challenges of autonomous government are to prevent Zapatista authorities from becoming corrupt and stealing the money of the communities, from becoming authoritarian and using their position to gain power and influence, and from perpetuating gendered forms of oppression that place economic and political power in the hands of men and exclude women from full participation and self-determination in the Zapatista organization. This chapter examines the intricacies of these three challenges, the solutions that have been developed to address them, and the relative successes of these solutions throughout the five Caracoles. However, before we can address these challenges, we first must lay out the most basic mechanism that makes Zapatista authorities accountable to their communities: the process of democratic elections in the assembly.

Elections through the Assembly and the Obligations of Zapatista Authorities

How do the communities choose people to fulfill the responsibilities of autonomous government? This process is very different in each of the five Caracoles; however, there is a common logic that unites all their diverse practices. Some of the most in-depth descriptions of the process of choosing authorities are given in the testimonies from Caracol IV Morelia. Manuel, a former member of the consejo of the autonomous municipality 17 de Noviembre, describes the process of choosing authorities at the three levels of autonomous government:

> The way that we choose our authorities in Caracol IV is through the assembly. If in the communities they are going to choose a local authority, it could be a comisariado, comisariada, agenta, agente, consejo de vigilancia, conseja de vigilancia, or some other local authority, we do it by means of a local general assembly. There they choose from among the compañeras and compañeros. They name two or three compañeros and propose them as authorities. Once there is this proposal a vote is carried out. The assembly will defend who they would like to be their authority.
>
> When the proposed compañero or compañera is named, everyone raises their hand, if it is a majority, they become an authority. This is how it is done in the community, in the ejidos. Once the local authorities are named, the comisariada or comisariado, the agenta or the agente, or the cargo that each person has received, this compañero or compañera has to go and present themselves to the autonomous municipality to go and bring the news, the work they are going to share with the Autonomous Consejo. This is their work.
>
> Choosing a municipal authority is done in the same way. Everyone is gathered. We convoke a municipal assembly. All the authorities gather so that they can make proposals to choose an authority. For example, if we are naming the Municipal Consejo, they make proposals in the same way, three, four, or five compas, then the majority of the assembly choose who will be the president, who will be consejo, like that until all the commissions are

filled. Some compañeros who are present in the municipal assembly are chosen, but there are also some compañeros who aren't in the municipal assembly, who are working in their community without knowing that they are now named as an authority. When this happens the comisariado or the comisariada, the responsable, goes to the community of this compañero or compañera and informs them that they have been named in the municipality as an authority. So this compañero or compañera wasn't at their election, but they do accept the cargo, because it is clear where it is coming from and what is their duty as a member of the organization.

In the zone they also have municipal assemblies, each municipality carries out its responsibility of naming its delegate for the Good Government Council. When a compañero or compañera is chosen, it depends on their discipline, their behavior. This is what we have done in our zone when we choose the three levels of government.... This is how the work is done, the government at the three levels. When the authority . . . is in their cargo, we respect them because they are an authority that we chose.[1]

Other Caracoles do things similarly. The testimonies in the escuelita textbooks from La Realidad, Oventik, La Garrucha, and Roberto Barrios all describe choosing authorities using a similar assembly process.[2] Furthermore, the testimonies describing this process go beyond describing electoral practices, they strike at the core of what it means to be a Zapatista authority. They make clear that being an authority is an onerous obligation not a privileged source of power. The idea of a Zapatista authority arises from long traditions of indigenous community governance, but these traditions have themselves been significantly altered by the democratic principles of Zapatismo. The knowledge of how to govern as an authority should never be held by a select group of specialists but must be shared equally among the people.

Those who are chosen as Zapatista authorities have a duty to accept their cargo and carry out their responsibilities as best they can. The autonomous authorities do not ask the people to elect them and certainly do not run election campaigns. Rosa Isabel, a member of one of the communities in the municipality 17 de Noviembre in Caracol IV Morelia, emphasizes the difference between elections in the autonomous government and the official government:

Compared with the official government . . . we see that they spend many millions of pesos to do their campaigns. The worst is that they offer many things at the time of their campaign, and when they are in government they don't fulfill them. So the difference is that the compañeros who are part of our autonomous governments are in their cargo because the people offered it to them not because they themselves offered to do it. They were chosen, and so they have to accept the work that our communities need.[3]

I have heard this critique of the Mexican electoral system expressed by many Zapatistas in many different public speeches. The idea of someone asking the people to elect them, let alone running a full-fledged electoral campaign, seems fundamentally wrong. Elections in the autonomous government are the opposite of those in the official government. Rather than candidates trying to convince the people to elect them, the people elect their autonomous authorities regardless of whether that authority wants to be elected or not and then must convince them to fulfill their duties. In fact, Caracol IV Morelia has its own agreement defining what to do if someone doesn't fulfill their cargo. For example, if someone is named as a member of the Good Government Council and they don't show up in the Caracol for their turn, a member of their municipality's consejo must fill in for them. Furthermore, an unnamed authority from Morelia says that they also receive the following sanctions per the agreement of the zone:

> First, they get a warning. They always get three chances. If the compañero didn't show up, they go and ask why he or she didn't show up, what problems they have. If it is because of sickness, it is justified that they didn't show up. If it is because they didn't want to show up, they got lazy, they receive a warning for the first time. The second time maybe they have to pay, but first we have to really see what their reason is, what is the problem. As it is, problems do come up. If someone didn't want to do the work, maybe it is because they don't want to do the work, but maybe also because their ideas and heart aren't in it. Sometimes it has come out like that.[4]

If someone doesn't want to show up to fulfill their responsibilities as a member of the Good Government Council, the other authorities are responsible for figuring out why that person isn't doing the work and for convincing them that they need to fulfill their responsibilities. These testimonies reflect a sharp contrast between the Mexican state's understanding of governance and that of the indigenous Zapatista communities. For the Zapatistas, governing is not a way to seek power or prestige, it is a duty assigned by the democratic will of the communities. Furthermore, the existence of sanctions for those who don't show up to carry out their duties implies that a cargo in autonomous government can be so onerous that many people, far from running election campaigns, do their best to avoid fulfilling it. The work of governing is the obligation of everyone in the Zapatista organization, it is a duty rather than a privilege, and it requires a significant amount of work.

As with many things in Zapatismo, this understanding of government as obligation arises from long traditions of indigenous government that have also been significantly altered by the new political possibilities of the Zapatista movement. The escuelita textbooks give one example that strikingly illustrates this process of continuity and change. The testimonies from Caracol II Oventik describe how in the municipality of San Andrés Sakamchen de los Pobres for many years they used a traditional form of choosing authorities that did not involve the democratic process of an assembly. The testimonies are somewhat unclear, but they paint a general picture of this traditional form of choosing new authorities. In San Andrés the municipal authorities are split between one consejo that attends to the work of autonomous government and another called the "traditional authorities," which is responsible for organizing the religious rituals and festivals in the community. Until about a year before the escuelita, these traditional authorities would directly choose their replacements. The testimonies from Oventik describe how they would try to surprise their replacement in his or her home, because if the replacement saw the traditional authority coming to his or her house, he or she would hide and pretend no one was home so as not to be chosen to fulfill the cargo. The traditional authorities would use tricks, like sending someone else to the house and then following them once they got invited in so they could pass on their cargo.

However, around a year before the escuelita, the municipality has decided to change its approach and now chooses all of its authorities in an assembly of all of the communities. An unnamed authority from Oventik reflected on this decision: "[N]ow they changed [the way they name authorities in San Andrés], because we are understanding what democracy is. . . . [T]here are traditional things that are good that we should never lose, and there are traditional things that we should. We have to understand that now they don't work for us."[5] The understanding of the work of an authority as a fairly undesirable community obligation comes from a long tradition in San Andrés; however, the assembly as the sole form of carrying out elections is a new practice that has resulted from the political possibilities created by Zapatismo. As the authority from Oventik implies, Zapatismo has allowed San Andrés to critically reflect on their traditions and transform them in accordance with shared democratic principles. They are slowly transforming their understanding of the cargo of an authority from a traditional obligation to a duty shared by all members of the Zapatista organization that is assigned through the democratic process of an assembly.

The testimonies from La Realidad also mention a recent change in their process of choosing authorities. For many years, each community in the zone had to take turns filling the cargos of the Good Government Council. They would rotate among the communities, and when it was a certain community's turn they would have to choose someone that lived there to be one of the members of the Good Government Council. However, they recently changed this process and now choose the members of the Good Government Council from among all the communities in the zone so that they can find the people who will be the most committed to the work.[6] This case illustrates a potential problem implicit in an understanding of governance in which everyone has an obligation to carry out the work of government: the work of governing is difficult and not everyone is adequately prepared to carry it out. These difficulties encompass very real practical obstacles, such as not knowing how to read or not having basic math skills. This lack of preparation is very pervasive in the older Zapatista generations who grew up before the revolution and often did not have access to formal education. However, these older generations often have a great wealth of life experience and wisdom that is lacking in the younger generations who have learned reading and math in the Zapatista education system. Subcomandante Moisés says that there were many autonomous municipalities that elected only eighteen or nineteen-year-olds to their consejos, because they were the only ones who knew how to read, but this brought with it many other immediate problems, because these young people didn't have any previous experience carrying out responsibilities in the organization and had difficulty doing the work of governing.[7]

The authorities in La Realidad have taken concrete steps to address this issue and ensure that whoever is chosen to serve in autonomous government will be prepared for the work. They have organized trainings in the communities that help prepare people to become new members of the Good Government Council and assume their responsibilities. As an unnamed authority from La Realidad remarked:

What we saw . . . is that we had to have trainings, that is to say, that the compañeros and compañeras who were already members of the Good Government Council now have the experience of what it was like when they were working, what problems they encountered, or what they did so that things would work well. Now they can share with the rest of the compañeros. We've already given a first training for all the authorities, where the compañeros and compañeras who were already members of the Council shared their experience. These compañeros who are authorities also go to the communities and explain to them how things function within the Good Government Council, how to write a denunciation, everything that is done there.

These steps are being taken, they are in process, because what we want is that afterward those that become members of the Council won't say, "I don't know, I'm not prepared for this." For this reason, they are being trained now. When they come to be there and they need to address an issue, if they need to make a denunciation, if they need to perform a service, to call for someone's testimony, now they won't say that they don't know how to do it, because now they are prepared. They will know what work they need to do in health, in education, in transit, in justice.

At this point this is the plan that we have to continue with this training, and this is for everyone. We aren't only going to train the authorities, because, as we say, we are democratic, and the people are who decide who will be an authority. They won't choose someone just because they are trained. When the people choose a compañero or compañera it will be because they decided to do so, but they will know that this compañera is prepared. This is why the training will be for everyone. This is what we are doing so that the future generations will have ideas and experience for when they are an authority, whether as Good Government Council or as municipal consejo, or even as a local authority in their community.[8]

The Good Government Council hopes that one day everyone in the zone will not only know how the autonomous government functions but also be prepared to do the day-to-day work of a member of the Good Government Council, municipal consejo, or local autonomous government. This is a pragmatic aspiration with deep political implications. It aims to make it easier for members of the Zapatista communities to work in the autonomous government when they are chosen as authorities, and also aspires to a form of political existence in which there is no separation between the autonomous government and the communities, where everyone participates in governance and is prepared to take a turn in a governing body in the Caracol, the municipality, and the community, and where this knowledge will be passed on and grow in the future generations of the Zapatista movement. It reflects the Zapatista understanding of the work of governance: it is an obligation that is democratically assigned by the communities, but which is also shared by everyone in the communities. This initiative in La Realidad prevents the formation of a separate class of experts or specialists responsible for governing by disseminating the knowledge of governance equally among all members of the communities. The goal of autonomous government is that everyone know how to govern. As one authority put it, "The people are the books we use to learn autonomy. And among the people, with the work of our cargo, we are taught to be an authority. And so that the knowledge is not kept in the head of those who have experience and knowledge. We must give the wisdom to others."[9]

The Zapatista process of electing authorities reflects their understanding of work in the autonomous government. It is a democratically assigned duty that is shared by all members of the Zapatista organization. It is a'mtel not a source of personal power or prestige. However, this system confronts two problems: first, the problem of preexisting forms of choosing community authorities that do not follow the democratic principles of the Zapatista organization; second, the problem of Zapatistas who don't want to fulfill their duty because they lack the necessary skills or simply because they do not feel motivated. The process of creating the autonomous government system necessitates the creation of functioning democratic structures that may alter traditional structures of decision-making to redefine the role of an authority as a democratically assigned duty to the Zapatista organization. Furthermore, this duty and the commitment to the organization it implies is the only thing motivating members of the communities to carry out the work of autonomous government. Those who work as Zapatista authorities cannot be motivated by a desire for power in their communities or by personal material gain, because the system is designed to place all power and resources under the direct democratic control of the communities not their authorities. As we have already seen, the role of authorities is to make proposals to the communities not to decide for them. There is no motivation to carry out the difficult work of a cargo other than a sense of duty to the communities and the organization, and sometimes this motivation is not enough to sustain an authority through the difficulties of the day-to-day work. The Zapatistas' answer to this problem has been to attempt to integrate the work of governance into the daily life of the communities by training them to govern, but also, as we shall see, by finding ways to make it easier for Zapatista authorities to fulfill their cargos without accumulating forms of economic or political power.

Preventing the Formation of Political and Economic Elites

The structure of the autonomous government itself is designed to prevent the somewhat onerous work of governing from becoming a desirable privilege and source of power. Inherent in any administrative system is the danger of creating a separate class of administrators who have privileged access to power and who are always in danger of becoming corrupt. As Raúl Zibechi has argued, using the example of Aymara forms of governance in Bolivia, the task of social movements that aspire to communitarian democracy is to come up with governance systems that both recognize the inherent dangers that could create a governing elite and include mechanisms that minimize or eliminate these dangers. In a Zapatista context, the problem is to create structures that insure the work of governance remains work for the collective (a'mtel) and never becomes work for money and personal gain (kanal).

Those who work in autonomous government could accumulate two forms of power: economic and political. Due to their hard work outside of their community, they could be compensated with a salary that would make them wealthier than the other people in their community. But even more significantly, since they are responsible for watching over the funds and resources of the zone, they could easily embezzle funds. These are the two potential sources of economic power. These two dangers exist alongside the possibility of accumulating political power through personal connections and relationships, for example, with outside NGOs, or even with other communities, that increase political influence and could result in forms of corruption and bribery. We have already seen an example of the concrete benefits of this accumulation of political power in the case of the Zapatista who worked with the NGO SHOXEL building dry latrines. He received a salary from the NGO, making him one of richest people in his community, and he made sure that his relatives were the first to receive the dry latrines.

The first step that Zapatista autonomous government has taken to prevent the accumulation of economic power is to eliminate monetary compensation for those who govern. Zapatista authorities are not paid for their work. The food and funds that sustain them during their work as authorities comes from the trabajos colectivos of the communities. Doroteo, a former member of the Good Government Council of La Realidad, describes the support for Good Government Council members in his zone:

> When [the Good Government Council] was starting our work, the communities and the municipalities started to discuss how to support this group of compañeros, because they are doing their work full-time. They started to organize, and the communities decided to give a contribution of ten pesos each, ten pesos per member in the zone, to give these compañeros the support of thirty pesos per day while they were taking their turn.
>
> We did it like this for a few months. Each compañero who covered a turn had to receive thirty pesos per day. These were the agreements of the communities, but a few months later, one of the military commanders . . . explained to us the advantages and disadvantages of this form of support. Analyzing the advantages and disadvantages that they explained to us, as members of the Good Government Council we decided to suspend this support and informed the people why we decided to suspend it.
>
> We thought that it was not a viable path for us to become accustomed to working in that way, so we informed the people, and each community, each region, each municipality discussed another type of support. Some were supported in one way, some in another, but now it wasn't with money. . . . [S]ome receive support from their community in work, in staple grains, different forms of support according to how the community comes to an agreement, but never

money, and this is how we have been working these nine years in the Good Government Council.[10]

The other Caracoles have similar agreements. For example, in the zone of Caracol II Oventik the costs of transportation to the Caracol and the cost of purchasing rice, beans, and salt are covered. However, the Good Government Council members do not receive any monetary payment and are responsible for bringing their own tostadas—the central staple of their diet during their time in the Caracol.[11] The Good Government Council is not the only part of the Zapatista organization that functions with this form of voluntary work. The testimonies in the escuelita textbooks from all five Caracoles mention that people responsible for cargos in the Zapatisa organization never receive a salary for their work. They often receive limited support for their travel costs or some of their food from the trabajos colectivos in their community, municipality, or zone, through small donations from the compañeros that they serve, or through agreements in their community, for example, to work their land while they are away fulfilling their cargo. These forms of support only go toward feeding and sustaining them during their work. Fanny, a member of the Good Government Council of La Realidad at the time of the escuelita, makes clear that the work of autonomous government is always done as a service to the people and never in the interest of making money:

> In the autonomous government, in the work of being a local, municipal, or Good Government Council authority, you do the work from your consciousness. In the autonomous government we are working thanks to our consciousness and without any interest in making a salary, because everyone needs to participate for the autonomous government to work well. Service to the people is done with the consciousness that we each have. It is not done for money, it is not in the interest of making a salary, but rather of serving our people. With support or without support we are doing the work to build autonomy.[12]

The autonomous government functions thanks to the strong commitment to the Zapatista organization of every authority, and every community in all the zones. Although the resources generated by trabajos colectivos are very important in supporting the work of autonomous government, what truly sustains their work is their commitment to the

Zapatista organization. For example, the testimonies from La Realidad mention that some members of the Good Government Council are not supported at all by their communities, because they could not reach an agreement, but they still fulfill their cargo as best they can,[13] while the testimonies from La Garrucha describe how during the early years of the autonomous municipalities there was no money to pay for transportation and food for the municipal consejos, so they had to walk for hours and sometimes days, carrying their food with them, in order to arrive at the municipal center and fulfill their cargo.[14] This is the work of a'mtel. It is a constant process of collective decision-making in which different tasks and responsibilities are divided among the people of the communities, with everyone fulfilling different roles to sustain the collective heart of the organization and never for their own personal gain, their own kanal. These people work to sustain the Zapatista organization and are in turn sustained by the work of the other cargos and trabajos colectivos at the different levels of the organization.

The Government and Communities Are One and the Same: Rotation Systems in the Five Caracoles

However, even a group of people who do their work through the strength of their commitment rather than for money could transform into a new form of revolutionary governing elite with disproportionate influence and power. In fact, this was exactly the danger inherent in the military structure of the EZLN, which threatened to subsume the democratic processes of the communities due to its intense political legitimacy after the 1994 revolution. The Caracoles have sought to combat this danger by developing complex rotation systems for the members of the Good Government Councils, with part of the council doing the work of governing in the Caracol, while the rest work in their communities. These systems ensure that no one is governing long enough to develop disproportionate power and influence. Furthermore, since members aren't paid, they have to go home periodically to work their fields in order to survive. In his analysis of similar rotation systems in Aymara community governance, Zibechi argues that such rotation systems constitute "[a] social machinery that prevents the concentration of power or, similarly, prevents the emergence of a separate power from that of the community gathered in assembly."[15] In a very literal sense rotating systems of governance ensure that the government and the communities remain part of the same social body.

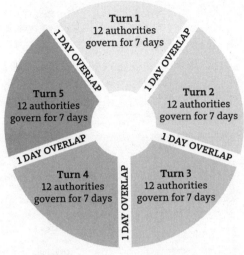

Figure 4: The Good Government Council of Morelia's Weekly Rotation System

Those who are chosen from the communities for cargos in the Zapatista autonomous government are never away long enough to become separate from the life of their communities. The work of governance remains as one of the many communal obligations of a'mtel in each community, rather than as a privilege that launches those who attain it into a different social sphere of power and influence. But how do these rotation systems function in practice in the five Caracoles, and what unforeseen problems have arisen?

The Good Government Council of Morelia is made up of a total of sixty members, but they do not all work in the Caracol at the same time. They are divided into five teams of twelve members that take turns fulfilling the responsibilities of the Good Government Council in the Caracol. Each team works in the Caracol one out of every five weeks and returns to their communities to work their fields and be with their families for four weeks. Each team's turn overlaps with the next by a day so that the team leaving can inform the next team about the work they have been doing and what still needs to be addressed. All the members of the Good Government Council, as well as the authorities at the other levels of autonomous government in Morelia, are elected for three-year terms. Each of the regions in the zone elects at least one member of the Good Government Council in each period, but each region's representation on the Council is proportional to its population, so some of the larger municipalities elect six or more members.[16]

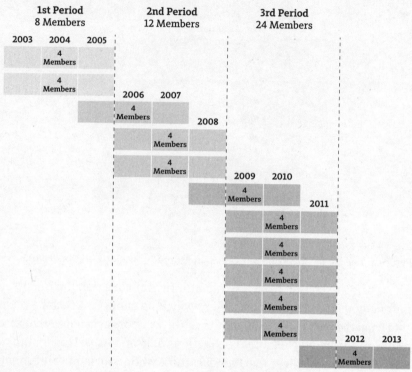

Figure 5: The Good Government Council of La Realidad's Three-Year Rotation System

The other four Caracoles also function according to similar rotation systems. The Good Government Council that was operating in La Realidad at the time of the escuelita had twenty-four members divided into two teams of twelve that would each spend fifteen days per month working in the Caracol. Members of the Good Government Council are also elected for three-year periods in La Realidad, although their elections are staggered so that at the end of the second year of every period four new members will be chosen whose three-year term will overlap with the first two years of the next period. They started staggering their elections like this because they saw that it was difficult for the council members to learn how to do their work when they arrived at the start of their period. By staggering their elections, they made sure that four new members would have a whole year to learn how the Good Government Council functioned from the old members. These four members could then teach the new members of the next period how to do the work. In the first three-year period there were eight members on the Council, in the second there was

	1st Period			2nd Period			3rd Period		
	2003	2004	2005	2006	2007	2008	2009	2010	2011
		2 Members			4 Members			4 Members	
		2 Members			4 Members			4 Members	
		2 Members			4 Members			4 Members	
	2 Members		2 Members			4 Members			4 Members	
	2 Members		2 Members			4 Members			4 Members	
	2 Members			2 Members			4 Members			4 Members
	2 Members			2 Members			4 Members			4 Members

Figure 6: The Good Government Council of Oventik's Three-Year Rotation System

twelve, while the third that was operating at the time of the escuelita had twenty-four. They increased the number of members each period, because they realized that there was too much work for a small team of people to accomplish.[17]

The Good Government Council of Caracol II Oventik is made up of twenty-eight members divided into two teams of nine and one team of ten who each take a one week turn working in the Caracol. Each of Oventik's seven municipalities is responsible for electing four members. They also are elected for three-year terms and have staggered elections so that there will be older members with experience who can teach the new authorities. Every year, eight members from two municipalities leave and are replaced by eight new members from these same municipalities (presumably since they have seven municipalities, every three years three municipalities switch out rather than two), so that every new period will still have twenty members who have experience.[18] The Good Government Council of Caracol III La Garrucha has twenty-four members divided into three teams of eight who each take a ten-day turn in the Caracol. They are also elected for three-year periods, but the escuelita textbooks don't mention whether their elections are staggered or not.[19]

The Good Government Council of Caracol V Roberto Barrios had gone through many recent changes at the time of the escuelita in 2013. At first, the Good Government Council was made up of members of the nine municipal consejos in the zone. Then, in 2008, the zone agreed that each municipality would provide three Council members for a total of twenty-seven members who were divided in teams of between five and seven people who would each take a four-month turn in the Caracol. These members only served on the Good Government Council and did not have to fulfill the double responsibility of working as a municipal consejo. Every four-month turn overlapped by one month so that the new group would be prepared to continue the work. However, in 2010, the zone altered the agreement to make every turn only last two months. They reached this decision to make the work easier for the Council members, because many members had been abandoning their cargo, but even after they reduced each turn to two months Council members were still abandoning the work. They tried to solve the problem by making sure that there were some more experienced members in each turn that could teach the newer members how to do the work. This agreement had just been made at the time of escuelita and the testimonies do not mention whether it worked or not.[20]

The most common problem with the rotation systems in the five Caracoles is providing enough continuity between rotations. There are many problems, for example, a complex land dispute, that take longer than one or two weeks to address. There must be some way of adequately preparing the next rotation to continue with the work. Most Caracoles address this issue by having their rotations overlap by at least a day so that they will have enough time to smoothly pass along the work to the new team. However, the more difficult problem has been providing continuity between three-year terms. In the course of three years working on the Good Government Council, members inevitably develop some specialized knowledge that helps them with their work. For example, they know how the trabajos colectivos at the level of the zone function, they know how to investigate an agrarian dispute or what to do if there is paramilitary or government aggression. The Caracoles have addressed this problem by overlapping their three-year terms, and through other means mentioned above, such as La Realidad's initiative to train everyone in the zone in the skills and knowledge needed to work on the Good Government Council.

The elimination of a political class does come at the expense of the elimination of the specialized knowledge of this class. However, this isn't a cause for concern since a separate political class tends to use this specialized knowledge more for its own benefit than for those they are supposedly there to serve. Ultimately, it is more important to the Zapatistas to prevent the concentration of political and economic power than to maximize the efficiency of the autonomous government. The guiding principle of governing by obeying aims to create a system of governance that has numerous concrete practices, such as the rotation systems and lack of monetary compensation, that prevent the separation of the governing authorities from the people. If the realization of this principle means that decisions take longer to make or problems take longer to solve, then everyone will have to be patient. The Zapatistas never sacrifice their fundamental principles of good government in the name of efficiency.

Watching over the Autonomous Governments: Accountability Structures in the Five Caracoles

Even if the members of the Good Government Councils only spend a limited amount of time in the Caracol, they are still governing far away from their home community, and there is ample time between assemblies of the zone for them stray from the agreements of the communities. Who watches over the Good Government Council to make sure they remain true to the communities' agreements and the principles of governing by obeying? Every Caracol has a separate body called the comisión de vigilancia whose sole purpose is to watch over the Good Government Council, and especially to monitor all the money handled by the Council, to make sure they are not corrupt or disobeying the agreements of the communities.[21] The testimonies in the escuelita textbooks also mention that the CCRI in each zone, sometimes called the comisión de información (commission of information), also serve as an additional accountability structure that watches over the work of the Good Government Council, provides ideas and advice, and makes sure the that they are following the agreements of the communities. However, the CCRIs are part of the EZLN military structure and, as such, do not have any defined responsibilities or powers in the autonomous government beyond giving recommendations and advice. Although the comisiónes de vigilancia in the five zones all have the same general purpose, in practice they work very differently in each of the five Caracoles.

In Caracol II Oventik the comisión de vigilancia has been in place since the formation of the Caracol in 2003. It is made up of teams of five people from all the communities in the zone who take one-week turns in the Caracol. Anyone who has visited Oventik has had to show them identification and state the purpose of their visit. They are responsible for taking down the information of everyone who enters the Caracol and recording every donation received by the Good Government Council. Their primary role is to watch over money from donations and to make sure that no one from the Mexican government enters the Caracol. Furthermore, there is an additional commission of eighteen people called the comisión general de vigilancia, formed in 2012. Some of the members are people from the communities, others are local authorities, and there are some who are part of the núcleo de resistencia (nucleus of resistance), which is not fully explained in the escuelita textbooks but seems to be a group of young people who receive training, including education in math and account-ing, from the CCRI.[22] The comisión general de vigilancia checks all the accounts of the Good Government Council, the municipal consejos, and the different trabajos colectivos—for example, health, education, agricul-ture, and the artisan and coffee cooperatives—to make sure there aren't any instances of corruption. They also send regular reports to all the com-munities in the zone to let them know how the autonomous government and trabajos colectivos are functioning.[23]

The comisión de vigilancia in Caracol V Roberto Barrios works in a similar way to that of Caracol II Oventik. The commission is made up of three people from each of the nine municipalities in the zone who serve for three years and are divided into teams that take one-month turns working in the Caracol. They are also responsible for recording the information of everyone who enters the Caracol and monitoring donations and expen-ditures. The testimonies in the escuelita textbooks say that a member of the comisión de vigilancia physically accompanies the members of the Good Government Council whenever they need to leave the Caracol to make a purchase using the funds of the zone. They are also responsible for making sure that the accounts add up. If any money is missing members of the comisión de vigilancia, the Good Government Council, and the CCRI must make up the difference out of their own pockets.[24]

In Caracol III La Garrucha the comisión de vigilancia is made up of people from all the communities in the zone who take turns working in the Caracol. The testimonies from La Garrucha make clear that their comisión de vigilancia is not just responsible for overseeing finances but is always present and part of the conversation, together with the CCRI, when the Good Government Council is deliberating on any issue that arises in their work. Cornelio, a former member of the Good Government Council, explains, "If there is a problem, if there is a trabajo of another area like health or education, we have to consult with the offices of vigilancia and information [the CCRI]. The Good Government Council can't decide on its own, because it is watched over by the people. This is why the vigilancia is there, they watch to make sure that we are respecting the agreement that we have in the zone."[25] At the time of the escuelita, Caracol III La Garrucha had recently agreed to form an additional comisión de vigilancia made up of two young people from the núcleo de resistencia in each municipality who take ten-day turns in the Caracol. It is their job to check all the Good Government Council's accounts and control the zone's funds. If the good Government Council needs to make a purchase they ask this commission, which gives them the amount needed for the purchase. Since they are the ones who control the funds, if any money goes missing the people in the núcleo de resistencia are responsible for replacing it from their own pockets.

Caracol I La Realidad did not have a functioning comisión de vigilancia until around the time of the escuelita. For the ten years since the formation of the Caracol the Good Government Council would send reports of their income and expenditures to all the communities and the CCRI but no authorities or communities fully checked these reports to make sure they were correct. The testimonies from La Realidad state that they had recently organized a group of compañeros and compañeras called "the filter." This group had only been functioning for a month and was made up of former members of the Good Government Council and municipal consejos, as well as other people with cargos in the organization. "The filter" works in collaboration with the CCRI and checks all the finance reports to make sure everything adds up and is correct.[26]

In Caracol IV Morelia, as well, the role of the comisión de vigilancia is to check all the accounts of the Good Government Council and keep track of how much money is coming in, how much is being spent, and how much is currently in their fund. From 2003 to 2008, like the Good Government Council, the comisión de vigilancia was a long-term cargo of three years, but this didn't work, because people would often abandon the cargo. In 2008, the zone agreed that the comisión de vigilancia would be made up of one person from each of the regions in the zone who would serve for a three-month period in the Caracol. They also made them responsible for providing a report on their work every six months in one of the assemblies of the zone. This new agreement solved the previous problem, and the commission was working well at the time of the escuelita.[27]

Caracol IV Morelia also has an additional unique accountability structure called the commission of elders. This commission is made up of the elders of each municipality whose central responsibility is to preside over the changing of authorities in the municipalities and the zone and to encourage the new authorities to respect the people and take their responsibilities seriously. Manuel, a former member of the municipal consejo of 17 de Noviembre, describes the role of the commission of elders:

> Once the levels of government are named, for example, in the municipality, they use our customs so that the new authorities go into effect. The elders, the new authorities, and the authorities that are going to leave use their traditional clothing. The elders make their presentation, they council the new authorities so that they will govern well for their three years. They also say goodbye to the authorities that are leaving and tell those that are entering to take care of their people. The elders use their custom, with their incense, their regional music, and all that; since in our zone and in our municipalities there are Tojolobal and Tzeltal customs, all the elders come together at the municipal level to do their work.[28]

Rosa Isabel, a member of one of the communities in the municipality 17 de Noviembre, further elaborates on this ceremony:

> [T]he elders, who are now very old, start to counsel the new authorities. At times they speak so that they will do their work well, because being an authority is not a game. The elders know, because they have also been authorities before. They served in their municipalities. The elders give us their counsel, as is our culture. Because we have to take being an authority seriously, the elders counsel us to be responsible. After they give counsel, the elders line up and give a blessing to the new authorities. The work of the elders is like this. We respect it very much. . . . When the old authorities are going to leave their cargo and the new ones are going to receive it, the compañeros, men and women, from the base communities are present, because they are the ones who will give their trust, they are the ones who will give legality to this change of authorities. Once everyone has received their cargo, all this finishes. Then all the base communities that are in the assembly go over to the new authorities. There is a gathering where we eat together. Once the gathering is finished,

sometimes we have a cultural event, we have a party and dance. This is how we change authorities in our municipalities, and also in the zone it is done like this.[29]

This ceremony provides a form of cultural accountability in the autonomous government structure of Caracol IV Morelia. The role of the commission of elders is to remind the authorities who they are, that they carry the trust and responsibility of the people, and that they should always respect this trust by doing their best work as an authority.

The accountability structures in Zapatista autonomous government, among them the comisiones de vigilancia in the five Caracoles and Morelia's commission of elders, provide an additional bridge between the communities and their authorities. These structures bring people from the communities into the Caracol and allow them to watch over their authorities in a very literal sense. In all the Caracoles, someone from the communities is present when the authorities are developing proposals, addressing problems, and, most importantly, handling the funds of the autonomous government. The organization of these accountability structures serve a dual purpose. First, they recognize the very real temptations of corruption for anyone working as a Zapatista authority and take concrete steps discourage it. Second, as Rosa Isabel points out, they are the means for the base communities to "give their trust" to their government. The rotations of the comisiones de vigilancia serve to insure that the autonomous authorities do not become corrupt and bring the assurance that these authorities are in fact honest back to the communities so that the people will trust their authorities, respect their work, and ultimately have faith that their system of autonomous government is fairly and justly serving the people.

The work of autonomous government functions according to the logic of a'mtel: it is never a means of gaining wealth, power, or prestige. Instead, it is a responsibility assigned by the collective of all the Zapatista communities. It is a duty and commitment to the Zapatista organization and struggle in accordance with the defined responsibilities that come with that particular cargo. Just as with all cargos, it fulfills a set of responsibilities but does not remove or separate those who assume them from the collective heart of the people. There are numerous concrete practices, such as the lack of a salary, the constant rotations of Good Government Council members, and the additional structures of accountability, including the comisión vigilancia, the CCRI, and the commission of elders, that ensure that the work of autonomous government does not create a separate class of administrators that governs rather than obeys. The logic of a'mtel defines government as a temporary responsibility that is shared by everyone and serves everyone. The goal of autonomous government is to make it possible for everyone to participate in every decision and share in the work of governing. This goal defines the structure of the Zapatista Caracoles.

The State of Women's Participation in Autonomous Government in the Five Caracoles

The structures of gendered oppression in the indigenous communities of Chiapas produce many barriers to women's full participation in the Zapatista autonomous government and reinforce a situation where men control most aspects of political and economic decision-making. The Caracoles have taken some steps to mitigate these barriers so women can participate equally in the autonomous government. For example, every Caracol has an agreement that half the members of the Good Government Council and the municipal consejo must be women. However, the only testimonies to this agreement actually functioning at all levels of autonomous government are from Caracol IV Morelia, and the escuelita textbooks give the impression that women's participation is more advanced in Morelia than in the other Caracoles. Additionally, in her 1997–2001 study of Zapatista women, Melissa Forbis cites a regional responsable from the zone of Morelia who comments on their relative progress compared to other zones.[30] For example, one of the testimonies from Morelia in the escuelita textbooks mentions that the first Zapatista women's cooperative was developed in their zone.[31] However, there is no clear explanation for the greater progress apparent in Morelia compared to the other Caracoles. It likely has to do with the particular history of the Zapatista women's struggle in that zone.

Morelia's Good Government Council is made up of thirty men and thirty women, and each of their five turns of twelve members is also split equally between six men and six women.[32] Furthermore, each of their three municipal consejos are made up of six men and six women.[33] They also mention that the majority of the communities in their zone have women participating as local authorities.[34] The testimonies from La Realidad do not mention whether their municipal consejos are gender-equal, although they do say that they are trying to promote women's participation at that level. However, they do make clear that the past two periods of the Good Government Council were split equally between men and women. Twelve men and twelve women participated in the Council that was working at the time of the escuelita, while six men and six women participated in the previous period.[35] They also mention that the majority of the communities in their zone have women working as local authorities, and that they have an agreement that any community with more than ten people must have a woman and a man as local authorities.[36] The Good Government Council of Oventik is made up of fourteen men and fourteen women, with each municipality responsible for naming two men and two women.[37] Although the testimonies in the escuelita textbooks do not mention whether the municipal consejos are gender-equal, they do make clear that there are women participating at this level. They also say that although some communities have local authorities who are women, this is not the case in a majority of the communities.[38]

Lack of women's participation in autonomous government is especially pervasive in Caracol III La Garrucha and Caracol V Roberto Barrios, to the point that these Caracoles had difficulties finding enough women to fill the spots reserved for women in the autonomous government. Caracol V Roberto Barrios has an agreement that the Good Government Council must be gender-equal but in practice has been unable to implement this agreement. The period of the Good Government Council that began in 2009 and was working at the time of the escuelita had six members who were women and twenty-one men.[39] Similarly, the testimonies from this zone state that there were very few women participating in the autonomous government at the municipal level.[40] The Good Government Council of Caracol III La Garrucha had similar problems. There are very few women participating in the municipal consejos in the zone or in the Good Government Council.[41] According to an unnamed authority from this zone:

> In the current [Good Government] Council it is half compañeros and half compañeras, but at times there are problems, the compañeras arrive and after two, three, or four months they abandon the work, because they say, "Well, I can't read" or "I have a boyfriend, I'm getting married," and then they go. This is the problem that we have, but the agreement of our zone is to share ... but at times this doesn't actually happen, because sometimes the parents or husbands of the women tell them no or because of other family problems, but

sometimes the compañeras also don't exercise their right. These are the problems that we have. . . . Now we are working in the Council, I believe that there are only about four compañeras. At the beginning they came like this, half compañeras and half compañeros, but then little by little they left and we had to find someone else, but instead of a woman we found a man, because no one wanted to enter into this work. But it was a lack of understanding. We have to try to go back to bring the compañeras into this work. Right now, the compañeros are a majority in the Council, because there are only four compañeras of a total of twenty-four members.[42]

This authority identifies the same issues as the Zapatista organization as obstacles to women's participation from the beginning of their struggle: first, a lack of autonomy due to control by fathers and husbands; second, a parallel lack of the self-confidence and skills needed to fulfill the work of autonomous government. However, focusing on this second issue runs the risk of excusing the overrepresentation of men in the autonomous government by focusing on women's lack of self-confidence, rather than the forms of gendered oppression that produce it. Overall, the women's testimonies collected in the escuelita textbook *The Participation of Women Participation in Autonomous Government* do not present the problem as a lack of self-confidence, but rather as a denial of freedom. They do not present their aspirations just in terms of participation but in terms of participation as means to create women's self-determination and autonomy in their communities. The general requirement of gender equality in all levels of autonomous government cannot fully address the root of the problem. The lack of women's participation arises from concrete barriers that prevent them from participating whether they want to or not, and these barriers in turn arise from deeply ingrained gender hierarchies in the Zapatista communities. Until these hierarchies are dismantled, the organization will never find a complete solution to the lack of women's participation in autonomous government.

"How Can We Change if the Compañeros Don't Know How to Make Tortillas?" Barriers to Women's Participation in Autonomous Government

Women's lack of confidence in their ability to fulfill the work of cargos as well as men's ability to prohibit them from doing this work are not just the product of a lack of experience or an inability to understand women's rights in the Zapatista organization. They are the product of pervasive social and economic systems that arise from the structure of the communities and families that make up the Zapatista organization. These systems are described again and again in the women's testimonies in the escuelita textbook *The Participation of Women in Autonomous Government*. For example, often when women claim they can't fulfill the work of their cargo due to lack of skills or education they may just be making an excuse and the real reason has to do with their husband's wishes. As an unnamed woman from Caracol II Oventik observes, "[A] compañera is named [in the assembly]. We say that this compañera will be a local authority, and before she says anything she just looks at her husband and the compa's face has changed. She looks at her husband and then she says, 'No, because I don't know how to read,' but she is looking at her husband. It's because he won't let her."[43] This unequal power often results from men's control of household resources and the resulting dependence of women on their husbands or fathers. As Ana, an education trainer from Caracol V Roberto Barrios, observes:

> Maybe one of the reasons the compañeras don't want to participate is because they depend on their husbands. This could be why some of them don't denounce the violence, the mistreatment, the abuse that they confront as compañeras, because they know they are dependent on their husbands. Maybe this is why they don't denounce it. They don't say anything about what he is doing. "If he leaves me, where will I go, if I depend on the compañero, depend on my husband?" It could be that this is one of the reasons for the lack of participation of the compañeras, because there still isn't equal participation in work. Maybe this is one of the reasons that on the surface it looks like there aren't problems; there are obstacles that don't show up on the surface.[44]

The underlying system producing women's apparent lack of self-confidence or reluctance to participate in the organization begins with an unequal distribution of social and economic power in the home and the community.

Hilary Klein has argued that this inequality results, at least in part, from women's exclusion from holding title to a share of collective lands. Although Zapatista land is owned collectively, in many communities each

family is given title to a parcel of the collective land for their own sustenance and pass this parcel on to their descendants. According to Klein's
research, control of the vast majority of these individual plots was given
to men during the process of Zapatista land redistribution. Furthermore,
these parcels are usually divided among the sons in a family, while the
daughters receive nothing, the assumption being that they will have
access to land once they marry a man.[45] Since access to land for cultivation
is the primary means of survival for members of a Zapatista community,
this reality serves to make women dependent either on their fathers or
their husbands for their survival.

Zapatista women recognize the injustice of this reality. For example,
one woman said in a collective interview conducted by Klein in Olga Isabel,
in the zone of Caracol IV Morelia, "Men and women are equal and should
have equal rights. Single women should receive their share of the land. If
a woman is not married and is not going to marry, she has the same right
as men to the land. Women can do all the same work as men in the fields."[46]
In fact, there is a proposal to expand the Revolutionary Law of Women that
includes a tenet guaranteeing women's land rights among its thirty-three
points.[47] However, this proposal has existed since 1996 and has yet to be
ratified by the Zapatista communities in the five zones. It was proposed
in a general assembly of all five zones and brought back to the communities for approval. However, not everyone agreed and the process stalled.[48]
I have not encountered a clear explanation of why the process stalled,
although it likely has to do with the same force that usually prevents such
processes from moving forward: men's resistance to the erosion of their
social and economic power over women.

Although this expansion to the Revolutionary Law of Women has
not been approved, women's economic dependence on men due to lack
of access to land title has been partially mitigated through the creation
of women's trabajos colectivos. As one woman stated in an interview
conducted by Melissa Forbis, "Women also have their collective land,
which is a form of autonomy. They now have their own land and are
doing projects and not only the men get to do projects."[49] The creation
of trabajos colectivos allows women to collectively control land, even if
they do not inherit land title from their fathers. It allows them to build
their economic autonomy from men. If a woman participates in a trabajo
colectivo, for example, selling her weaving and embroidery in a women's
cooperative or selling the products of a women's collective vegetable

garden, she can usually access sufficient resources to at least pay for her own transport to carry out the work of her cargo without relying on her husband.

However, in addition to economic dependence on men, women face other obstacles resulting from the gendered division of labor in the home, as well as men's tendency for suspicion and jealousy when women work outside the home. As Adamari, a member of the autonomous municipal consejo of Rubén Jaramillo in Caracol V Roberto Barrios, explains:

> There is very little participation of the compañeras . . . due to a lack of time for doing whatever work in the organization, because they dedicate all their time to household chores, like making the food, sweeping, washing the dishes and the clothes, feeding the animals, and taking care of their husbands. It's even worse if they have several small children. Also, the majority of men still don't help the compañeras with the household work. Their husbands' jealousy and mistrust sometimes stop the compañeras from taking their cargo. The same with girls, because the parents don't trust their daughters.[50]

Adamari identifies two fundamental barriers to women's participation in the Zapatista organization: the lack of men's participation in household work that makes women choose between fulfilling their cargo and letting their children and animals go hungry, and men's jealousy and suspicion that their wives might find another man when they leave to fulfill their cargo. Furthermore, one of the women interviewed by Melissa Forbis explains how this distrust can be reinforced by a women's community, even if their husband or father supports her. A seventeen-year-old Tzeltal woman interviewed by Forbis describes her experience going to women's gatherings and trainings in one of the Zapatista municipal centers: "I would hear rumors about how I was going there to be with men and not to work and learn. It made me cry. My father told me not to listen and to remember that I was doing important things, but I didn't like [the rumors]."[51] Another unnamed woman in the escuelita textbooks from Caracol IV Morelia characterizes these suspicions and jealousies as "psychological blows"that many women must constantly shrug off if they are to participate in the Zapatista organization.[52]

The gendered division of labor, jealousy and suspicion, and women's lack of economic autonomy are the three primary barriers to women's participation emphasized throughout women's testimonies in the escuel-ita textbooks. Ana, an education trainer from Caracol V Roberto Barrios, theorizes the origins of these three systems of oppression:

> Many years ago, there was equality between men and women, because there wasn't one that was more important than the other. Little by little inequality began with the division of labor, when the men were the ones to go out to the fields to cultivate the food, they went out to hunt to complement the sustenance of the families, and the women stayed in the house to dedicate themselves to domestic work, as well as spinning, weaving clothes, and making kitchen utensils, like clay pots, cups, and plates.
>
> Later another division of work arose with those who started raising cattle; cattle started to serve as a form of money. They used it to exchange their products. With time this activity became the most important, even more so with the rise of the bourgeoisie who buy and sell to accumulate profit. It was the men who dedicated themselves to all these tasks. Because of this the men are the ones who give the orders in the family. Because he was the only one who covered the family expenses, the work of women was not recognized as important. Because of this they were seen as lesser, as weak, unable to do any work.
>
> This was the custom, the way of life that the Spanish brought when they came to conquer our peoples. It was the friars who educated and instructed us in their customs and ways of thinking. They taught us that women have to serve men and obey them whenever they give orders, and that women have to cover their heads with a veil when they go to church, and that they can't look wherever they want, that they have to keep their heads lowered. They thought that women were the ones who made men sin. Because of this the church didn't allow women to go to school, and certainly didn't allow them to hold cargos. We, the indigenous peoples, took up the way the Spanish treated their women as our own culture. This is why the inequality between men and women arose in the communities and continues to this day.[53]

While Ana attributes the creation of gendered oppression in indigenous communities to processes of colonization and capitalism, she also makes clear that these oppressions are actively perpetuated by indigenous communities themselves. She identifies the source of gendered division of labor in practices in indigenous communities, emphasizing that this division gave men power over women due to the process of colonization and the later introduction of a capitalist economy. Furthermore, she implicitly connects men's jealousy and suspicion to the control of women's sexuality created by the forced introduction of Catholicism by the Spanish. Ultimately, she makes clear that although the indigenous communities learned this way of thinking and working from the Spanish, they are now the ones practicing it, and it is up to them to unlearn it.

What might this process of unlearning look like? We have already seen how the Zapatista struggle set in motion changes in gendered power relations, in particular through the creation of women's trabajos colectivos, which allow them to build their own economic autonomy. However, unequal power in the home cannot be overcome through economic independence alone, it also requires the creation of a new culture that values and supports women's work in the organization, with all labor, both domestic and agricultural, shared by men and women. As an unnamed woman from Caracol IV Morelia states:

> [H]ow can we change if the compañeros don't know how to make tortillas, if the compañeros still don't know how to prepare their corn, if the compañeros still don't know how to wash their clothes? How can we change these ideas, how can we be better? I always speak in my zone saying that education has to happen within the home. We have to teach boys to wash their clothes. Boys need to learn to take their food and wash their plate. Boys need to learn to work in the kitchen, and girls need to learn to work in the fields.
>
> If we don't do this, if we treat boys and girls differently, there will never be a change; it will remain the same. What happens when the compa stays and only drinks *pozol* [raw corn gruel], because he doesn't want to make his food, and the boys are going to continue like this? We have to put a different education into the heads of boys. If we are able to educate our boys like this, then we will make a change. Boys really can learn to do things in the home. So that the compañeros don't depend on us, but also so we won't depend on the compañeros. When the compañeros leave, we will do the work, we will weed the cornfield, we will bring the firewood, all the work that needs to be done, we can do. We just can't plow

or fell trees, I think because we've never had practice, but we can do the other work.

... I think that more years must pass before we can completely change our situation, the bad ideas that we have. What we are trying to create are equal rights between women and men, but there are many things left to do. There is still a lot of things we need to do in order to get it into the heads of the compañeros, of the compañeras. The home provides the best education. We are the teachers within the home. If we are able to teach our children, to educate them in a different way, things will be different; but if we aren't going to be good teachers, things will remain the same.[54]

The creation of a new culture where labor is shared in the home and the contributions of women are valued equally to those of men is a task that spans generations. In some Zapatista families, this process is already underway. I can attest that in the community in Caracol IV Morelia, where I stayed during the escuelita, the equal division of household and agricultural work between men and women was strikingly apparent. The same unnamed woman from Caracol IV also describes her experience of this change in her own family:

This is my experience: my compañero also doesn't know how to make his food. When he stays home he drinks pozol, that is he still has the idea from his mother that he should be served food at the table. This has not left, all of us here still have this. When I started to work the boys were very little.... I had three little boys, and now they are men. Since I wasn't always at home, I always went out to the meetings, to do other trabajos colectivos, I wouldn't always be at home, and what the boys did is they learned to cook on their own, because I wasn't always there.

... Now I see the difference with these boys. It is very different now. The wife of one of them is a health promoter. The day his compañera leaves he goes and brings in the corn, he goes and brings in firewood or cleans the place she has in the house, he does make tortillas. His wife is relaxed when she arrives. She doesn't worry, she doesn't feel unmotivated, because she feels this support. I am bringing up their experience, because I see it, it is very changed. When she is at a meeting her husband stays at home. When the wife arrives, the corn is already cooked, her coffee is ready. It is very different, and I think it is wonderful. That is why I tried to share it here.[55]

This experience shows the possibility for a new culture of gender equality that is being built in the Zapatista organization. Furthermore, it illustrates the deep importance of women's participation in the organization and the importance of men's support. If women can participate with men's support, the Zapatistas will one day create a culture where men and women have an equal right to work, govern, and live with dignity.

Women's participation remains a central concern for the Zapatistas. In the testimonies in the escuelita textbooks, when an authority is asked questions by the other authorities after finishing their testimony, by far the most common questions were those concerning women's participation in autonomous government in the zone. They constantly pressed the authorities to explain why women had difficulty participating and to explain what their zone was doing to address these issues. However, as we have seen, there are numerous systemic obstacles in Zapatista communities that block this participation. Dismantling these obstacles will likely be a long process that spans generations and that will be carried forward by the persistent struggle of Zapatista women to demand recognition of their rights and support for their work. Perhaps the experience of the escuelita itself has advanced this struggle. Hilary Klein noted that women coming together from different municipalities often motivates advancements in women's right to self-determination.[56] It allows women to see their shared experiences and be inspired by successes in other regions, for example, by the relative progress of Caracol IV Morelia. It brings Zapatista women together in a collective heart (ko'ontik). Hopefully, the experience of compiling testimonies from all five zones in *The Participation of Women in Autonomous Government* will inspire more advances for Zapatista women throughout the five Caracoles.

Conclusion

The work of autonomous government will likely always confront numerous challenges that threaten to reproduce old hierarchies or create new forms of oppression. The principles of Zapatista democracy, of governing by obeying, cannot be brought into reality simply by their assertion. These words must be made real through concrete forms of organization and constant struggle. The Zapatista pask'op must always produce new governing systems that both recognize existing and potential hierarchies and create processes that work to dismantle them.

The current system of autonomous government confronts three potential threats: the danger of corruption, the danger of creating a political and economic elite, and the danger of reproducing and entrenching men's power over women. The current system of autonomous government has developed several systems that are designed to confront and mitigate these problems and dismantle these hierarchies. The lack of monetary pay for Zapatista authorities and the accountability structures of the comisiones de vigilancia, the CCRI, and Morelia's commission of elders attempt to prevent corruption among Zapatista authorities and to ensure that they follow the will of the communities. The complex rotation systems in the five Caracoles prevent Zapatista authorities from separating themselves from the communities and becoming an elite governing class. Finally, the Zapatista autonomous government is attempting to redress the exclusion of women from autonomous government through the agreement that all levels of Zapatista authority be gender-equal. However, the real force that will dismantle this hierarchy is women's self-empowerment through the economic autonomy of trabajos colectivos and possibly through a future right to land, as well as through the slow process of educating future Zapatista generations in the practice of gender equality in the home. In all these cases, the Zapatista struggle (pask'op) advances not just through the power and truth of their words but also through the strength and imagination of their concrete practices of organization.

EPILOGUE

Another World Is Possible

We cannot forget the final exam of the escuelita, which Subcomandante Galeano frames as, "What is freedom according to you?"[1] The escuelita did not aim to instruct us in a new political doctrine or tell us how to organize ourselves in our own contexts, but it did provide certain lessons that are worth highlighting and reflecting on. First, this lack of political doctrine is a lesson in itself. It asserts that any organizational model or governing structure should arise through the mutual agreement and collective work of a people who take up the struggle to organize and govern themselves. The recent history of Zapatista autonomous government, and in fact of most of the many years of the Zapatista struggle, is defined by the constant creation and re-creation of governing structures, of new solutions to unforeseen problems, and, ultimately, of new forms of politics. This is the concrete work of a democracy of mutual respect (ichbail ta muk'). Such a democracy must constantly redefine the practice of democracy according to the agreements created by the collective heart of the communities through the constant passage from ko'onkutik to ko'ontik. The politics of Zapatismo is not a set doctrine, rather it is the product of the self-determination of multiple different communities that each have a voice in defining the future of their organization. These multiple voices have given rise to many different governing practices in their communities, autonomous municipalities, and each of the five Caracoles.

The politics of Zapatismo is more political orientation than organizational doctrine. All the communities ascribe to certain principles, including the seven principles of governing by obeying, the refusal of all involvement with the Mexican state, and a commitment to women's equality outlined in the Revolutionary Law of Women. However, each community, municipality, and Caracol brings these principles into reality through different political forms and governing practices. Each has its own way of making the collective word of the organization, of going forward with its collective pask'op. The right to self-determination is the consistent thread that runs throughout the history of the Zapatista struggle, from the aspiration to local democratic authorities in the Revolutionary Laws through the creation of the municipalities to the organization of the Caracoles and Good Government Councils. Zapatista democracy is a democracy of democratic forms, with the definition of democracy itself the product of a constant process of creation and re-creation undertaken by the Zapatista communities. This is the practice of governing by obeying.

Another lesson of the escuelita concerns the dangers of reproducing inequalities and hierarchies in these new governing systems. The central force that shapes Zapatista governing practices is the need to create systems that facilitate the practice of governing by obeying, while simultaneously preventing the autonomous government from accumulating power and transforming into a bad government that imposes its will on the democratic processes of the communities. The five Caracoles have developed numerous concrete practices that fulfill this need. The assembly of the zone is the highest and most inclusive governing body to ensure that the voices of all the communities participate in all decisions, while the Good Government Councils are watched over and tied to the communities by their rotation systems, as well as by various accountability structures, such as the comisiones de vigilancia. These practices aim to create a political system where those who govern remain part of the communities, and where the communities participate in all aspects of governance. They prevent the separation of the government from its people.

Similarly, the Zapatista organization aims to create an economic system that prevents the concentration of economic power and the formation of an economic elite. The Zapatista trabajos colectivos function according to the logic of a'mtel, or work that is democratically assigned and administered by the communities. The work of a'mtel is opposed to the work of kanal, or capitalist labor controlled by a boss, landowner, or anyone who has accumulated enough capital to exploit the labor of others for their own profit. The a'mtel of the trabajos colectivos does not eliminate the exchange of goods in local and global markets; however, it does aim to place the production of these goods under the egalitarian and democratic control of those who work to produce them. Furthermore, the trabajos colectivos of the Zapatista organization provide a means of sustaining their autonomy into the future. They represent a new form of economic relations and provide a means for the Zapatistas to become independent from outside funding. The practice of a'mtel is at the heart of Zapatismo. More than any ideology or principle, it is this shared practice of collective work that orients and defines the pask'op of the Zapatista organization.

The a'mtel of the trabajos colectivos and of the work of autonomous government itself create social and political systems that prevent the accumulation of power and the formation of an elite. A'mtel implicitly recognizes that this concentration is always an inherent danger that haunts any social system. Doing away with the hierarchies of power created by colonialism not only requires dismantling colonial systems, it requires the construction of new systems with specific mechanisms that prevent the formation of new hierarchies and inequalities and attempt to undo existing ones, such as women's oppression by men. One of the central lessons in the Zapatista practices of autonomous government is that the struggle against capitalism not only requires the creation of freedom from the capitalist class but also constant struggle against existing and potential forms of inequality, hierarchy, and oppression within the community in struggle. The Zapatista system of autonomous government has created numerous concrete practices that advance this internal struggle.

However, these mechanisms are far from perfect. The escuelita textbooks are full of self-criticism and honestly lay out their numerous mistakes and setbacks. In fact, this honesty is a central part of the principles of Zapatismo. The work of Zapatista autonomous government remains true to the heart of the Zapatista struggle by honestly taking responsibility for mistakes made. The Zapatista struggle does not aim for one goal that would constitute success; their struggle is the never-ending path of pask'op, of bringing the words of the collective heart of the communities into the world, a path composed of little besides mistakes. Every time the Zapatista authorities are honest about the mistakes they have made, we can see the strength of the Zapatista struggle. Because it is this honesty that shows the power of their commitment to truly obeying the democratic agreements of the communities. The Zapatistas did not form their autonomous government to construct a perfect world, but instead so that they would have the right to make their own mistakes, to make them together, and to celebrate when they find a solution.

This politics is a central aspect not only of the testimonies describing the work of autonomous government but also of the day-to-day tasks of that government. The word of the communities creates the cargos that make up the work of a'mtel. These cargos do not exist without their approval. The communities bestow them and can take them away, and the cargo itself can be altered at any time by a new agreement. The collective democratic practices of the communities determine the course of the Zapatista struggle. They are the ones that have the final say on whether something is working or not, and they are the ones who must ultimately come up with a solution. As Subcomandantes Moisés and Galeano write:

> How do we know if we are going in the right direction or not? Well for us Zapatistas it is very simple: the communities speak, the communities decide, the communities do, the communities undo. At the moment that someone takes the wrong path, the collective quickly gives them what we call a *zape* [a knock on the head], and either they correct it or they leave. This is our autonomy: it is our path. We will walk it, we will get it right, we will make our mistakes, and we will solve them.[2]

This is the core aspiration of autonomous government: a system where everyone is responsible for their successes as well as for their mistakes. This aspiration cannot be realized in a single set system but can only be created by the constant creation and re-creation of governing systems that respond to the desires and problems experienced by the communities. Autonomous government is a constant attempt to create governing structures in which the voices of the communities express themselves and come to agreement without being stifled by their government. It is the constant pursuit of a government that governs by obeying.

The pask'op of the Zapatista communities forces us to reflect on our own understandings of work, government, democracy, and political struggle. Zapatismo is an ethical orientation that defines what it means for a community to govern itself. If we distill the words and practices shared by the Zapatista communities through the escuelita, there are several core principles that might be relevant for those of us who struggle in other contexts. As I understand the lesson of the Zapatista communities, in a government that governs by obeying:

1. Everyone participates in all aspects of the decision-making process: an assembly of all the people creates the proposals, approves them, and reviews the resulting initiatives to make sure they are functioning as intended.

2. There is no set constitution, only agreements that are constantly being modified, such that the structure of government itself is up to constant democratic determination. Furthermore, each individual community defines its own governing structure so that there are almost always multiple local forms of government within the larger organization.

3. The responsibility of serving as a governing authority is an onerous obligation, rather than a source of economic or political power. Authorities are not paid and receive no special privileges.

4. The government and the people are one and the same. Those who govern do not garner their means of survival from governing and are not a separate class of specialists. Everyone is prepared to do the work of governing, and those who govern are like everyone else.

5. There are separate accountability structures made up of people from the communities for the sole purpose of making sure the authorities do not become corrupt and to assure the people that their government is honest and transparent.

6. There are no police. Administering justice is not a means of consolidating economic or political power, but rather an attempt to heal harm done to the community. Disputes or issues of justice are resolved according to the principles "to convince not defeat" and "to propose not impose."

7. Democracy extends to all spheres of life, including the economic. The means of production, such as land for cultivation, the form of production, such as the decision whether to grow corn or raise cattle, and the work of production itself are democratically controlled by those who do the work.

8. Democracy functions as a form of empowerment that breaks down long-standing hierarchies, among them the power of men over women. For example, the government recognizes the existing gender hierarchies in their community and seeks to break them down, not only by encouraging women's participation but

also by identifying and attacking the socioeconomic structures
that deny women the right to self-determination.
9. The people have the right to defend themselves and their autonomy by any means. The government does not have a monopoly
on the legitimate use of force and no organized armed forces has
power over the government.
10. No one believes that they are perfect and mistakes are reflected
upon publicly and in good faith.

These ten principles may sound hopelessly utopian, but that was the prov-
ocation of the escuelita: to invite us to imagine the possibility of another
world, to imagine how we might create forms of democratic self-government in our own contexts.

Notes

Dedication

1   Zapatista Autonomous Communities, *Resistencia autónoma*, August 2013, 44.

Foreword

1   In the German original of Marx's "A Contribution to the Critique of Hegel's Philosophy of Right: Introduction," the passage reads: "Die Religion ist der Seufzer der bedrängten Kreatur, das Gemüt einer *herzlosen* Welt, wie sie der *Geist geistloser* Zustände ist. Sie ist das Opium des Volkes." Emphasis added.

2   *Gemüt*, the word that is translated as "heart" also connotes "mind" or "soul," but here it clearly means "heart," in contrast to the "heartless" world. The word *Geist* means both "mind" or "spirit," and, in this case, connotes "spirit" in contrast to the "spiritless" conditions in that world.

3   Gustav Landauer, *Revolution and Other Writings*, ed. and trans. Gabriel Kuhn (Oakland: PM Press, 2010), 263.

4   Landauer, *Revolution and Other Writings*, 132. Landauer invokes these words of the Medieval Council of Florence, borrowing a citation from Peter Kropotkin, *Mutual Aid: A Factor in Evolution* (Boston: Porter Sargent Publishers, 1955), 106.

5   Gustav Landauer, *For Socialism* (St. Louis, MO: Telos Press, 1978), 102.

6   Joel Kovel, *History and Spirit: An Inquiry into the Philosophy of Liberation* (Boston: Beacon Press, 1991), 1.

7   Kovel, *History and Spirit*, 46.

8   Using these terms in a more objective and empirical sense than in Durkheim's classic Eurocentric version.

9   Dorothy Lee, *Freedom and Culture* (Upper Saddle River, NJ: Prentice-Hall, 1963), 131–40. This essay and the complementary one "Linguistic Reflection of Wintu Thought" are available online, accessed September 7, 2018, https://www.scribd.com/document/50059829/Freedom-and-culture.

10   Ibid., 134.

11   Pierre Clastres, *Society against the State* (New York: Urizen Books, 1977).

12   Dylan Fitzwater, personal correspondence. There is a large body of ecofeminist literature on the ethics and politics of care and the radical implications of recognizing the importance of caring labor, especially by women and indigenous people across the globe. See Ariel Salleh's analysis of "regenerative labor" in "From Eco-Sufficiency to Global Justice," in *Eco-Sufficiency & Global Justice: Women Write Political Ecology*, ed. Ariel Salleh (London: Pluto Press, 2009), 291–312, and her discussion of caring and "meta-industrial" labor in her groundbreaking work *Ecofeminism as Politics* (London: Zed Books, 2017), throughout the work, but especially Chapter 10.

13   See "ProArbol," *REDD Desk*, 2016, accessed September 7, 2018, https://theredddesk.org/countries/initiatives/proarbol.

Introduction

1   El Comité Clandestino Revolucionario Indígena and Subcomandante Insurgente Marcos, "Comunicado del Comité Clandestino Revolucionario Indígena–Comandancia General del Ejército Zapatista de Liberación Nacional del 21 de Diciembre del 2012," *Enlace Zapatista*, December 21, 2012, accessed September 7, 2018, http://enlacezapatista.ezln.org.mx/2012/12/21/comunicado-del-comite-clandestino-revolucionario-indigena-comandancia-general-del-ejercito-zapatista-de-liberacion-nacional-del-21-de-diciembre-d-el-2012/.

2   In the original Spanish the seventh principle of good government is "*Bajar y no subir.*" It could also be translated as "Lower yourself, don't raise yourself up."

3   Gloria Muñoz Ramírez, *The Fire and the Word: A History of the Zapatista Movement* (San Francisco: City Lights Books, 2008), 21.

4   John Womack, ed., *Rebellion in Chiapas: An Historical Reader* (New York: New Press, 1999), 195.

5   Muñoz Ramírez, *The Fire and the Word*, 47–277.

6   Hilary Klein, *Compañeras: Zapatista Women's Stories* (New York: Seven Stories Press, 2015), 84–87.

7   Subcomandante Insurgente Marcos, "Coloquio Aubry: Parte VII. (y última) sentir el rojo," *Enlace Zapatista*, December 17, 2007, accessed September 7, 2018, http://enlacezapatista.ezln.org.mx/2007/12/17/parte-vii-y-ultima-sentir-el-rojo-el-calendario-y-la-geografia-de-la-guerra/.

8   Subcomandante Insurgente Moisés, "Ellos y nosotros. VI.–las miradas. Parte 6: él somos," *Enlace Zapatista*, February 14, 2013, accessed September 7, 2018, http://enlacezapatista.ezln.org.mx/2013/02/14/ellos-y-nosotros-vi-las-miradas-parte-6-el-somos/.

9   Subcomandante Insurgente Moisés, "Cupo completo para el primer grado de la escuelita Zapatista en las vueltas de diciembre 2013 y enero 2014," *Enlace Zapatista*, November 26, 2013, accessed September 7, 2018, http://enlacezapatista.ezln.org.mx/2013/11/26/cupo-completo-para-el-primer-grado-de-la-escuelita-zapatista-en-las-vueltas-de-diciembre-2013-y-enero-2014/.

10   Promoter is the name given to all Zapatistas who work in health, education, and collective production, rather than "teacher," "doctor," or "specialist."

11   Carlos Lenkersdorf, *Los hombres verdaderos: voces y testimonios tojolabales: lengua y sociedad, naturaleza y cultura, artes y comunidad cósmica (Antropología)* (Mexico, DF: Siglo XXI, 1996), 24.

12   Subcomandante Insurgente Galeano, "El muro y la grieta: primer apunte sobre el método Zapatista: SupGaleano," *Enlace Zapatista*, May 3, 2015, accessed September 7, 2018, http://enlacezapatista.ezln.org.mx/2015/05/03/el-muro-y-la-grieta-primer-apunte-sobre-el-metodo-zapatista-supgaleano-3-de-mayo/.

Chapter 1

1   In May 2014, Subcomandante Marcos ceased to exist and was reborn as Subcomandante Galeano. Galeano is the name of a Zapatista from the community of La Realidad who was killed on May 2, 2014 in a paramilitary attack. This choice to symbolically "kill" Subcomandante Marcos also coincided with the announcement that Subcomandante Moisés would now be the sole official spokesperson for the EZLN. See Subcomandante Insurgente Galeano, "Entre la luz y la sombra," *Enlace Zapatista*, May 25, 2014, accessed September 7, 2018, http://enlacezapatista.ezln.org.mx/2014/05/25/entre-la-luz-y-la-sombra/.

2   Subcomandante Insurgente Galeano, "En el tablón de avisos: el conserje," *Enlace Zapatista*, March 4, 2015, accessed September 7, 2018, http://enlacezapatista.ezln.org.mx/2015/03/04/en-el-tablon-de-avisos-el-conserje/.

3   Moisés and Galeano wrote that the reason it would take place in the form of a video was to make sure that the escuelita would "not only be for those who don't have conflicts in their calendar or who have enough money to travel." They further announced that there will be a total of six grades and that they will be timed with other public initiatives to make sure that students don't have to come to Zapatista territory more than once a year. Subcomandante Insurgente Moisés and Subcomandante Insurgente Galeano, "Segundo nivel escuela Zapatista," *Enlace Zapatista*, July 27, 2015, accessed September 7, 2018, http://enlacezapatista.ezln.org.mx/2015/07/27/segundo-nivel-escuela-zapatista/.

4   There is no good English translation of "*responsable*." It literally means "person responsible for" and could be translated as "head." But this has too much of a connotation of unilateral decision-making power that would not be true to the meaning of "responsable" in a Zapatista context. The essence of this position in the Zapatista process of clandestine organization is a sense of responsibility for things such as security, recruiting new members, and organizing military training, education, health services, clandestine meetings, and the transport of food, equipment, and information. Since it is so awkward in English, I have left it untranslated as "responsable," which is close to the English word "responsible" and might still convey the centrality of the idea and practice of responsibility in this position.

5   Zapatista Autonomous Communities, "Video segundo nivel de la escuelita Zapatista," 2015, accessed September 7, 2018, http://enlacezapatista.ezln.org.mx/video-segundo-nivel/.

6   Ibid.

7   Ibid.

8   Ibid.

9   Ibid.

10   Adela Cedillo Cedillo, "El fuego y el silencio: historia de las Fuerzas de Liberación Nacional Mexicanas (1969–1974)" (Bachelor's thesis, Universidad Nacional Autónoma de México, 2008); Adela Cedillo Cedillo, "El suspiro del silencio: de la reconstrucción de las Fuerzas de Liberación Nacional a La fundación del Ejército Zapatista de Liberación Nacional (1974–1983)" (Master's thesis, Universidad Nacional Autónoma de México, 2010).

11   John Womack, ed., *Rebellion in Chiapas: An Historical Reader* (New York: New Press, 1999), 195.

12   Ibid.

13   The actual reality of the Cuban Revolution was much more complex than this simple formula. However, in the early period of the revolution this quickly became the image that the Cuban government set forward as its own political aspirations, which in turn was taken up by other groups throughout Latin America, including the founders of the FLN.

14   Womack, *Rebellion in Chiapas*, 252; Gloria Muñoz Ramírez, *The Fire and the Word: A History of the Zapatista Movement* (San Francisco: City Lights Books, 2008), 53; For a description of the passage of the Revolutionary Laws in the context of the Revolutionary Law of Women, see Subcomandante Insurgente Marcos, "Heroísmo cotidiano hace posible que existan los destellos," *Enlace Zapatista*, January 26, 1994, accessed September 7, 2018, http://enlacezapatista.ezln.org.mx/1994/01/26/heroismo-cotidiano-hace-posible-que-existan-los-destellos/.

15   Although there is one mention of a Law of Revolutionary Government in point eight of the "Instructions for Commanders and Officials of the EZLN." This law has never been published, presumably because it was never passed by the Zapatista communities. See Womack, *Rebellion in Chiapas*.

16   Ejército Zapatista de Liberación Nacional, "Ley de Derechos y Obligaciones de los Pueblos en Lucha," *Enlace Zapatista*, December 31, 1993, accessed September 7, 2018, http://enlacezapatista.ezln.org.mx/1993/12/31/ley-de-derechos-y-obligaciones-de-los-pueblos-en-lucha/. Emphasis added.

17   The law states: "The Law of War Taxes is obligatory for all those civilians who live from the exploitation of the labor power of others or who obtain some form of profit from the people in their activities." These taxes would consist of 7 percent of monthly income for small businesses and landlords and 10 percent of monthly income for professionals, as long as these taxes do not affect the means or materials for reproduction of these individuals. Medium landlords would be charged 15 percent of monthly income and large capitalists would be charged 20 percent. In both cases their property would be affected by the respective Revolutionary Law of Expropriation. Under the

Law of War Taxes, funds collected through taxation would not go to a national revolutionary government nor to the forces of the EZLN, but rather to the democratically elected authorities in each locale. As the Law of War Taxes makes clear, "All war taxes collected by the revolutionary armed forces or by the organized people will become collective property of the respective populations and will be administered according to the popular will of the democratically elected civil authorities, giving to the EZLN only what is necessary to aid the material necessities of the regular troops and to continue the liberation movement according to the Law of Rights and Obligations of The Peoples in Struggle." Ejército Zapatista de Liberación Nacional, "Ley de Impuestos de Guerra," *Enlace Zapatista*, December 31, 1993, accessed September 7, 2018, http://enlacezapatista.ezln.org.mx/1993/12/31/ley-de-impuestos-de-guerra/.

18   The law states, "Foreign companies will pay their workers an hourly wage in national currency equivalent to what they pay in dollars in their own countries." Ejército Zapatista de Liberación Nacional, "Ley del Trabajo," *Enlace Zapatista*, December 31, 1993, accessed September 7, 2018, http://enlacezapatista.ezln.org.mx/1993/12/31/ley-del-trabajo/.

19   Ejército Zapatista de Liberación Nacional, "Ley de Reforma Urbana," *Enlace Zapatista*, December 31, 1993, accessed September 7, 2018, http://enlacezapatista.ezln.org.mx/1993/12/31/ley-de-reforma-urbana/; Ejército Zapatista de Liberación Nacional, "Ley de Industria y Comercio," *Enlace Zapatista*, December 31, 1993, accessed September 7, 2018, http://enlacezapatista.ezln.org.mx/1993/12/31/ley-de-industria-y-comercio/; Ejército Zapatista de Liberación Nacional, "Ley del Trabajo," *Enlace Zapatista*, December 31, 1993, accessed September 7, 2018, http://enlacezapatista.ezln.org.mx/1993/12/31/ley-del-trabajo/; Ejército Zapatista de Liberación Nacional, "Ley de Seguridad Social," *Enlace Zapatista*, December 31, 1993, accessed September 7, 2018, http://enlacezapatista.ezln.org.mx/1993/12/31/ley-de-seguridad-social/. This law also states that the local civilian authorities have the obligation to care for orphans until they reach the age of thirteen.

20   Comité Clandestino Revolucionario Indígena, "Primera declaración de la Selva Lacandona," *Enlace Zapatista*, January 1, 1994, accessed September 7, 2018, http://enlacezapatista.ezln.org.mx/1994/01/01/primera-declaracion-de-la-selva-lacandona/.

21   Comité Clandestino Revolucionario Indígena, "Condiciones y agenda para el diálogo," *Enlace Zapatista*, January 20, 1994, accessed September 7, 2018, http://enlacezapatista.ezln.org.mx/1994/01/20/condiciones-y-agenda-para-el-dialogo/; Comité Clandestino Revolucionario Indígena, "Respuesta a Manuel Camacho," *Enlace Zapatista*, January 31, 1994, accessed September 7, 2018, http://enlacezapatista.ezln.org.mx/1994/01/31/respuesta-a-manuel-camacho/.

22   Ricardo Alemán, "Conferencia de prensa: Para que se dé una democracia, la mesa tiene que ser más grande: del país entero," *La Jornada*, February 22, 1994, accessed September 7, 2018, http://enlacezapatista.ezln.org.mx/1994/02/23/conferencia-de-prensa-para-que-se-de-una-democracia-la-mesa-tiene-que-ser-mas-grande-del-pais-entero/.

23 Subcomandante Insurgente Marcos, "Heroísmo cotidiano hace posible que existan los destellos."

24 See point four: "Women have the right to participate in the affairs of the community and to serve as local authorities if they are freely and democratically elected." Ejército Zapatista de Liberación Nacional, "Ley Revolucionaria de Mujeres," *Enlace Zapatista*, December 31, 1993, accessed September 7, 2018, http://enlacezapatista.ezln.org.mx/1993/12/31/ley-revolucionaria-de-mujeres/.

25 See point nine: "Women can hold positions of leadership in the organization and obtain military ranks in the revolutionary armed forces." Ibid.

26 See point one: "Women, regardless of race, creed, color, or political affiliation have the right to participate in the revolutionary struggle in the ways and to the degree that their desire and capacity determines." And point ten: "Women will have all the rights and obligations outlined in the revolutionary laws and regulations." Ibid.

27 Ibid.

28 Ejército Zapatista de Liberación Nacional, "Ley de Derechos y Obligaciones de los Pueblos en Lucha." Emphasis added.

29 Nicholas P. Higgins, *Understanding the Chiapas Rebellion: Modernist Visions and the Invisible Indian* (Austin: University of Texas Press, 2004), 162–63.

30 In jpojvanejetik the prefix j- denotes a social role or profession, poj is the root of the verb pojel to defend, the suffix -vanej modifies pojel to mean a person who defends, and the suffix -etik is a pluralizer. A more literal translation would be the social role (j-) of people who defend (poj-vanej-etik). The grammar of jmilvanejetik is the same with the exception of the root mil from the verb milel to kill that replaces poj.

Chapter 2

1 Comité Clandestino Revolucionario Indígena, "Al consejo 500 años de resistencia indígena: que nuestros corazones junten sus pasos," *Enlace Zapatista*, February 1, 1994, accessed September 7, 2018, http://enlacezapatista.ezln.org.mx/1994/02/01/al-consejo-500-anos-de-resistencia-indigena-que-nuestros-corazones-junten-sus-pasos/.

2 They may also be direct translations of similar expressions in the other Zapatista language groups Chol, Tojolobal, Mam, or even the non-Mayan language Zoque. However, I do not know these languages well enough to say for sure.

3 Xuno López Intzín, "Senti-pensar el género: perspectivas desde los pueblos originarios," Lecture, Smith College Lewis Global Studies Center, April 7, 2016.

4 Josías López K'ana et al., *Diccionario multilingue = svunal bats'i k'opetik* (Mexico, DF: Siglo XXI, 2005).

5 Pedro Pitarch Ramón, *The Jaguar and the Priest: An Ethnography of Tzeltal Souls* (Austin: University of Texas Press, 2010), 22.

6 Ibid., 202.

7 Manuel Delanda provides a succinct summary of Deleuze's understanding of the virtual: "Deleuzian ontology is flat: the world of actual assemblages

forming a *plane of reference*, that is, a world of individual singularities operating at different spatio-temporal scales, to which we can refer by giving them, for example, a proper name; and the world of virtual diagrams . . . forming a *plane of immanence*, a plane that does not exist above the other plane . . . but is like its reverse side. A single flat ontology with two sides, one side populated by virtual problems and the other by a divergent set of actual solutions to those problems." Manuel Delanda, *Deleuze: History and Science* (New York: Atropos, 2010), 104.

8   Xuno López Intzín, "La noción de Ch'ulel-Ch'ulelal y la urgencia de Re-Ch'ulel-Izarnos," in *Colección Snajtaleltik: Sna'el jkoleltik sok xnichimal ko'tantik* (Kolektivo Snajtaleltik, 2015).

9   "Ch-cha'y" is the third person intransitive conjugation of the verb "cha'yel," meaning to be mistaken, to ruin, or to spoil. The subject of this verb is "svoko-lik," which means their sadness (the prefix s- is the third person possessive for words beginning in a consonant and the suffix -ik is the third person possessive pluralizer, which in combination translate as "their" in English), ta is a particle that in this context means "in," and yo'onik means "their hearts" (this time with the third person possessive y- for words beginning with a vowel) and is the location where their sadness (svokolik) mistakes itself (ch-cha'y). In general, you always use the construction "cha'yel ta o'onil" (something mistaking itself in the heart) when in English we would use the verb "to forget."

10   While it is possible that here "o'on" is a form of mass noun in Tsotsil I have seen other examples where "o'on" is pluralized, for example, the phrase *"tol hk'ak'al-wonetik ta htoholtik"* (We are surrounded by envious people) in Robert M. Laughlin, *The Great Tzotzil Dictionary of San Lorenzo Zinacantán*, Contributions to Anthropology no. 19 (Washington, DC: Smithsonian Institution Press, 1975), implying that there is a meaningful distinction between referring to multiple hearts with the pluralizer -etik and referring to them without it.

11   Marion M. Cowan, "Expresiones formadas con -o'ton corazón," *SIL*, 1999, accessed September 7, 2018, http://www.sil.org/resources/archives/58622.

12   In "smuk'ul" the prefix s- is the third person possessive for words beginning in a consonant, muk' means greatness in size, and the suffix -ul is one of several that mark something that is in generalized but nonspecific relation, in this case to a general collective heart rather than a single heart. In "ko'ontik" the prefix k- is the first person possessive for words beginning in a vowel, o'on is heart and the suffix -tik is the first person inclusive pluralizer. Lastly, in Tsotsil the possessor follows the thing possessed, so the third person possessive in "smuk'ul" refers to the possession of greatness in size (muk') by the heart (o'on), while the prefix k- and the suffix -tik mark that this heart is possessed by a collective "us" that includes the speaker.

13   Explicitly stating that the heart is big can have a more specific connotation in Tsotsil, including happiness, contentedness, patience, and hope.

14   "Ichil" is the verb to bring oneself, and the suffix -ba- denotes an action that is reciprocal.

15   López K'ana et al., *Diccionario multilingue = svunal bats'i k'opetik.*

16   "Lek" means good, the suffix -il denotes something that is generalized or applicable to everyone, and kuxlejal means life.

17   Zapatista Autonomous Communities, "Video segundo nivel de La escuelita Zapatista," *Enlace Zapatista*, 2015, accessed September 7, 2018, http://enlacezapatista.ezln.org.mx/video-segundo-nivel/.

18   Ibid. Gender is ambiguous in the original Spanish.

19   Ibid.

20   Manuel is from the autonomous municipality of San Pedro de Michoacan, which is predominantly Tojolabal. However, it borders the autonomous municipality Tierra y Libertad to the south, which includes several predominantly Tsotsil communities situated along the frontier highway that parallels the Guatemalan border. See Jan de Vos, *Una tierra para sembrar sueños: historia teciente de la Selva Lacandona, 1950–2000* (Mexico: Fondo de Cultura Económica, 2002), 157–60.

21   Once again the suffix -ba- is used here to denote reciprocity, "ta" means in or into, and "venta" is an importation of the Spanish word *cuenta* meaning account in the sense of "taking into account."

22   Hilary Klein, *Compañeras: Zapatista Women's Stories* (New York: Seven Stories Press, 2015), 141.

23   Ibid., 144.

24   Subcomandante Insurgente Galeano, "Sherlock Holmes, Euclides, los errores de dedo y las ciencias sociales," in *El pensamiento crítico frente a La hidra capitalista* (Mexico: Ediciones México, 2015), 263.

25   Klein, *Compañeras*.

26   Ibid., 146.

27   Ibid., 61. These contemporary forms of collective work are discussed in depth in Chapter Five.

28   Ibid., 44.

29   Zapatista Autonomous Communities, "Video segundo nivel de La escuelita Zapatista."

30   Isaac Sánchez, "En estos tiempos de escuelita," in *La escuelita Zapatista* (Guadalajara, MX: Grietas Editores, 2014), 84.

31   Zapatista Autonomous Communities, "Video segundo nivel de la escuelita Zapatista."

32   It is somewhat difficult to translate "k'in" into English. In English the primary connotation of "party" is having fun, and while this is a big part of the Tsotsil understanding of "k'in," there is an added element in which the party is an offering to the territory of the community, the earth, and to the whole world. In Tsotsil they say *sk'in osil balumil*, which means party or festival for the territory/earth/world. Another way to translate "k'in" would be "festival," but I am wary of this word being overly tied to religion and ideas of tradition or ritual at the expense of emphasizing the importance of having fun. In English, "k'in" is best translated through a combination of "party" and "festival," a combination that is much closer to the connotations of the Mexican word "fiesta."

33 Subcomandante Insurgente Marcos, "Votán II: L@s Guardian@s," *Enlace Zapatista*, July 30, 2013, accessed September 7, 2018, http://enlacezapatista. ezln.org.mx/2013/07/30/votan-ii-ls-guardians/.

34 Comité Clandestino Revolucionario Indígena, "Primera declaración de la Selva Lacandona," *Enlace Zapatista*, January 1, 1994, accessed September 7, 2018, http://enlacezapatista.ezln.org.mx/1994/01/01/ primera-declaracion-de-la-selva-lacandona/.

35 Klein, *Compañeras*, 84–87.

36 Comité Clandestino Revolucionario Indígena, "Creación de Municipios Autónomos," *Enlace Zapatista*, December 19, 1994, accessed September 7, 2018, http://enlacezapatista.ezln.org.mx/1994/12/19/creacion-de-municipios-autonomos/.

37 Hermann Bellinghausen, "Comandante Tacho: creación de Municipio Zapatista," *Enlace Zapatista*, December 19, 1994, accessed September 7, 2018, http://enlacezapatista.ezln.org.mx/1994/12/19/comandante-tacho-creacion-de-municipio-zapatista/.

Chapter 3

1 "Others" is a translation of "l@s otr@s," a Zapatista term meaning others in a gender-inclusive sense, but which also refers to queer and trans* people, or otherness or queerness in a more general sense.

2 Subcomandante Insurgente Marcos, "Votán II: L@s Guardian@s," *Enlace Zapatista*, July 30, 2013, accessed September 7, 2018, http://enlacezapatista. ezln.org.mx/2013/07/30/votan-ii-ls-guardians/.

3 Zapatista Autonomous Communities, *Resistencia autónoma*, August 2013, 72.

4 These suffixes are -al, -il and -ol depending on the noun. For example, "ch'ulelal" means a potentiality of the heart that is abstract or without a specific relation, and "o'onil" means a heart that is abstract or without a specific relation.

5 Promotores de la Escuela Secundaria Rebelde Zapatista "Primero de Enero," *Nuestra lengua, nuestra memoria: ideas para clases de Tsotsil* (Edición ESRAZ, 2001).

6 Subcomandante Insurgente Marcos, "Chiapas: la treceava estela: Quinta parte: una historia," *Enlace Zapatista*, July 21, 2003, accessed September 7, 2018, http://enlacezapatista.ezln.org.mx/2003/07/21/chiapas-la-treceava-estela-quinta-parte-una-historia/.

7 Ibid.

8 These are three areas of traditional Mayan medicine that constitute a special initiative of the Zapatista health system throughout all five Caracoles. Women are specifically targeted for training as health promoters in these three areas.

9 There is no good translation of the Zapatista idea of trabajos collectivos in English. The meaning of trabajo in this context is a combination of the English verb "to work" and the noun "works" and includes connotations similar to those of "project" or "initiative." All of these words could provide adequate translations in different contexts. However, this would create a false separation, and ultimately a bad translation, since the unification of all these connotations in the Zapatista trabajos collectivos is essential to the meaning of

the phrase. This phrase encompasses various forms of work and projects in the communities as well as the processes of collective decision-making that go along with them as a cohesive activity. This cohesion would be lost if I were to translate "trabajos colectivos" using multiple English words. I have chosen to leave it untranslated, also leaving trabajo untranslated when it clearly refers to the work of the trabajos colectivos.

10 Zapatista Autonomous Communities, *Gobierno autónomo I*, August 2013, 6.

11 Subcomandante Insurgente Marcos, "Chiapas: la treceava estela: Quinta parte."

12 Subcomandante Insurgente Marcos, "Chiapas: la treceava estela: Segunda parte: una muerte," *Enlace Zapatista*, July 21, 2003, accessed September 7, 2018, http://enlacezapatista.ezln.org.mx/2003/07/21/chiapas-la-treceava-estela-segunda-parte-una-muerte/.

13 Ibid.

14 Ibid.

15 Subcomandante Insurgente Marcos, "Chiapas: la treceava estela: Quinta parte."

16 Zapatista Autonomous Communities, *Gobierno autónomo I*, 58–59.

17 Subcomandante Insurgente Marcos, "Chiapas: la treceava estela: Quinta parte."

18 "Consejo" can best be translated as "council" in English. However, I have chosen to leave it untranslated, because "*junta*" can also only be translated as "council." There are two distinct words in Spanish, while there is only one in English. Thus, in order to avoid confusion where testimonies make reference both to consejos and juntas, with the former clearly referencing the autonomous authorities at the municipal level and the latter the autonomous authorities in the Good Government Council, I have chosen to maintain this distinction by leaving consejo untranslated. In my descriptions of Zapatista autonomous authorities "council" always refers to the Good Government Council, while "consejo" always refers to the autonomous municipal authorities.

19 Zapatista Autonomous Communities, *Gobierno autónomo I*, 59.

20 Ibid., 8.

21 Zapatista Autonomous Communities, *Gobierno autónomo I*, 44.

22 Ibid.

23 Ibid., 22.

Chapter 4

1 In a broad sense cargo means "role of responsibility in the community." The system of community cargos defines the concrete practice of direct communitarian democracy that existed long before the birth of the EZLN in the Mayan indigenous communities of Chiapas. In essence, it consists of the following: the community gives a certain person a set of responsibilities, sometimes regardless of whether this person volunteers for them or even particularly wants them, and then they must work to carry them out to the best of their abilities. For example, they might have the cargo of fulfilling a certain role

in one of the community festivals and would be required to provide food and perform part of the rituals in the festival. Or, in the case of a Zapatista community, a person might have the cargo of being an education promoter and be responsible for teaching classes at the autonomous school in their community.

2   Subcomandante Insurgente Moisés, "Resistencia y rebeldía III," *Enlace Zapatista*, May 8, 2015, accessed September 7, 2018, http://enlacezapatista. ezln.org.mx/2015/05/08/resistencia-y-rebeldia-iii-subcomandante-insurgente-moises-8-de-mayo/.

3   Ibid.

4   López K'ana et al., *Diccionario multilingue = svunal bats'i k'opetik* (Mexico, DF: Siglo XXI, 2005), 545.

5   Zapatista Autonomous Communities, *Gobierno autónomo I*, August 2013, 15.

6   Sandoval does not say which Caracol these teachers are from or what experience they have in the autonomous government. However, at least one of them, Doroteo, whose testimonies are included in the escuelita textbooks, is a former member of the Good Government Council of Caracol I La Realidad.

7   Rafael Sandoval, "Escuchar, pensar y comprender las prácticas de la autonomía Zapatista exige colocarse desde la perspectiva del sujeto Zapatista," in *La escuelita Zapatista* (Guadalajara, MX: Grietas Editores, 2014), 49.

8   Zapatista Autonomous Communities, *Gobierno autónomo I*, 52.

9   Ibid., 63–64.

10 Ibid., 77–78.

11 Ibid., 38.

12 Oventik education promoter, personal conversation, July 2018.

13 Zapatista Autonomous Communities, *Resistencia autónoma*, August 2013, 18–21.

14 Ibid., 16–17.

15 Zapatista Autonomous Communities, *Gobierno autónomo II*, August 2013, 4–5.

16 Zapatista Autonomous Communities, *Gobierno autónomo I*, 19.

17 Zapatista Autonomous Communities, *Gobierno autónomo II*, 11–13.

18 Zapatista Autonomous Communities, *Gobierno Autónomo I*, 19.

19 Zapatista Autonomous Communities, *Gobierno autónomo II*, 10–11.

20 Ibid., 11.

21 Ibid., 12.

22 Ibid., 13.

23 Ibid., 35.

24 Ibid., 44.

25 Zapatista Autonomous Communities, *Gobierno autónomo I*, 22.

26 Ibid., 59–60.

27 Rafael Sandoval says that his teachers in the escuelita listed the major problems addressed by the Good Government Council as "murder, land invasions, theft of coffee, cattle rustling, rape, and migrant trafficking," while minor problems addressed by the municipal councils are "intrafamilial violence, theft of animals, alcoholism, and infidelity." Sandoval, "Escuchar, pensar y comprender las prácticas de la autonomía Zapatista," 44–45.

28 Zapatista Autonomous Communities, *Gobierno autónomo II*, 6–7.
29 Sandoval, "Escuchar, pensar y comprender las prácticas de la autonomía Zapatista," 45.
30 Ibid., 46.
31 Zapatista Autonomous Communities, *Gobierno autónomo II*, 6–7.

Chapter 5
1   Zapatista Autonomous Communities, *Gobierno autónomo II*, August 2013, 13.
2   "Finca" refers to a large agricultural estate. In the Chiapan context, it often connotes the full system of labor exploitation and social domination carried out on these estates.
3   Ejidos are collectively held land, which in the context of Chiapas usually means land collectively held by indigenous subsistence farmers.
4   Andrés Aubry, *Chiapas a contrapelo* (Chiapas: Centro de estudios información y documentación Immanuel Wallerstein, 2005), 161–63.
5   Hilary Klein, *Compañeras: Zapatista Women's Stories* (New York: Seven Stories Press, 2015), 7.
6   Ibid., 12.
7   Aubry, *Chiapas a contrapelo*.
8   Mercedes Olivera Bustamente, "Acteal: Effects of the Low Intensity War," in *The Other Word: Women and Violence in Chiapas before and after Acteal*, ed. Rosalva Aída Hernández Castillo (Copenhagen: International Work Group for Indigenous Affairs, 2001).
9   Rosalva Aída Hernández Castillo and Anna Maria Garza Caligaris, "Encounters and Conflicts of the Tzotzil People with the Mexican State: A Historical-Anthropological Perspective for Understanding Violence in San Pedro Chenalhó, Chiapas," in Hernández Castillo, *The Other Word*.
10 Subcomandante Insurgente Moisés and Subcomandante Insurgente Galeano, "Y mientras tanto en . . . las comunidades partidistas," *Enlace Zapatista*, February 21, 2016, accessed September 7, 2018, http://enlacezapatista.ezln.org.mx/2016/02/21/y-mientras-tanto-en-las-comunidades-partidistas/.
11 Ibid.
12 REDD desk, "ProArbol," 2016, accessed September 7, 2018, http://theredddesk.org/countries/initiatives/proarbol.
13 Subcomandante Insurgente Moisés and Subcomandante Insurgente Galeano, "Y mientras tanto en."
14 Klein, *Compañeras*, 91.
15 Subcomandante Insurgente Moisés and Subcomandante Insurgente Galeano, "Y mientras tanto en."
16 Niels Barmeyer, *Developing Zapatista Autonomy: Conflict and NGO Involvement in Rebel Chiapas* (Albuquerque: University of New Mexico Press, 2009), 207–9.
17 Zapatista Autonomous Communities, *Gobierno autónomo I*, August 2013, 64.
18 Zapatista Autonomous Communities, *Gobierno autónomo II*, 43.
19 Zapatista Autonomous Communities, *Gobierno autónomo I*, 67.
20 Ibid., 68.

21   Barmeyer, *Developing Zapatista Autonomy*, 226–27.

22   Zapatista Autonomous Communities, *Resistencia autónoma*, August 2013, 11.

23   Ibid., 11.

24   Ibid., 8–9.

25   Ibid., 9.

26   Comité Clandestino Revolucionario Indígena and Subcomandante Insurgente
     Marcos, "El retiro militar de la comunidad de Amador Hernández es una
     buena señal," *Enlace Zapatista*, December 22, 2001, accessed September 7,
     2018, http://enlacezapatista.ezln.org.mx/2000/12/22/el-retiro-militar-de-la-
     comunidad-de-amador-hernandez-es-una-buena-senal/.

27   Zapatista Autonomous Communities, *Resistencia autónoma*, 11.

28   Karl Marx, *Capital: A Critique of Political Economy*, vol. 1, trans. Ben Fowkes,
     (New York: Penguin Books, 1981), 125; John Holloway, "La primera frase de
     el capital comienza con la riqueza, no con la mercancía," in *Contra el dinero*,
     (Buenos Aires, AR: Ediciones Herramienta, 2015).

29   Ibid., 7–8.

30   Zapatista Autonomous Communities, *Gobierno autónomo II*, 9.

31   Zapatista Autonomous Communities, *Resistencia autónoma*, 12.

32   Zapatista Autonomous Communities, *Gobierno autónomo II*, 48.

33   Zapatista Autonomous Communities, *Gobierno autónomo I*, 79.

34   Ibid., 79.

35   Zapatista Autonomous Communities, *Gobierno autónomo II*, 48.

36   Zapatista Autonomous Communities, *Resistencia autónoma*, 82.

37   Zapatista Autonomous Communities, *Gobierno autónomo I*, 78; Zapatista
     Autonomous Communities, *Resistencia autónoma*, 81.

38   Zapatista Autonomous Communities, *Gobierno autónomo II*, 46.

39   Zapatista Autonomous Communities, *Resistencia autónoma*, 84.

40   Zapatista Autonomous Communities, *Gobierno autónomo II*, 36–38.

41   Zapatista Autonomous Communities, *Resistencia autónoma*, 48; Zapatista
     Autonomous Communities, *Gobierno autónomo II*, 36–37.

42   Zapatista Autonomous Communities, *Resistencia autónoma*, 54–60.

43   Ibid., 57.

44   Zapatista Autonomous Communities, *Gobierno autónomo II*, 43.

45   Ibid., 21–22.

46   Zapatista Autonomous Communities, *Gobierno autónomo I*, 40.

47   Ibid., 37–38.

48   Ibid., 26.

49   Zapatista Autonomous Communities, *Resistencia autónoma*, 33.

50   Subcomandante Insurgente Moisés, "Resistencia y rebeldía I," *Enlace
     Zapatista*, May 6, 2015, accessed September 7, 2018, http://enlacezapatista.
     ezln.org.mx/2015/05/06/resistencia-y-rebeldia-i-subcomandante-
     insurgente-moises-6-de-mayo/.

51   Jan Rus, Rosalva Aída Hernández Castillo, and Shannan L. Mattiace, introduc-
     tion to *Mayan Lives, Mayan Utopias: The Indigenous Peoples of Chiapas and the
     Zapatista Rebellion*, Latin American Perspectives in the Classroom (Lanham,
     MD: Rowman & Littlefield, 2003); Aubry, *Chiapas a contrapelo*, 159–64.

52 Klein, *Compañeras*, 85.

53 Zapatista Autonomous Communities, *Resistencia autónoma*, 29.

54 Subcomandante Insurgente Moisés, "Resistencia y rebeldía I"; Zapatista Autonomous Communities, *Gobierno autónomo II*, 8.

55 Subcomandante Insurgente Moisés and Subcomandante Insurgente Galeano, "¿Y en las comunidades Zapatistas?" *Enlace Zapatista*, February 23, 2015, accessed September 7, 2018, http://enlacezapatista.ezln.org.mx/2016/02/23/y-en-las-comunidades-zapatistas/.

56 Subcomandante Insurgente Moisés, "Resistencia y rebeldía I."

57 Subcomandante Insurgente Moisés, "Economía política desde las comunidades I," *Enlace Zapatista*, May 4, 2015, accessed September 7, 2018, http://enlacezapatista.ezln.org.mx/2015/05/04/economia-politica-desde-las-comunidades-i-subcomandante-insurgente-moises-4-de-mayo/.

Chapter 6

1 Zapatista Autonomous Communities, *Resistencia autónoma*, August 2013, 61.

2 Zapatista Autonomous Communities, *Gobierno autónomo I*, August 2013, 11, 27, 43, 73.

3 Zapatista Autonomous Communities, *Resistencia autónoma*, 63.

4 Zapatista Autonomous Communities, *Gobierno autónomo I*, 65.

5 Ibid., 31.

6 Ibid., 11.

7 Subcomandante Insurgente Moisés, "Resistencia y rebeldía III," *Enlace Zapatista*, May 8, 2015, accessed September 7, 2018, http://enlacezapatista.ezln.org.mx/2015/05/08/resistencia-y-rebeldia-iii-subcomandante-insurgente-moises-8-de-mayo/.

8 Zapatista Autonomous Communities, *Gobierno autónomo I*, 17–18.

9 Rafael Sandoval, "Escuchar, pensar y comprender las prácticas de la autonomía Zapatista exige colocarse desde la perspectiva del sujeto Zapatista," in *La escuelita Zapatista* (Guadalajara, MX: Grietas Editores, 2014), 25.

10 Zapatista Autonomous Communities, *Gobierno autónomo I*, 9–10.

11 Ibid., 25.

12 Ibid., 14.

13 Ibid., 10.

14 Ibid., 43.

15 Raúl Zibechi, *Dispersing Power: Social Movements as Anti-State Forces*, trans. Ramor Ryan (Oakland: AK Press, 2010), 16.

16 Zapatista Autonomous Communities, *Gobierno autónomo I*, 65–66.

17 Zapatista Autonomous Communities, *Resistencia autónoma*, 61.

18 Zapatista Autonomous Communities, *Gobierno autónomo I*, 24–25.

19 Ibid., 48–49.

20 Ibid., 71.

21 There is no good English translation of "comisión de vigilancia" in this context. The best literal translation would be "commission of watching over." However, this sounds very awkward so I have decided to leave it untranslated.

22   Zapatista Autonomous Communities, *Gobierno autónomo I*, 54. There is no description of what "training" the nucleus of resistance receives from the CCRI beyond education in math and accounting. However, I think we could speculate that it includes training them for the work of political-military leadership carried out by the CCRI.

23   Ibid., 39.

24   Ibid., 80–81.

25   Ibid., 53–54.

26   Ibid., 20.

27   Ibid., 68.

28   Zapatista Autonomous Communities, *Resistencia autónoma*, 61.

29   Ibid., 62.

30   Melissa Forbis, "Hacía la Autonomía: Zapatista Women Developing a New World," in *Women in Chiapas: Making History in Times of Struggle and Hope*, ed. Christine Engla Eber and Christine Marie Kovic (New York: Routledge, 2003), 243.

31   Zapatista Autonomous Communities, *Resistencia autónoma*, 59.

32   Zapatista Autonomous Communities, *Participación de las mujeres en el gobierno autónomo*, August 2013, 53.

33   Zapatista Autonomous Communities, *Gobierno autónomo I*, 64–65, 67.

34   Zapatista Autonomous Communities, *Participación de las mujeres en el gobierno autónomo*, 50.

35   Zapatista Autonomous Communities, *Gobierno autónomo I*, 14.

36   Zapatista Autonomous Communities, *Participación de las mujeres en el gobierno autónomo*, 8.

37   Zapatista Autonomous Communities, *Gobierno autónomo I*, 24.

38   Zapatista Autonomous Communities, *Participación de las mujeres en el gobierno autónomo*, 20–21.

39   Zapatista Autonomous Communities, *Gobierno autónomo I*, 72.

40   Ibid., 77.

41   Ibid., 45–46.

42   Ibid., 54–55.

43   Zapatista Autonomous Communities, *Participación de las mujeres en el gobierno autónomo*.

44   Ibid., 69.

45   Klein, *Compañeras*, 94–95.

46   Ibid., 97.

47   Zapatista Autonomous Communities, *Participación de las mujeres en el gobierno autónomo*, 29–30.

48   Ibid., 31.

49   Forbis, "Hacía la Autonomía," 245.

50   Zapatista Autonomous Communities, *Participación de las mujeres en el gobierno autónomo*, 74.

51   Forbis, "Hacía la Autonomía," 248.

52   Zapatista Autonomous Communities, *Participación de las mujeres en el gobierno autónomo*, 57.

53   Ibid., 62.
54   Ibid., 60.
55   Ibid., 60.
56   Klein, *Compañeras*, 158–61.

Epilogue

1   Subcomandante Insurgente Marcos, "Votán II: L@s Guardian@s," *Enlace Zapatista*, July 30, 2013, accessed September 7, 2018, http://enlacezapatista. ezln.org.mx/2013/07/30/votan-ii-ls-guardians/.
2   Subcomandante Insurgente Moisés and Subcomandante Insurgente Galeano, "¿Y en las comunidades Zapatistas?" *Enlace Zapatista*, February 23, 2015, accessed September 7, 2018, http://enlacezapatista.ezln.org. mx/2016/02/23/y-en-las-comunidades-zapatistas/.

Bibliography

Alemán, Ricardo. "Conferencia de prensa: Para que se dé una democracia, la mesa tiene que ser más grande: del país entero." *La Jornada*, February 22, 1994. Accessed September 7, 2018. http://enlacezapatista.ezln.org.mx/1994/02/23/conferencia-de-prensa-para-que-se-de-una-democracia-la-mesa-tiene-que-ser-mas-grande-del-pais-entero/.

Aubry, Andrés. *Chiapas a contrapelo*. Chiapas: Centro de estudios información y documentación Immanuel Wallerstein, 2005.

Barmeyer, Niels. *Developing Zapatista Autonomy: Conflict and NGO Involvement in Rebel Chiapas*. Albuquerque: University of New Mexico Press, 2009.

Bellinghausen, Hermann. "Comandante Tacho: creación de municipio Zapatista." *Enlace Zapatista*, December 19, 1994. Accessed September 7, 2018. http://enlacezapatista.ezln.org.mx/1994/12/19/comandante-tacho-creacion-de-municipio-zapatista/.

Cedillo, Adela Cedillo. "El fuego y el silencio: historia de las Fuerzas de Liberación Nacional Mexicanas (1969–1974)." Bachelor's thesis, Universidad Nacional Autónoma de México, 2008.

———. "El Suspiro del silencio: de la reconstrucción de Las Fuerzas de Liberación Nacional a la fundación del Ejército Zapatista de Liberación Nacional (1974–1983)." Master's thesis, Universidad Nacional Autónoma de México, 2010.

Clastres, Pierre. *Society against the State*. New York: Urizen Books, 1977.

Comité Clandestino Revolucionario indígena. "Al consejo 500 años de resistencia indígena: que nuestros corazones junten sus pasos." *Enlace Zapatista*, February 1, 1994. Accessed September 7, 2018. http://enlacezapatista.ezln.org.mx/1994/02/01/al-consejo-500-anos-de-resistencia-indigena-que-nuestros-corazones-junten-sus-pasos/.

———. "Condiciones y agenda para el diálogo." *Enlace Zapatista*, January 20, 1994. Accessed September 7, 2018. http://enlacezapatista.ezln.org.mx/1994/01/20/condiciones-y-agenda-para-el-dialogo/.

———. "Creación de Municipios Autónomos." *Enlace Zapatista*, December 19, 1994. Accessed September 7, 2018. http://enlacezapatista.ezln.org.mx/1994/12/19/creacion-de-municipios-autonomos/.

———. "Primera declaración de la Selva Lacandona." *Enlace Zapatista*, January 1, 1994. Accessed September 7, 2018. http://enlacezapatista.ezln.org.mx/1994/01/01/primera-declaracion-de-la-selva-lacandona/.

———. "Respuesta a Manuel Camacho." *Enlace Zapatista*, January 31, 1994. Accessed September 7, 2018. http://enlacezapatista.ezln.org.mx/1994/01/31/respuesta-a-manuel-camacho/.

Comité Clandestino Revolucionario Indígena and Subcomandante Insurgente Marcos. "Comunicado del Comité Clandestino Revolucionario Indígena-Comandancia General del Ejército Zapatista de Liberación Nacional del 21 de Diciembre del 2012." *Enlace Zapatista*, December 21, 2012. Accessed September 7, 2018. http://enlacezapatista.ezln.org.mx/2012/12/21/comunicado-del-comite-clandestino-revolucionario-indigena-comandancia-general-del-ejercito-zapatista-de-liberacion-nacional-del-21-de-diciembre-del-2012/.

———. "El retiro militar de la comunidad de Amador Hernández es una buena señal." *Enlace Zapatista*, December 22, 2001. Accessed September 7, 2018. http://enlacezapatista.ezln.org.mx/2000/12/22/el-retiro-militar-de-la-comunidad-de-amador-hernandez-es-una-buena-senal/.

Congreso Nacional Indígena and Ejército Zapatista de Liberación Nacional. "Declaración del V Congreso Nacional Indígena." *Enlace Zapatista*, January 1, 2017. Accessed September 7, 2018. http://enlacezapatista.ezln.org.mx/2017/01/01/y-retemblo-informe-desde-el-epicentro/.

Cowan, Marion M. "Expresiones formadas con-o'ton corazón." *SIL*, 1999. Accessed September 7, 2018. http://www.sil.org/resources/archives/58622.

de Vos, Jan. *Una tierra para sembrar sueños: historia reciente de la Selva Lacandona.* Mexico: Fondo de Cultura Económica, 2002.

Delanda, Manuel. *Deleuze: History and Science.* New York: Atropos Press, 2010.

Ejército Zapatista de Liberación Nacional. "Ley Agraria Revolucionaria." *Enlace Zapatista*, December 31, 1993. Accessed September 7, 2018. http://enlacezapatista.ezln.org.mx/1993/12/31/ley-agraria-revolucionaria/.

———. "Ley de Derechos y Obligaciones de las Fuerzas Armadas Revolucionarias." *Enlace Zapatista*, December 31, 1993. Accessed September 7, 2018. http://enlacezapatista.ezln.org.mx/1993/12/31/ley-de-derechos-y-obligaciones-de-las-fuerzas-armadas-revolucionarias/.

———. "Ley de Derechos y Obligaciones de los Pueblos en Lucha." *Enlace Zapatista*, December 31, 1993. Accessed September 7, 2018. http://enlacezapatista.ezln.org.mx/1993/12/31/ley-de-derechos-y-obligaciones-de-los-pueblos-en-lucha/.

———. "Ley de Impuestos de Guerra." *Enlace Zapatista*, December 31, 1993. Accessed September 7, 2018. http://enlacezapatista.ezln.org.mx/1993/12/31/ley-de-impuestos-de-guerra/.

———. "Ley de Industria y Comercio." *Enlace Zapatista*, December 31, 1993. Accessed September 7, 2018. http://enlacezapatista.ezln.org.mx/1993/12/31/ley-de-industria-y-comercio/.

———. "Ley de Justicia." *Enlace Zapatista*, December 31, 1993. Accessed September 7, 2018. http://enlacezapatista.ezln.org.mx/1993/12/31/ley-de-justicia/.

———. "Ley de Reforma Urbana." *Enlace Zapatista*, December 31, 1993. Accessed September 7, 2018. http://enlacezapatista.ezln.org.mx/1993/12/31/ley-de-reforma-urbana/.

———. "Ley Revolucionaria de Mujeres." *Enlace Zapatista*, December 31, 1993. Accessed September 7, 2018. http://enlacezapatista.ezln.org.mx/1993/12/31/ley-revolucionaria-de-mujeres/.

———. "Ley de Seguridad Social." *Enlace Zapatista*, December 31, 1993. Accessed September 7, 2018. http://enlacezapatista.ezln.org.mx/1993/12/31/ley-de-seguridad-social/.

———. "Ley del Trabajo." *Enlace Zapatista*, December 31, 1993. Accessed September 7, 2018. http://enlacezapatista.ezln.org.mx/1993/12/31/ley-del-trabajo/.

Forbis, Melissa. "Hacía la Autonomía: Zapatista Women Developing a New World." In *Women in Chiapas: Making History in Times of Struggle and Hope*. Edited by Christine Engla Eber and Christine Marie Kovic. New York: Routledge, 2003.

Hernández Castillo, Rosalva Aída, and Anna Maria Garza Caligaris. "Encounters and Conflicts of the Tzotzil People with the Mexican State: A Historical-Anthropological Perspective for Understanding Violence in San Pedro Chenalhó, Chiapas." In *The Other Word: Women and Violence in Chiapas before and after Acteal*. Edited by Rosalva Aída Hernández Castillo. Copenhagen: International Work Group for Indigenous Affairs, 2001.

Higgins, Nicholas P. *Understanding the Chiapas Rebellion: Modernist Visions and the Invisible Indian*. Austin: University of Texas Press, 2004.

Holloway, John. "La primera frase de el capital comienza con la riqueza, no con la mercancía." In *Contra el dinero*. Buenos Aires, AR: Ediciones Herramienta, 2015.

Klein, Hilary. *Compañeras: Zapatista Women's Stories*. New York: Seven Stories Press, 2015.

Kovel, Joel. *History and Spirit: An Inquiry into the Philosophy of Liberation*. Boston: Beacon Press, 1991.

Kropotkin, Peter. *Mutual Aid: A Factor in Evolution*. Boston: Porter Sargent Publishers, 1955.

Landauer, Gustav. *For Socialism*. St. Louis, MO: Telos Press, 1978.

Landauer, Gustav. *Revolution and Other Writings*. Edited and translated by Gabriel Kuhn. Oakland: PM Press, 2010.

Laughlin, Robert M. *The Great Tzotzil Dictionary of San Lorenzo Zinacantan*. Smithsonian Contributions to Anthropology no. 19. Washington, DC: Smithsonian Institution Press, 1975.

Lee, Dorothy. *Freedom and Culture*. Upper Saddle River, NJ: Prentice-Hall, 1963.

Lenkersdorf, Carlos. *Los hombres verdaderos: voces y testimonios tojolabales: lengua y sociedad, naturaleza y cultura, artes y comunidad cósmica (Antropología)*. Mexico, DF: Siglo XXI, 1996.

López Intzín, Xuno. "La noción de Ch'ulel-Ch'ulelal y la urgencia de Re-Ch'ulel-Izarnos." In *Sna'el jkoleltik sok xnichimal ko'tantik*. Kolektivo Snajtaleltik, 2015.

———. "Senti-pensar el género: perspectivas desde los pueblos originarios." Lecture, Smith College Lewis Global Studies Center, April 7, 2016.

López K'ana, Josías, Miguel Sántiz Méndez, Bernabe Montejo López, Pablo Gómez Jiménez, and Pablo González Casanova. *Diccionario multilingue = svunal bats'i k'opetik.* Mexico, DF: Siglo XXI, 2005.

Marx, Karl. *Capital: A Critique of Political Economy.* Vol. 1. Translated by Ben Fowkes. London: Penguin Books, 1981.

Muñoz Ramírez, Gloria. *The Fire and the Word: A History of the Zapatista Movement.* San Francisco: City Lights Books, 2008.

Olivera Bustamente, Mercedes. "Acteal: Effects of the Low Intensity War." In *The Other Word: Women and Violence in Chiapas before and after Acteal.* Edited by Rosalva Aída Hernández Castillo. Copenhagen: International Work Group for Indigenous Affairs, 2001.

Pitarch Ramón, Pedro. *The Jaguar and the Priest: An Ethnography of Tzeltal Souls.* Austin: University of Texas Press, 2010.

"ProArbol." *REDD Desk,* 2016. Accessed September 7, 2018. http://theredddesk.org/countries/initiatives/proarbol.

Promotores de la Escuela Secundaria Rebelde Zapatista "Primero de enero." *Nuestra lengua, nuestra memoria: ideas para clases de Tsotsil.* Edición ESRAZ, 2001.

Rus, Jan, Rosalva Aída Hernández Castillo, and Shannan L. Mattiace. Introduction to *Mayan Lives, Mayan Utopias: The Indigenous Peoples of Chiapas and the Zapatista Rebellion.* Latin American Perspectives in the Classroom. Lanham, MD: Rowman & Littlefield, 2003.

Salleh, Ariel. *Ecofeminism as Politics.* London: Zed Books, 2017.

———. "From Eco-Sufficiency to Global Justice." In *Eco-Sufficiency & Global Justice: Women Write Political Ecology.* Edited by Ariel Salleh. London: Pluto Press, 2009.

Sánchez, Isaac. "En estos tiempos de escuelita." In *La escuelita Zapatista.* Guadalajara, MX: Grietas Editores, 2014.

Sandoval, Rafael. "Escuchar, pensar y comprender las prácticas de la autonomía Zapatista exige colocarse desde la Perspectiva del sujeto Zapatista." In *La escuelita Zapatista.* Guadalajara, MX: Grietas Editores, 2014.

Subcomandante Insurgente Galeano. "En el tablón de avisos: el conserje." *Enlace Zapatista,* March 4, 2015. Accessed September 7, 2018. http://enlacezapatista.ezln.org.mx/2015/03/04/en-el-tablon-de-avisos-el-conserje/.

———. "Entre la luz y la sombra." *Enlace Zapatista,* May 25, 2014. Accessed September 7, 2018. http://enlacezapatista.ezln.org.mx/2014/05/25/entre-la-luz-y-la-sombra/.

———. "El muro y la grieta: primer apunte sobre el método Zapatista: SupGaleano." *Enlace Zapatista,* May 3, 2015. Accessed September 7, 2018. http://enlacezapatista.ezln.org.mx/2015/05/03/el-muro-y-la-grieta-primer-apunte-sobre-el-metodo-zapatista-supgaleano-3-de-mayo/.

———. "Sherlock Holmes, Euclides, los errores de dedo y las ciencias sociales." In *El pensamiento crítico frente a la hidra capitalista.* Mexico: Ediciones México, 2015.

Subcomandante Insurgente Marcos. "Chiapas: la treceava estela: Quinta parte: una historia." *Enlace Zapatista,* July 21, 2003. Accessed September 7, 2018. http://enlacezapatista.ezln.org.mx/2003/07/21/chiapas-la-treceava-estela-quinta-parte-una-historia/.

———. "Chiapas: la treceava estela. Segunda parte: una muerte." *Enlace Zapatista*, July 21, 2003. Accessed September 7, 2018. http://enlacezapatista.ezln.org.mx/2003/07/21/chiapas-la-treceava-estela-segunda-parte-una-muerte/.

———. "Coloquio Aubry: Parte VII: (y última) sentir el rojo." *Enlace Zapatista*, December 17, 2007. Accessed September 7, 2018. http://enlacezapatista.ezln.org.mx/2007/12/17/parte-vii-y-ultima-sentir-el-rojo-el-calendario-y-la-geografia-de-la-guerra/.

———. "Heroísmo cotidiano hace posible que existan los destellos." *Enlace Zapatista*, January 26, 1994. Accessed September 7, 2018. http://enlacezapatista.ezln.org.mx/1994/01/26/heroismo-cotidiano-hace-posible-que-existan-los-destellos/.

———. "Votán II: l@s guardian@s." *Enlace Zapatista*, July 30, 2013. Accessed September 7, 2018. http://enlacezapatista.ezln.org.mx/2013/07/30/votan-ii-ls-guardians/.

Subcomandante Insurgente Moisés. "Cupo completo para el primer grado de La escuelita Zapatista en las vueltas de Diciembre 2013 y Enero 2014." *Enlace Zapatista*, November 26, 2013. Accessed September 7, 2018. http://enlacezapatista.ezln.org.mx/2013/11/26/cupo-completo-para-el-primer-grado-de-la-escuelita-zapatista-en-las-vueltas-de-diciembre-2013-y-enero-2014/.

———. "Economía política desde las comunidades I." *Enlace Zapatista*, May 4, 2015. Accessed September 7, 2018. http://enlacezapatista.ezln.org.mx/2015/05/04/economia-politica-desde-las-comunidades-i-subcomandante-insurgente-moises-4-de-mayo/.

———. "Ellos y nosotros. VI.–las miradas: Parte 6: él somos." *Enlace Zapatista*, February 14, 2013. Accessed September 7, 2018. http://enlacezapatista.ezln.org.mx/2013/02/14/ellos-y-nosotros-vi-las-miradas-parte-6-el-somos/.

———. "Resistencia y rebeldía I." *Enlace Zapatista*, May 6, 2015. Accessed September 7, 2018. http://enlacezapatista.ezln.org.mx/2015/05/06/resistencia-y-rebeldia-i-subcomandante-insurgente-moises-6-de-mayo/.

———. "Resistencia y rebeldía III." *Enlace Zapatista*, May 8, 2015. Accessed September 7, 2018. http://enlacezapatista.ezln.org.mx/2015/05/08/resistencia-y-rebeldia-iii-subcomandante-insurgente-moises-8-de-mayo/.

Subcomandante Insurgente Moisés and Subcomandante Insurgente Galeano. "Segundo nivel escuela Zapatista." *Enlace Zapatista*, July 27, 2015. Accessed September 7, 2018. http://enlacezapatista.ezln.org.mx/2015/07/27/segundo-nivel-escuela-zapatista/.

———. "¿Y en las comunidades Zapatistas?" *Enlace Zapatista*, February 23, 2015. Accessed September 7, 2018. http://enlacezapatista.ezln.org.mx/2016/02/23/y-en-las-comunidades-zapatistas/.

———. "Y mientras tanto en . . . las comunidades partidistas." *Enlace Zapatista*, February 21, 2016. Accessed September 7, 2018. http://enlacezapatista.ezln.org.mx/2016/02/21/y-mientras-tanto-en-las-comunidades-partidistas/.

Womack, John, ed. *Rebellion in Chiapas: An Historical Reader*. New York: New Press, 1999.

Zapatista Autonomous Communities. *Gobierno autónomo I*. August 2013.

———. *Gobierno autónomo II*. August 2013.

———. *Participación de las mujeres en el gobierno autónomo*. August 2013.

———. *Resistencia autónoma*. August 2013.

———. "Video segundo nivel de la escuelita Zapatista." *Enlace Zapatista*, 2015. Accessed September 7, 2018. http://enlacezapatista.ezln.org.mx/video-segundo-nivel/.

Zibechi, Raúl. *Dispersing Power: Social Movements as Anti-State Forces*. Translated by Ramor Ryan. Oakland: AK Press, 2010.

Index

"Passim" (literally "scattered") indicates intermittent discussion of a topic over a cluster of pages.

About the Authors

Dylan Eldredge Fitzwater has encountered the Zapatistas as a human rights observer, as a participant in several international gatherings, and as a student at the Zapatista language school in Oventik. His most recent permanent residence was Portland, OR, where he worked at Burgerville, a regional fast-food chain, and organized for the Burgerville Workers Union, an affiliate of the Industrial Workers of the World. He is currently on the road, living out of a van and selling Zapatista coffee through MonkeyBear Coop.

John P. Clark is a philosopher, activist, and educator. He lives and works in New Orleans, where his family has been for twelve generations. He is director of La Terre Institute for Community and Ecology, located on Bayou La Terre in the forest of coastal Mississippi. He is the author or editor of over a dozen books, including *The Anarchist Moment; Anarchy, Geography, Modernity;* and *The Impossible Community*.

ABOUT PM PRESS

PM Press was founded at the end of 2007 by a small collection of folks with decades of publishing, media, and organizing experience. PM Press co-conspirators have published and distributed hundreds of books, pamphlets, CDs, and DVDs. Members of PM have founded enduring book fairs, spearheaded victorious tenant organizing campaigns, and worked closely with bookstores, academic conferences, and even rock bands to deliver political and challenging ideas to all walks of life. We're old enough to know what we're doing and young enough to know what's at stake.

We seek to create radical and stimulating fiction and nonfiction books, pamphlets, T-shirts, visual and audio materials to entertain, educate, and inspire you. We aim to distribute these through every available channel with every available technology—whether that means you are seeing anarchist classics at our bookfair stalls, reading our latest vegan cookbook at the café, downloading geeky fiction e-books, or digging new music and timely videos from our website.

PM Press is always on the lookout for talented and skilled volunteers, artists, activists, and writers to work with. If you have a great idea for a project or can contribute in some way, please get in touch.

PM Press
PO Box 23912
Oakland, CA 94623
www.pmpress.org

PM Press in Europe
europe@pmpress.org
www.pmpress.org.uk

FRIENDS OF PM PRESS

These are indisputably momentous times—the financial system is melting down globally and the Empire is stumbling. Now more than ever there is a vital need for radical ideas.

In the years since its founding—and on a mere shoestring— PM Press has risen to the formidable challenge of publishing and distributing knowledge and entertainment for the struggles ahead. With over 300 releases to date, we have published an impressive and stimulating array of literature, art, music, politics, and culture. Using every available medium, we've succeeded in connecting those hungry for ideas and information to those putting them into practice.

Friends of PM allows you to directly help impact, amplify, and revitalize the discourse and actions of radical writers, filmmakers, and artists. It provides us with a stable foundation from which we can build upon our early successes and provides a much-needed subsidy for the materials that can't necessarily pay their own way. You can help make that happen—and receive every new title automatically delivered to your door once a month—by joining as a Friend of PM Press. And, we'll throw in a free T-shirt when you sign up.

Here are your options:

- **$30 a month** Get all books and pamphlets plus 50% discount on all webstore purchases

- **$40 a month** Get all PM Press releases (including CDs and DVDs) plus 50% discount on all webstore purchases

- **$100 a month** Superstar—Everything plus PM merchandise, free downloads, and 50% discount on all webstore purchases

For those who can't afford $30 or more a month, we have **Sustainer Rates** at $15, $10 and $5. Sustainers get a free PM Press T-shirt and a 50% discount on all purchases from our website.

Your Visa or Mastercard will be billed once a month, until you tell us to stop. Or until our efforts succeed in bringing the revolution around. Or the financial meltdown of Capital makes plastic redundant. Whichever comes first.

DEPARTMENT OF ANTHROPOLOGY & SOCIAL CHANGE

Anthropology and Social Change, housed within
the California Institute of Integral Studies, is a small
innovative graduate department with a particular focus
on activist scholarship, militant research, and social change. We offer both masters
and doctoral degree programs.

Our unique approach to collaborative research methodology dissolves traditional
barriers between research and political activism, between insiders and outsiders,
and between researchers and protagonists. Activist research is a tool for "creating
the conditions we describe." We engage in the process of co-research to explore
existing alternatives and possibilities for social change.

Anthropology and Social Change
anth@ciis.edu
1453 Mission Street
94103
San Francisco, California
www.ciis.edu/academics/graduate-programs/anthropology-and-social-change

Wobblies and Zapatistas: Conversations on Anarchism, Marxism and Radical History

Staughton Lynd and Andrej Grubačić

ISBN: 978-1-60486-041-2
$20.00   300 pages

Wobblies and Zapatistas offers the reader an encounter between two generations and two traditions. Andrej Grubačić is an anarchist from the Balkans. Staughton Lynd is a lifelong pacifist, influenced by Marxism. They meet in dialogue in an effort to bring together the anarchist and Marxist traditions, to discuss the writing of history by those who make it, and to remind us of the idea that "my country is the world." Encompassing a Left libertarian perspective and an emphatically activist standpoint, these conversations are meant to be read in the clubs and affinity groups of the new Movement.

The authors accompany us on a journey through modern revolutions, direct actions, anti-globalist counter summits, Freedom Schools, Zapatista cooperatives, Haymarket and Petrograd, Hanoi and Belgrade, 'intentional' communities, wildcat strikes, early Protestant communities, Native American democratic practices, the Workers' Solidarity Club of Youngstown, occupied factories, self-organized councils and soviets, the lives of forgotten revolutionaries, Quaker meetings, antiwar movements, and prison rebellions. Neglected and forgotten moments of interracial self-activity are brought to light. The book invites the attention of readers who believe that a better world, on the other side of capitalism and state bureaucracy, may indeed be possible.

"There's no doubt that we've lost much of our history. It's also very clear that those in power in this country like it that way. Here's a book that shows us why. It demonstrates not only that another world is possible, but that it already exists, has existed, and shows an endless potential to burst through the artificial walls and divisions that currently imprison us. An exquisite contribution to the literature of human freedom, and coming not a moment too soon."
—David Graeber, author of *Fragments of an Anarchist Anthropology* and *Direct Action: An Ethnography*

"I have been in regular contact with Andrej Grubačić for many years, and have been most impressed by his searching intelligence, broad knowledge, lucid judgment, and penetrating commentary on contemporary affairs and their historical roots. He is an original thinker and dedicated activist, who brings deep understanding and outstanding personal qualities to everything he does."
—Noam Chomsky

Between Earth and Empire: From the Necrocene to the Beloved Community

John P. Clark
with a Foreword by Peter Marshall

ISBN: 978-1-62963-648-1
$22.95   352 pages

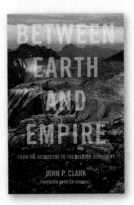

Between Earth and Empire focuses on the crucial position of humanity at the present moment in Earth History. We have left the Cenozoic, the "new period of life," and are now in the midst of the Necrocene, a period of mass extinction and reversal of the course of evolution of life on Earth. We are now nearing the end of the long history of Empire and domination, faced with the alternatives of either continuing the path of social and ecological disintegration or initiating a new era of social and ecological regeneration.

The book shows that conventional approaches to global crisis on both the right and the left have succumbed to processes of denial and disavowal, either rejecting the reality of crisis entirely or substituting ineffectual but comforting gestures and images for deep, systemic social transformation. It is argued that an effective response to global crisis requires attention to all major spheres of social determination, including the social institutional structure, the social ideology, the social imaginary, and the social ethos. Large-scale social and ecological regeneration must be rooted in communities of liberation and solidarity, in which personal and group transformation take place in all these spheres, so that a culture of awakening and care can emerge.

Between Earth and Empire explores examples of significant progress in this direction, including the Zapatista movement in Chiapas, the Democratic Autonomy Movement in Rojava, indigenous movements in defense of the commons, the solidarity economy movement, and efforts to create liberated base communities and affinity groups within anarchism and other radical social movements. In the end, the book presents a vision of hope for social and ecological regeneration through the rebirth of a libertarian and communitarian social imaginary, and the flourishing of a free cooperative community globally.

"Whether in Rojava where women are fighting for their people's survival, or in the loss and terror of New Orleans after the Katrina flood, Clark finds models of communality, care, and hope. Finely reasoned and integrative, tracing the dialectical play of institution and ethos, ideology and imaginary, this book will speak to philosophers and activists alike."
—Ariel Salleh, author of *Ecofeminism as Politics*

Anarchy, Geography, Modernity: Selected Writings of Elisée Reclus

Edited by John P. Clark and Camille Martin

ISBN: 978-1-60486-429-8

$22.95   304 pages

Anarchy, Geography, Modernity is the first comprehensive introduction to the thought of Elisée Reclus, the great anarchist geographer and political theorist. It shows him to be an extraordinary figure for his age. Not only an anarchist but also a radical feminist, anti-racist, ecologist, animal rights advocate, cultural radical, nudist, and vegetarian. Not only a major social thinker but also a dedicated revolutionary.

The work analyzes Reclus' greatest achievement, a sweeping historical and theoretical synthesis recounting the story of the earth and humanity as an epochal struggle between freedom and domination. It presents his groundbreaking critique of all forms of domination: not only capitalism, the state, and authoritarian religion, but also patriarchy, racism, technological domination, and the domination of nature. His crucial insights on the interrelation between personal and small-group transformation, broader cultural change, and large-scale social organization are explored. Reclus' ideas are presented both through detailed exposition and analysis, and in extensive translations of key texts, most appearing in English for the first time.

"For far too long Elisée Reclus has stood in the shadow of Godwin, Proudhon, Bakunin, Kropotkin, and Emma Goldman. Now John Clark has pulled Reclus forward to stand shoulder to shoulder with Anarchism's cynosures. Reclus' light brought into anarchism's compass not only a focus on ecology, but a struggle against both patriarchy and racism, contributions which can now be fully appreciated thanks to John Clark's exegesis and [his and Camille Martin's] translations of works previously unavailable in English. No serious reader can afford to neglect this book."
—Dana Ward, Pitzer College

"Finally! A century after his death, the great French geographer and anarchist Elisée Reclus has been honored by a vibrant selection of his writings expertly translated into English."
—Kent Mathewson, Louisiana State University

"Maintaining an appropriately scholarly style, marked by deep background knowledge, nuanced argument, and careful qualifications, Clark and Martin nevertheless reveal a passionate love for their subject and adopt a stance of political engagement that they hope does justice to Reclus' own commitments."
—Historical Geography

Anthropocene or Capitalocene? Nature, History, and the Crisis of Capitalism

Edited by Jason W. Moore

ISBN: 978-1-62963-148-6
$21.95   304 pages

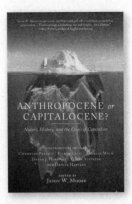

The Earth has reached a tipping point. Runaway climate change, the sixth great extinction of planetary life, the acidification of the oceans—all point toward an era of unprecedented turbulence in humanity's relationship within the web of life. But just what is that relationship, and how do we make sense of this extraordinary transition?

Anthropocene or Capitalocene? offers answers to these questions from a dynamic group of leading critical scholars. They challenge the theory and history offered by the most significant environmental concept of our times: the Anthropocene. But are we living in the Anthropocene, literally the "Age of Man"? Is a different response more compelling, and better suited to the strange—and often terrifying—times in which we live? The contributors to this book diagnose the problems of Anthropocene thinking and propose an alternative: the global crises of the twenty-first century are rooted in the Capitalocene; not the Age of Man but the Age of Capital.

Anthropocene or Capitalocene? offers a series of provocative essays on nature and power, humanity, and capitalism. Including both well-established voices and younger scholars, the book challenges the conventional practice of dividing historical change and contemporary reality into "Nature" and "Society," demonstrating the possibilities offered by a more nuanced and connective view of human environment-making, joined at every step with and within the biosphere. In distinct registers, the authors frame their discussions within a politics of hope that signal the possibilities for transcending capitalism, broadly understood as a "world-ecology" that joins nature, capital, and power as a historically evolving whole.

Contributors include Jason W. Moore, Eileen Crist, Donna J. Haraway, Justin McBrien, Elmar Altvater, Daniel Hartley, and Christian Parenti.

"We had best start thinking in revolutionary terms about the forces turning the world upside down if we are to put brakes on the madness. A good place to begin is this book, whose remarkable authors bring together history and theory, politics and ecology, economy and culture, to force a deep look at the origins of global transformation."
—Richard Walker, professor emeritus of geography, UC Berkeley, and author of *The Capitalist Imperative, The New Social Economy, The Conquest of Bread,* and *The Country in the City*

Re-enchanting the World: Feminism and the Politics of the Commons

Silvia Federici
with a Foreword by Peter Linebaugh

ISBN: 978-1-62963-569-9
$19.95   240 pages

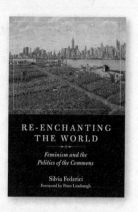

Silvia Federici is one of the most important contemporary theorists of capitalism and feminist movements. In this collection of her work spanning over twenty years, she provides a detailed history and critique of the politics of the commons from a feminist perspective. In her clear and combative voice, Federici provides readers with an analysis of some of the key issues and debates in contemporary thinking on this subject.

Drawing on rich historical research, she maps the connections between the previous forms of enclosure that occurred with the birth of capitalism and the destruction of the commons and the "new enclosures" at the heart of the present phase of global capitalist accumulation. Considering the commons from a feminist perspective, this collection centers on women and reproductive work as crucial to both our economic survival and the construction of a world free from the hierarchies and divisions capital has planted in the body of the world proletariat. Federici is clear that the commons should not be understood as happy islands in a sea of exploitative relations but rather autonomous spaces from which to challenge the existing capitalist organization of life and labor.

"*Silvia Federici's theoretical capacity to articulate the plurality that fuels the contemporary movement of women in struggle provides a true toolbox for building bridges between different features and different people.*"
—Massimo De Angelis, professor of political economy, University of East London

"*Silvia Federici's work embodies an energy that urges us to rejuvenate struggles against all types of exploitation and, precisely for that reason, her work produces a common: a common sense of the dissidence that creates a community in struggle.*"
—Maria Mies, coauthor of *Ecofeminism*

The Battle for the Mountain of the Kurds: Self-Determination and Ethnic Cleansing in the Afrin Region of Rojava

Thomas Schmidinger
with a Preface by Andrej Grubačić

ISBN: 978-1-62963-651-1
$19.95   176 pages

In early 2018, Turkey invaded the autonomous Kurdish region of Afrin in Syria and is currently threatening to ethnically cleanse the region. Between 2012 and 2018, the "Mountain of the Kurds" (Kurd Dagh) as the area has been called for centuries, had been one of the quietest regions in a country otherwise torn by civil war.

After the outbreak of the Syrian civil war in 2011, the Syrian army withdrew from the region in 2012, enabling the Party of Democratic Union (PYD), the Syrian sister party of Abdullah Öcalan's outlawed Turkish Kurdistan Workers' Party (PKK) to first introduce a Kurdish self-administration and then, in 2014, to establish the Canton Afrin as one of the three parts of the heavily Kurdish Democratic Federation of Northern Syria, which is better known under the name Rojava.

This self-administration—which had seen multiparty municipal and regionwide elections in the summer and autumn of 2017, which included a far-reaching autonomy for a number of ethnic and religious groups, and which had provided a safe haven for up to 300,000 refugees from other parts of Syria—is now at risk of being annihilated by the Turkish invasion and occupation.

Thomas Schmidinger is one of the very few Europeans to have visited the Canton of Afrin. In this book, he gives an account of the history and the present situation of the region. In a number of interviews, he also gives inhabitants of the region from a variety of ethnicities, religions, political orientations, and walks of life the opportunity to speak for themselves. As things stand now, the book might seem to be in danger of becoming an epitaph for the "Mountain of the Kurds," but as the author writes, "the battle for the Mountain of the Kurds is far from over yet."

"Preferable to most journalistic accounts that reduce the Rojava revolution to a single narrative. It will remain an informative resource even when the realities have further changed."
—Martin van Bruinessen, Kurdish Studies on *Rojava: Revolution, War and the Future of Syria's Kurds*

Practical Utopia: Strategies for a Desirable Society

Michael Albert
with a preface by Noam Chomsky

ISBN: 978-1-62963-381-7
$20.00   288 pages

Michael Albert's latest work, *Practical Utopia* is a
succinct and thoughtful discussion of ambitious
goals and practical principles for creating a desirable
society. It presents concepts and their connections to
current society; visions of what can be in a preferred, participatory future; and an
examination of the ends and means required for developing a just society. Neither
shying away from the complexity of human issues, nor reeking of dogmatism,
Practical Utopia presupposes only concern for humanity.

Part one offers conceptual tools for understanding society and history, for
discerning the nature of the oppressions people suffer and the potentials they
harbor. Part two promotes a vision for a better way of organizing economy, polity,
kinship, culture, ecology, and international relations. It is not a blueprint, of course,
but does address the key institutions needed if people are to be free to determine
their own circumstances. Part three investigates the means of seeking change
using a variety of tactics and programs.

"Practical Utopia *immediately struck me because it is written by a leftist who is
interested in the people winning and defeating oppression. The book is an excellent
jumping off point for debates on the framework to look at actually existing capitalism,
strategy for change, and what we need to do about moving forward. It speaks to many
of the questions faced by grassroots activists who want to get beyond demanding
change but who, instead, want to create a dynamic movement that can bring a just
world into existence. As someone who comes out of a different part of the Left than
does Michael Albert, I was nevertheless excited by the challenges he threw in front of
the readers of this book. Many a discussion will be sparked by the arguments of this
work."*
—Bill Fletcher Jr., author of *"They're Bankrupting Us!" And 20 Other Myths about
Unions*

"*Albert mulls over the better society that we may create after capitalism, provoking
much thought and offering a generous, hopeful vision of the future. Albert's
prescriptions for action in the present are modest and wise, his suggestions for building
the future are ambitious and humane.*"
—Milan Rai

We Are the Crisis of Capital: A John Holloway Reader

John Holloway

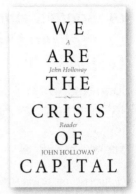

ISBN: 978-1-62963-225-4
$22.95   320 pages

We Are the Crisis of Capital collects articles and excerpts written by radical academic, theorist, and activist John Holloway over a period of forty years.

Different times, different places, and the same anguish persists throughout our societies. This collection asks, "Is there a way out?" How do we break capital, a form of social organisation that dehumanises us and threatens to annihilate us completely? How do we create a world based on the mutual recognition of human dignity?

Holloway's work answers loudly, "By screaming NO!" By thinking from our own anger and from our own creativity. By trying to recover the "We" who are buried under the categories of capitalist thought. By opening the categories and discovering the antagonism they conceal, by discovering that behind the concepts of money, state, capital, crisis, and so on, there moves our resistance and rebellion.

An approach sometimes referred to as Open Marxism, it is an attempt to rethink Marxism as daily struggle. The articles move forward, influenced by the German state derivation debates of the seventies, by the CSE debates in Britain, and the group around the Edinburgh journal *Common Sense*, and then moving on to Mexico and the wonderful stimulus of the Zapatista uprising, and now the continuing whirl of discussion with colleagues and students in the Posgrado de Sociología of the Benemérita Universidad Autónoma de Puebla.

"Holloway's work is infectiously optimistic."
—Steven Poole, the *Guardian* (UK)

"Holloway's thesis is indeed important and worthy of notice."
—Richard J.F. Day, *Canadian Journal of Cultural Studies*

In, Against, and Beyond Capitalism: The San Francisco Lectures

John Holloway
with a Preface by Andrej Grubačić

ISBN: 978-1-62963-109-7
$14.95   112 pages

In, Against, and Beyond Capitalism is based on three recent lectures delivered by John Holloway at the California Institute of Integral Studies in San Francisco. The lectures focus on what anticapitalist revolution can mean today—after the historic failure of the idea that the conquest of state power was the key to radical change—and offer a brilliant and engaging introduction to the central themes of Holloway's work.

The lectures take as their central challenge the idea that "We Are the Crisis of Capital and Proud of It." This runs counter to many leftist assumptions that the capitalists are to blame for the crisis, or that crisis is simply the expression of the bankruptcy of the system. The only way to see crisis as the possible threshold to a better world is to understand the failure of capitalism as the face of the push of our creative force. This poses a theoretical challenge. The first lecture focuses on the meaning of "We," the second on the understanding of capital as a system of social cohesion that systematically frustrates our creative force, and the third on the proposal that we are the crisis of this system of cohesion.

"His Marxism is premised on another form of logic, one that affirms movement, instability, and struggle. This is a movement of thought that affirms the richness of life, particularity (non-identity) and 'walking in the opposite direction'; walking, that is, away from exploitation, domination, and classification. Without contradictory thinking in, against, and beyond the capitalist society, capital once again becomes a reified object, a thing, and not a social relation that signifies transformation of a useful and creative activity (doing) into (abstract) labor. Only open dialectics, a right kind of thinking for the wrong kind of world, non-unitary thinking without guarantees, is able to assist us in our contradictory struggle for a world free of contradiction."
—Andrej Grubačić, from his Preface

"Holloway's work is infectiously optimistic."
—Steven Poole, the *Guardian* (UK)

"Holloway's thesis is indeed important and worthy of notice"
—Richard J.F. Day, *Canadian Journal of Cultural Studies*

Archive That, Comrade! Left Legacies and the Counter Culture of Remembrance

Phil Cohen

ISBN: 978-1-62963-506-4
$19.95   160 pages

Archive That, Comrade! explores issues of archival theory and practice that arise for any project aspiring to provide an open-access platform for political dialogue and democratic debate. It is informed by the author's experience of writing a memoir about his involvement in the London underground scene of the 1960s, the London street commune movement, and the occupation of 144 Piccadilly, an event that hit the world's headlines for ten days in July 1969.

After a brief introduction that sets the contemporary scene of 'archive fever,' the book considers what the political legacy of 1960s counter culture reveals about the process of commemoration. The argument then opens out to discuss the notion of historical legacy and its role in the 'dialectic of generations'. How far can the archive serve as a platform for dialogue and debate between different generations of activists in a culture that fetishises the evanescent present, practices a profound amnesia about its past, and forecloses the sociological imagination of an alternative future? The following section looks at the emergence of a complex apparatus of public fame and celebrity around the spectacle of dissidence and considers whether the Left has subverted or merely mirrored the dominant forms of reputation-making and public recognition. Can the Left establish its own autonomous model of commemoration?

The final section takes up the challenge of outlining a model for the democratic archive as a revisionary project, creating a resource for building collective capacity to sustain struggles of long duration. A postscript examines how archival strategies of the alt-right have intervened at this juncture to elaborate a politics of false memory.

"Has the Left got a past? And if so, is that past best forgotten? Who was it who said, 'Let the dead bury their dead'? Phil Cohen's book is a searing meditation on the politics of memory, written by someone for whom 'the '60s' are still alive—and therefore horrible, unfinished, unforgivable, tremendous, undead. His book brings back to life the William Faulkner cliché. The past for Cohen is neither dead nor alive. It's not even past, more's the pity."
—T.J. Clark, author of *The Sight of Death*

Occult Features of Anarchism: With Attention to the Conspiracy of Kings and the Conspiracy of the Peoples

Erica Lagalisse
with a Foreword by Barbara Ehrenreich

ISBN: 978-1-62963-579-8
$15.95   160 pages

In the nineteenth century anarchists were accused of conspiracy by governments afraid of revolution, but in the current century various "conspiracy theories" suggest that anarchists are controlled by government itself. The Illuminati were a network of intellectuals who argued for self-government and against private property, yet the public is now often told that they were (and are) the very group that controls governments and defends private property around the world. Intervening in such misinformation, Lagalisse works with primary and secondary sources in multiple languages to set straight the history of the Left and illustrate the actual relationship between revolutionism, pantheistic occult philosophy, and the clandestine fraternity.

Exploring hidden correspondences between anarchism, Renaissance magic, and New Age movements, Lagalisse also advances critical scholarship regarding leftist attachments to secular politics. Inspired by anthropological fieldwork within today's anarchist movements, her essay challenges anarchist atheism insofar as it poses practical challenges for coalition politics in today's world.

Studying anarchism as a historical object, *Occult Features of Anarchism* also shows how the development of leftist theory and practice within clandestine masculine public spheres continues to inform contemporary anarchist understandings of the "political," in which men's oppression by the state becomes the prototype for power in general. Readers behold how gender and religion become privatized in radical counterculture, a historical process intimately linked to the privatization of gender and religion by the modern nation-state.

"This is surely the most creative and exciting, and possibly the most important, work to come out on either anarchism or occultism in many a year. It should give rise to a whole new field of intellectual study."
—David Graeber, professor of anthropology at the London School of Economics and Political Science, author of *Debt: The First 5000 Years*